Microsoft Dynamics AX 2012 R2 Services

Harness the power of Microsoft Dynamics AX 2012 R2 to create and use your own services effectively

Klaas Deforche

Kenny Saelen

[PACKT] enterprise
professional expertise distilled
PUBLISHING

BIRMINGHAM - MUMBAI

Microsoft Dynamics AX 2012 R2 Services

Copyright © 2014 Packt Publishing

First published: March 2014

Production Reference: 1190314

Published by Packt Publishing Ltd.
Livery Place
35 Livery Street
Birmingham B3 2PB, UK.

ISBN 978-1-78217-672-5

www.packtpub.com

Cover Image by Klaas Deforche (klaasdeforche@gmail.com)

Credits

About the Authors

Klaas Deforche started working as a developer on Microsoft Dynamics AX in 2007 for the Belgian ICT company RealDolmen, primarily working with Dynamics AX 4.0. He gained experience with AX 2009 while working on projects for some well-known Belgian fashion retailers, especially on the integration side of things. He is currently working on AX 2012 projects for customers in the healthcare sector. Klaas likes to share his knowledge with the community, which is why he started his AX-oriented blog `artofcreation.be` in 2009. This is also why, in 2012, Klaas co-authored the book *Microsoft Dynamics AX 2012 Services*, *Packt Publishing*, to help spread knowledge on the subject.

Writing this book is a team effort, so I would like to thank everyone involved — co-author Kenny, everyone at Packt Publishing, and the reviewers. Without all of you, this book would not have been possible.

I would also like to thank the readers of the previous edition for supporting us and providing feedback. It has been a great motivation and inspiration for this book. Also, a big thanks to the readers of my blog, fellow bloggers, and the Dynamics community.

Last but not least, thank you my family, colleagues, friends, and girlfriend for their support. The time spent on this book could not have been spent with you, so thanks for your patience.

Kenny Saelen is a Dynamics AX MVP who works for the Belgian ICT company RealDolmen. He started as a developer on Microsoft Dynamics AX in 2004, primarily working on a European customer implementation with Dynamics AX 3.0. At RealDolmen, he gained experience with Dynamics AX 2009 while implementing AX internally, followed by an implementation at a book wholesale company. Currently, he is working as a technical architect for a worldwide customer implementation with Microsoft Dynamics AX 2012 R2, mainly working towards integrating Dynamics AX with other technologies such as SharePoint, BizTalk, and AgilePoint. He can be reached through his blog `ksaelen.be`.

I would like to thank everyone involved in making this book happen, starting with my co-author Klaas, for all the hours we've spent together writing it. Many thanks to everyone at Packt Publishing for the opportunity they have given us, and to the technical reviewers for providing us with the right alternative insights.

Special thanks to my girlfriend and my little son. Writing this book has proven to be much harder than I initially thought, but they have been patiently supporting me all the way.

About the Reviewers

Palle Agermark has worked as a developer and technical consultant with Concorde XAL and Microsoft Dynamics AX for more than 20 years. Palle has worked for a number of years at Microsoft Development Center Copenhagen, primarily developing the financial, accounts payable, and accounts receivable modules; he has also worked on other things such as the unit test framework.

In 2006, Palle wrote a chapter named *Extending Microsoft Dynamics AX* for *Inside Microsoft Dynamics AX 4.0, Microsoft Press*.

Currently, Palle works for one of Scandinavia's largest Microsoft Dynamics AX partners — EG.

Palle lives in Copenhagen, Denmark, with his wife Rikke and daughter Andrea.

Janet E. Blake was introduced to Axapta 3.0 in 2006 by a friend who promised her that she "would never get bored" and kept that promise. She is now a Technical Solutions Architect on the mcaConnect team. She has two degrees from New York University and spends her free time blogging at http://janeteblake.wordpress.com, searching for AX books, and pondering over her next certification.

Janet was a reviewer for *Microsoft Dynamics AX 2012 R2 Administration Cookbook, Packt Publishing*, which was published in November 2013.

I'd like to thank the authors and publishers for the opportunity to review this terrific book. Also, endless thanks to my colleagues and clients for keeping it interesting and fun!

Mohit Rajvanshy has spent nearly 10 years working on Microsoft Dynamics AX. He started his career working with Microsoft Axapta 3.0 in 2004 and since then, he has continued his professional journey working with various Microsoft Dynamics AX releases. He worked as technical lead and developer, delivering various customizations, upgrades, and integration projects in Microsoft Dynamics AX. He is certified in Microsoft Dynamics AX 4.0 and AX 2012. More details about him can be found at `https://www.mcpvirtualbusinesscard.com/VBCServer/mohit.rajvanshy/profile`.

Currently, Mohit is working for Avanade Inc. and is based in Seattle, USA. Avanade is Microsoft's largest Dynamics AX delivery partner.

Mohit has a passion for photography (`http://www.flickr.com/photos/mohitrajvanshy/`) and likes to travel. Mohit also contributes to the Microsoft Dynamics Community via his blog at `http://daxer-dynamicsax.blogspot.com/`.

Tom Van Dyck is a software engineer and technical consultant for Dynamics AX and is currently working with an MS partner in Belgium. After completing a degree in Computer Science and a few years of Visual Basic, ASP, and SQL programming, he began working with AX in 2004.

Being part of different project teams and building a variety of solutions based on AX Versions 3, 4, 2009, and 2012, he has built wide practical experience for himself.

Tom is a certified professional for AX with expertise in X++ development and a special interest in performance issues and optimization.

I've been privileged to work closely with both Kenny and Klaas and have got to know them as dedicated and experienced professionals.

To me, the two new and excellent chapters added complete the picture. The one on tracing and debugging is my favorite by far. My sincere congratulations on the added value you guys created in this second edition!

www.PacktPub.com

Support files, eBooks, discount offers and more

You might want to visit www.PacktPub.com for support files and downloads related to your book.

Did you know that Packt offers eBook versions of every book published, with PDF and ePub files available? You can upgrade to the eBook version at www.PacktPub.com and as a print book customer, you are entitled to a discount on the eBook copy. Get in touch with us at service@packtpub.com for more details.

At www.PacktPub.com, you can also read a collection of free technical articles, sign up for a range of free newsletters and receive exclusive discounts and offers on Packt books and eBooks.

PACKTLIB™

http://PacktLib.PacktPub.com

Do you need instant solutions to your IT questions? PacktLib is Packt's online digital book library. Here, you can access, read and search across Packt's entire library of books.

Why Subscribe?

- Fully searchable across every book published by Packt
- Copy and paste, print and bookmark content
- On demand and accessible via web browser

Free Access for Packt account holders

If you have an account with Packt at www.PacktPub.com, you can use this to access PacktLib today and view nine entirely free books. Simply use your login credentials for immediate access.

Instant Updates on New Packt Books

Get notified! Find out when new books are published by following @PacktEnterprise on Twitter, or the *Packt Enterprise* Facebook page.

Table of Contents

Preface

Enterprise Resource Planning (ERP) systems such as Microsoft Dynamics AX 2012 play a central role in an organization, and therefore, there will always be the need to integrate them with other applications. In many cases, services are the preferred way to do this, and Microsoft Dynamics AX 2012 is now more flexible than ever when it comes to the creation and use of these services. Understanding these services will help you effectively identify where they can be used.

Microsoft Dynamics AX 2012 R2 Services is a hands-on guide that provides you with all the knowledge that you need to implement services with Microsoft Dynamics AX 2012 and 2012 R2. The step-by-step examples will walk you through many of the tasks that you need to frequently perform when creating and using services. This book has been updated to include features of the R2 release while staying relevant to other versions of Microsoft Dynamics AX 2012.

What this book covers

Chapter 1, Getting Started with Microsoft Dynamics AX 2012 Services, introduces the concept of services and explores the new features and enhancements made to services in Microsoft Dynamics AX 2012.

Chapter 2, Service Architecture and Deployment, dives deeper into the service architecture and explores the different options that are available when deploying services.

Chapter 3, AIF Document Services, focuses on the creation, deployment, and consumption of the AIF document services.

Chapter 4, Custom Services, shows you how to create and deploy custom services and consume them using a Windows Communication Foundation (WCF) application using new concepts such as attributes.

Chapter 5, The SysOperation Framework, builds upon the knowledge gained from developing custom services to demonstrate how you can run the business logic in Microsoft Dynamics AX 2012 using services and the SysOperation framework.

Chapter 6, Web Services, walks you through all the steps that are needed to consume an external web service in Microsoft Dynamics AX 2012 using the Visual Studio integration.

Chapter 7, System Services, demonstrates how powerful the system services that are provided out of the box can be and how they allow you to build applications faster.

Chapter 8, High Availability, shows you how you can go from a very basic architecture to one that allows for the high availability of services.

Chapter 9, Tracing and Debugging, guides you through the many different debugging and tracing options that are available to troubleshoot services.

Appendix, Installing the Demo Application, describes how to install and use the demo application that you need to perform most of the examples in this book.

What you need for this book

- Microsoft Dynamics AX 2012 R2 CU7 is used in this book, but almost all the content applies to all versions of Microsoft Dynamics AX 2012

- Microsoft Visual Studio 2010

- WCF Service Configuration Editor and Microsoft Service Trace Viewer, which you can download as part of the Windows SDK and comes with some versions of Visual Studio

A full list of software requirements can be found in the *Microsoft Dynamics AX 2012 System Requirements* document available for download at http://www.microsoft.com/en-us/download/details.aspx?id=11094.

Who this book is for

When you are developing for Microsoft Dynamics AX 2012, you will certainly come in contact with services, even when you are not doing integration scenarios. Because of that, this book is aimed at all Microsoft Dynamics AX developers, both new and experienced.

This book assumes no other knowledge than a basic understanding of MorphX and X++. Even beginners will be able to understand and complete the examples in this book. Those new to services will get the most out of this book by doing a complete read-through, but those who are experienced can jump right in. The idea is that this book can be used both to educate yourself and as a resource that can be consulted during development.

Some examples use C#.NET, so experience with Visual Studio is a plus but not a must. This book is not aimed at .NET developers.

Conventions

In this book, you will find a number of styles of text that distinguish between different kinds of information. Here are some examples of these styles, and an explanation of their meaning.

Code words in text, database table names, folder names, filenames, file extensions, pathnames, dummy URLs, user input, and Twitter handles are shown as follows: "The service contract is a reflection of the DocumentHandlingService class that can be found in the AOT."

A block of code is set as follows:

```
public static void main(Args args)
{
    SysOperationServiceController controller;
    controller = new SysOperationServiceController();
    controller.initializeFromArgs(args);
    controller.startOperation();
}
```

Any command-line input or output is written as follows:

```
T000000007 The Dark Knight 119
T000000008 The Lord of the Rings: The Return of the King 112
```

New terms and **important words** are shown in bold. Words that you see on the screen, in menus or dialog boxes for example, appear in the text like this: "Go to the **Service Groups** node, right-click on it, and click on **New Service Group**".

[Warnings or important notes appear in a box like this.]

[Tips and tricks appear like this.]

Reader feedback

Feedback from our readers is always welcome. Let us know what you think about this book—what you liked or may have disliked. Reader feedback is important for us to develop titles that you really get the most out of.

To send us general feedback, simply send an e-mail to feedback@packtpub.com, and mention the book title via the subject of your message.

If there is a topic that you have expertise in and you are interested in either writing or contributing to a book, see our author guide on www.packtpub.com/authors.

Customer support

Now that you are the proud owner of a Packt book, we have a number of things to help you to get the most from your purchase.

Downloading the example code

You can download the example code files for all Packt books you have purchased from your account at http://www.packtpub.com. If you purchased this book elsewhere, you can visit http://www.packtpub.com/support and register to have the files e-mailed directly to you.

Errata

Although we have taken every care to ensure the accuracy of our content, mistakes do happen. If you find a mistake in one of our books—maybe a mistake in the text or the code—we would be grateful if you would report this to us. By doing so, you can save other readers from frustration and help us improve subsequent versions of this book. If you find any errata, please report them by visiting `http://www.packtpub.com/submit-errata`, selecting your book, clicking on the **errata submission form** link, and entering the details of your errata. Once your errata are verified, your submission will be accepted and the errata will be uploaded on our website, or added to any list of existing errata, under the Errata section of that title. Any existing errata can be viewed by selecting your title from `http://www.packtpub.com/support`.

Piracy

Piracy of copyright material on the Internet is an ongoing problem across all media. At Packt, we take the protection of our copyright and licenses very seriously. If you come across any illegal copies of our works, in any form, on the Internet, please provide us with the location address or website name immediately so that we can pursue a remedy.

Please contact us at `copyright@packtpub.com` with a link to the suspected pirated material.

We appreciate your help in protecting our authors, and our ability to bring you valuable content.

Questions

You can contact us at `questions@packtpub.com` if you are having a problem with any aspect of the book, and we will do our best to address it.

1
Getting Started with Microsoft Dynamics AX 2012 Services

Microsoft Dynamics AX 2012 introduces a lot of new features that are related to the **Application Integration Framework** (**AIF**) and services in general. Many of the existing concepts have been radically changed. This chapter unveils these new features and enhancements made to the services in Microsoft Dynamics AX 2012.

At the end of this chapter, you will have a clear picture of what services mean in the context of Microsoft Dynamics AX 2012. This should enable you to identify where and when to use services in your solution and what type of service to use.

The following topics are covered in this chapter:

- **Introducing services and SOA**: We will start by defining what services are and what SOA has to offer, and derive from that the scenarios in which they can be used.

- **Architecture overview**: We will look at an overview of the services and AIF architecture and familiarize ourselves with the key components of the architecture.

- **New and enhanced features**: We will discuss the new features and enhancements that have been made compared to Microsoft Dynamics AX 2009. This is also an opportunity to find out why some of these changes were made.

- **Types of services and comparison**: There are several types of services available to choose from when implementing your solution. Therefore, it is important to be able to distinguish between these different types and choose the type that suits your needs best.

Introducing services and SOA

So what is a service? The best way to understand what a service is, is understanding why you would need a service. Typically, there are a lot of different applications being used in an enterprise. Sometimes this is by design; for example, because a specialized functionality is needed that is not implemented in the ERP system. In other cases, legacy systems are not replaced when implementing an ERP system, simply because they do their jobs well. Whatever the reasons, these or others, the result is the same: a growing number of different applications.

One of the problems with these applications is that they are likely to have been built using different technologies. Because they speak a different language, it makes them unable to communicate with each other. This is a problem that services address by providing a means by which applications can communicate, independent of their technology. They achieve this by adhering to standards and protocols so that, in essence, they start speaking the same language.

A service should have many of the same qualities as modern applications. Applications should be modular, components should be reusable, and everything should be loosely coupled. These principles also apply when developing services. Your services should have a well-defined functionality and should be able to autonomously execute that functionality without interaction with other services.

Services should also be abstract. By this we mean that other applications should not have to know the inner workings of the provider in order to use the service. This can be attained by hiding details such as how data is stored, what technologies are used, and how the business logic is implemented. Abstraction is not an end goal, but a way to achieve loose coupling and reusability.

A service is also self-describing, meaning it can provide other applications with metadata about itself. This metadata describes what operations can be used and what the input and output is. In the case of Microsoft Dynamics AX, this information is published using the **Web Service Description Language (WSDL)**.

All of these qualities make services usable in a **Service-Oriented Architecture (SOA)**. In an SOA, services are published and made discoverable. Services are then composed to create loosely coupled applications.

Example implementations

To make the previous explanation about services more concrete, we will take a look at three very different scenarios in which services can be used.

Bing API

Microsoft provides an API for Bing Maps and Search that is available to developers in various ways, including a web service. Developers can use this service for things such as calculating a route between two addresses, locating an address on a map, getting search results for a certain query, and so on. It's not hard to imagine this service being used in a logistics application; for example, to calculate the most efficient route for delivering goods to customers.

Mobile application

Let's look at a scenario where a mobile application has to be developed for Microsoft Dynamics AX 2012. Even if your mobile application contains business logic to work offline, data will have to be sent back to the **Application Object Server** (**AOS**) at some point. The mobile application could use services to execute business logic and send data to the AOS when a network is available. A mobile application can also be built without containing business logic, in a way that it only renders a **Graphical User Interface** (**GUI**). In this scenario, the application will have to stay connected to the AOS over the network because the AOS will drive the application and tell it what to do using services.

Business Process Modeling (BPM)

You can use services in an SOA to model business processes. When all requirements for the business processes are available as services, it is possible to compose processes entirely using services. When done right, this is very powerful because of the great flexibility that the combination of BPM and SOA provides.

Architectural overview

Depending on the requirements of your projects, a different architectural approach will be needed. To make the right decisions when designing your solutions, it is important to understand the services and AIF architecture.

Compared to Microsoft Dynamics AX 2009, there have been a lot of improvements made to the service architecture in Microsoft Dynamics AX 2012. The biggest improvement is the native **Windows Communications Foundation** (**WCF**) support. As a result, the proprietary **Microsoft Message Queuing** (**MSMQ**) and BizTalk adapters that were available in Microsoft Dynamics AX 2009 have been deprecated and replaced by adapters that use WCF. The MSMQ adapter in particular is replaced by an adapter that uses the WCF NetMsmq binding. The filesystem adapter remains intact and still allows you to import and export messages from and to the filesystem.

All services are WCF services and are hosted on the AOS. When an application wants to consume these services on the local network, no further deployment is needed because it can connect directly to the AOS. Just like with Microsoft Dynamics AX 2009, deployment on **Internet Information Services (IIS)** is needed for consumers that are not on the intranet. However, the services themselves are no longer deployed on IIS; instead, a WCF routing service on the IIS routes everything to the AOS.

If you want to modify messages before they are received or after they are sent, you can use pipelines and transformations. **Pipelines** only apply to the body of a message and are handled by the **request preprocessor** and **response postprocessor**. You can use **transformations** to transform a complete message, including the header. This allows you to exchange messages in a non-XML format.

The following diagram depicts the architecture as it is in Microsoft Dynamics AX 2012 and clearly shows the central role of WCF:

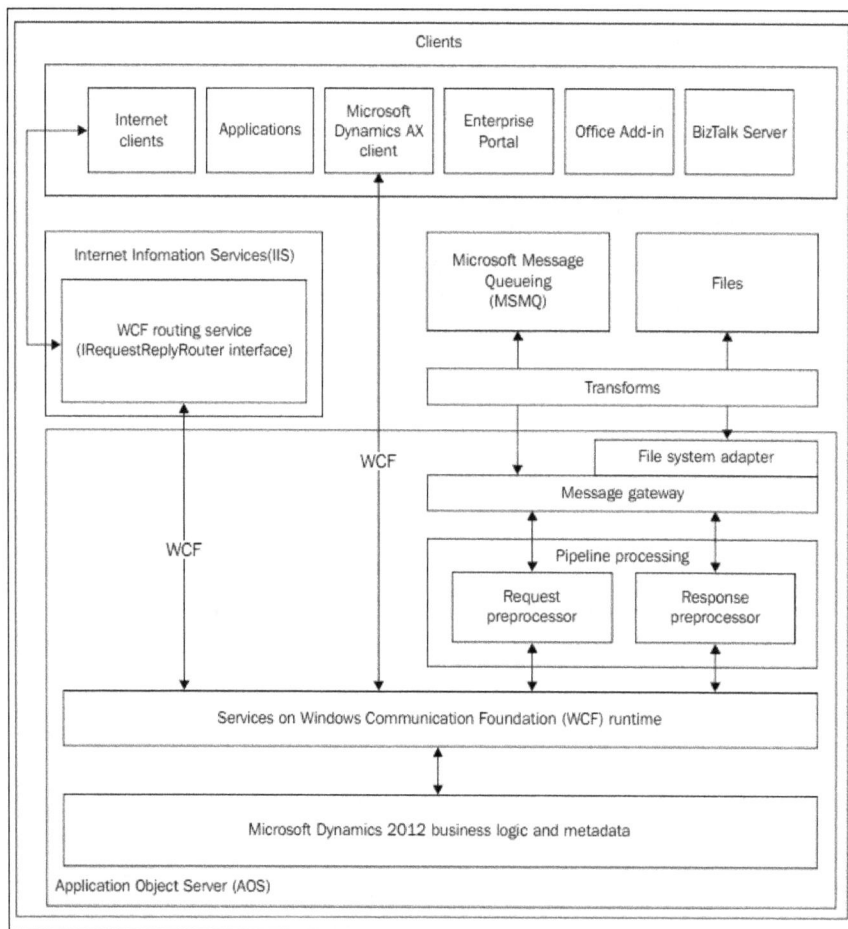

While not displayed in the diagram, there is now load balancing support for services using Windows Server **Network Load Balancing** (**NLB**). Combined with NLB for IIS, which was already available, this enables high availability and load balancing for services.

New and enhanced features

Services have been around for some time in Microsoft Dynamics AX. AIF was initially introduced with the release of Microsoft Dynamics AX 4.0, with Microsoft Dynamics AX 2009 continuing to build on that. But with the release of Microsoft Dynamics AX 2012, Microsoft has really succeeded in bringing the service functionality to a whole new level. Occasionally, even more features and enhancements are added in new releases and cumulative updates. Let us take a walk through the major changes that Microsoft Dynamics AX 2012 brings to the table.

The AOS WCF service host

The first major feature that has been added to this release is that the AOS is now the host for the Microsoft Dynamics AX 2012 services. In previous releases, the exchange of messages was either through adapters such as the filesystem, BizTalk, and MSMQ adapter, or services that were exposed as WCF 3.5 services through IIS. With the latter, IIS was acting as the host for the WCF services.

With this new release of Microsoft Dynamics AX, services will be exposed as WCF 4.0 services hosted directly in the AOS Windows service. As long as intranet users and applications are consuming these services, no IIS is needed.

WCF adapters

Microsoft Dynamics AX 2012 provides a lot more support for WCF. Proprietary adapters such as BizTalk and MSMQ that were previously available are now obsolete and no longer available. Instead, support for MSMQ and BizTalk is provided by a native WCF equivalent of these adapters.

This does not mean that creating custom adapters using the AIF adapter framework is not supported anymore. Custom adapters can still be added by implementing the `AifIntegrationAdapter` interface.

Out of the box, Microsoft Dynamics AX 2012 comes with the following adapters:

- **NetTcp**: This is the default adapter used when creating a new integration port. This adapter type corresponds to the WCF NetTcpBinding. It provides synchronous message exchanges by using WS-* standards over the **Transmission Control Protocol (TCP)**.

- **Filesystem**: This can be used for asynchronous exchange of XML messages stored in the filesystem directories.

- **MSMQ**: This is used when support for queuing is needed. Message exchange is asynchronous and uses MSMQ. Note that choosing this adapter type actually uses the WCF NetMsmq binding.

- **HTTP**: This supports synchronous message exchanges over the HTTP and HTTPS protocols. This was already available in Microsoft Dynamics AX 2009, but there is a difference in the deployment to the IIS. The business connector is no longer used for services hosted on the IIS; instead, a WCF routing service is used. There is more about routing services later in this chapter.

> More information about the bindings that are used in these adapters can be found on MSDN at http://msdn.microsoft.com/en-us/library/ms733027.aspx. If you want to learn more about WS-* standards, check out the **Web Services Specification Index Page** at http://msdn.microsoft.com/en-us/library/ms951274.aspx.

Integration ports

In Microsoft Dynamics AX 2009, there was a lot of configuration required to get AIF up and running. This included configuration of the following:

- Endpoints
- Local endpoints
- Channels
- Endpoint users
- Endpoint constraints

Now, integration ports have been added and they provide a simpler way to configure services. There are two types of integration ports: inbound and outbound. Which type you should use for your service depends on whether the message originates from outside or inside of Microsoft Dynamics AX.

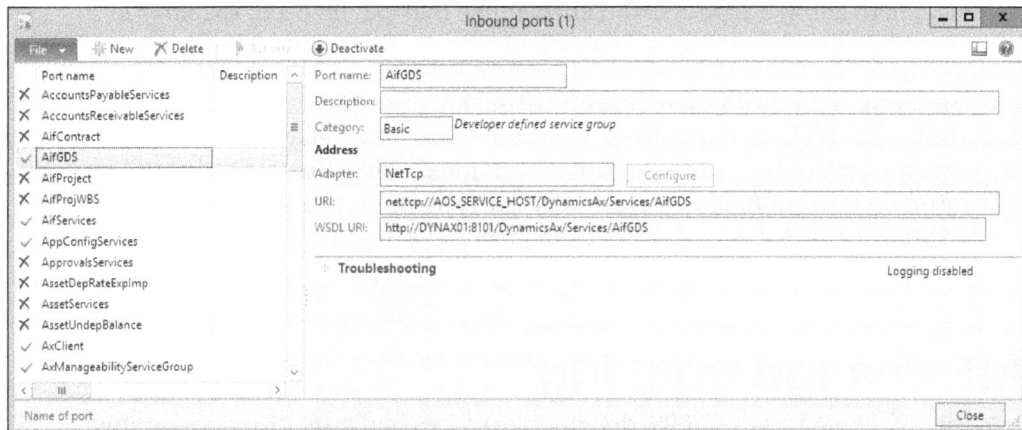

The inbound integration ports can be divided into two types: **basic** and **enhanced**. Out of the box, Microsoft Dynamics AX 2012 already has some services that are associated with basic integration ports. These have been deployed and enabled by default. We will discuss how these basic ports differ from enhanced ports in later chapters.

Instead of having Microsoft-Dynamics-AX-specific endpoints and channels, integration ports use native WCF to deploy services and therefore endpoints, security, behaviors, bindings, and so on. All of this is configured using the WCF Configuration utility. By default, integration ports are hosted on the AOS using the NetTcp binding.

IIS hosting without Business Connector

Previously, when services were deployed on IIS, they used the .NET Business Connector to communicate with the AOS. This has been replaced by a WCF routing service that implements the IRequestReplyRouter interface. Regardless of whether services are consumed from the intranet or the Internet, they are always processed by the AOS. So, when services are deployed to be used on the Internet, they will be deployed both on the AOS and on the IIS. The AOS hosts the service using the NetTcp binding, and the IIS has a WCF routing service that will forward service requests to the internal services hosted on the AOS.

Non-XML support

Using transformations, Microsoft Dynamics 2012 can transform inbound messages from a variety of formats into a format AIF can understand. Likewise, outbound messages can be transformed from the AIF format into a format required by external systems. There are two types of transformations that can be used: **Extensible Stylesheet Language Transformations (XSLT)** and **.NET assemblies**.

You can create XSLT transformations by using any text editor, but tools such as BizTalk MAPPER, Visual Studio, or Altova MapForce make it very easy. .NET assemblies are DLL files that can be compiled using Visual Studio and do transformations in code. This is especially convenient for transforming from or into a non-XML format. Some of the tools available can actually generate both the XSLT and the managed code needed to compile a .NET assembly.

AIF change tracking

In Microsoft Dynamics AX 2009, document services had a set of six operations available for use. They are as follows:

- Create
- Delete
- Find
- FindKeys
- Read
- Update

In Microsoft Dynamics AX 2012, there are two additional operations available for developers:

- GetKeys: This can be used in combination with a document filter to only obtain the keys of the documents that were the result of the filter.
- GetChangedKeys: This does the same as the GetKeys operation with the addition of a date and time being passed to the action. This way, only the keys of documents that have actually changed since that time are returned.

Custom services

One of the major changes in Microsoft Dynamics AX 2012 is the ease and flexibility by which you can create custom services. Instead of having to provide all the technical details on how the documents need to be serialized by implementing `AifSerializable`, you can now easily attribute class instance methods. These attributes are used to identify service operations and data contract members.

The SysOperation framework

Prior to Microsoft Dynamics AX 2012, the RunBase framework was used to provide a generic way to create processes and batch jobs in the system.

In Microsoft Dynamics AX 2012, the SysOperation framework allows you to leverage the power of services to execute your business logic in Microsoft Dynamics AX. When you create a service, it encapsulates the business logic so other components within the system can use the service instead of accessing the business logic themselves.

The SysOperation framework makes use of the **Model-view-controller** (**MVC**) pattern by using multiple components that each have their own responsibilities. These components separate the business logic from the code that is responsible for rendering the GUI and the classes that represent the data model. This is a great leap forward from Microsoft Dynamics AX 2009, where everything was written in one class that extended Runbase.

Also important to note is that, when a service has been created for the SysOperation framework, it requires little effort to expose the same service to the outside world. You can simply expose it using an integration port.

So the advantages of the SysOperation framework can be summarized as follows:

- It facilitates a service-oriented approach within Microsoft Dynamics AX
- It implements the MVC pattern for more efficient client/server communication and separation of responsibilities
- The GUI is automatically generated based on data contracts
- Less effort in exposing business functionality externally using services

Types of services

Microsoft Dynamics AX 2012 already provides a number of services out of the box. These services, together with additional services that can be developed, can be divided into three types. Each of the service types has its own characteristics and a different approach to create it.

Document services

Document services use documents to represent business objects such as purchase and sales orders, customers, and vendors.

A document service is composed of the following components:

- **Document query**: This is a query that is created in the **Application Object Tree (AOT)** and contains all the tables that are related to the business object that you want to expose. Based on this query, the Document Service Generation Wizard can be used to generate the other artifacts that make up the document service.

- **AxBC classes**: This class is a wrapper for a table and contains business logic that is needed for the **Create, Read, Update, and Delete (CRUD)** operations.

- **Document class**: The purpose of this class is to contain business logic that is associated with the creation and modification of the business entity itself. For example, the AxdCustomer class could contain logic to handle a customer's party information.

- **Document service class**: This is the actual service implementation class and extends the AifDocumentService class. This class implements the service operations that are published through the service contract.

When creating document services, developers need to make sure that the business object is mapped correctly to the document query. The document services framework will handle all other things, such as the serialization and deserialization of XML and date effectiveness.

Document services can be deployed using the integration ports and all available adapters can be used.

Custom services

Custom services were already available in Microsoft Dynamics AX 2009, but support for **Extended Data Types** (**EDTs**) was limited, which resulted in developers having to provide custom serialization and deserialization logic. Microsoft Dynamics AX 2012 introduces the concept of attributes. **Attributes** provide a way to specify metadata about classes and methods. Two of these attributes are used when creating data contracts: the `DataContractAttribute` and `DataMemberAttribute` attributes.

The `DataContractAttribute` attribute is used to define that a class is a data contract. The `DataMemberAttribute` attribute is added to methods of data contracts representing data members that have to be exposed. This way of defining data contracts is very similar to other programming languages such as C#.

Support for more complex datatypes such as collections and tables has been added so that these types can be serialized and deserialized without developers having to provide the logic themselves.

In a typical custom service, you will find the following components:

- **Service contract**: A service contract is an X++ class that contains methods with the `SysEntryPointAttribute` attribute. This identifies methods that will result in a service operation contract when the service is exposed.

- **Data contracts**: A data contract is an X++ class that is attributed with the `DataContractAttribute` attribute. It contains parameter methods that will be attributed as data members for each member variable that needs to be part of the data contract.

Custom services can be deployed using the integration ports and any available adapter can be used.

System services

These services are new since the release of Microsoft Dynamics AX 2012. The main difference between these services and the previous two types is that they are not customizable and are not mapped to a query or X++ code. They are not customizable because they are written by Microsoft in managed code. One exception is the user session service, which is written in X++ code but is generally considered as a system service.

There are four system services available for use in Microsoft Dynamics AX 2012: the query service, the metadata service, the user session service, and the OData query service.

The query service

The query service provides the means to run queries of the following three types:

- Static queries defined in the AOT.

- User-defined queries by using the `QueryMetaData` class in the service.

- Dynamic queries that are written in X++ classes. These classes need to extend the `AIFQueryBuilder` class.

When queries are called by a service, the AOS authorization ensures that the caller has the correct permissions to retrieve the information. This means that unpermitted fields will be omitted from the query result. Furthermore, when joined data sources are not allowed to be used, the query call will result in an error that can be caught by the calling application.

The resulting rows will be returned as an ADO.NET DataSet object. This can be very useful when you make use of controls in your application that can be bound to a DataSet object.

The query service can be found at the following link:
`net.tcp://<hostname:port>/DynamicsAX/Services/QueryService`

The metadata service

This system service can be used to retrieve metadata information about the AOT. Consumers of this service can get information such as which tables, classes, forms, and menu items are available in the system. An example use case for this service is when retrieving information about the AOT and using it in a dashboard application running on the Microsoft .NET Framework. We will create an example dashboard application in *Chapter 7, System Services*, where we will use this service to look up queries in the AOT.

The metadata service can be found at `net.tcp://<hostname:port>/DynamicsAX/Services/MetaDataService`.

The user session service

The third system service is the user session service. With this service, you can retrieve information about the caller's user session. This information includes the user's default company, language, preferred calendar, time zone, and currency.

The user session service can be found at the following link:
`net.tcp://<hostname:port>/DynamicsAX/Services/UserSessionService`

The OData query service

The OData query service is a REST-based service that uses the OData protocol to expose the results of a query object in the AOT in an Atom feed. **Open Data Protocol (OData)** is a web protocol that allows CRUD operations, but the Microsoft Dynamics AX 2012 implementation only supports reading data.

The OData query service can be found at the following link:
`http://<hostname:port>/DynamicsAX/Services/ODataQueryService`

> **What is a RESTful web service?**
>
> **Representational State Transfer (REST)** represents a set of design principles by which web services are developed. For more details about REST, you can go to the following link: `http://www.ibm.com/developerworks/webservices/library/ws-restful/`

Choosing the right service for the job

Now that it is clear what types of services Microsoft Dynamics AX 2012 has to offer, the question arises as to when each type of service should be used. There is no simple answer for this due to the fact that every type has its strengths and weaknesses. Let us take a look at two factors that may help you make the right decision.

Complexity

Both document services and custom services can handle any business entity complexity. The document services framework parses the incoming XML and validates it against an **XML Schema Definition (XSD)** document. After validation, the framework calls the appropriate service action.

Custom services, on the other hand, use the .NET XMLSerializer class and no validation of data is done. This means that any validations of the data in the data contract need to be written in code. Using custom services, you not only have to code all validation, but also all the other business logic. When working with data from the database, this puts custom services at a disadvantage because document services use AxBC and document classes that already contain a lot of the logic needed for CRUD operations.

Flexibility

Document services have service contracts that are tightly coupled with the AOT Query object. This means that when the query changes, the schema also changes. Data policies allow you to control which fields are exposed. When using custom services, this cannot be done by setup, but has to be done at design time.

Custom services have flexibility towards the service contract, while document services lack such flexibility. Here, the developer is in full control of what is in the contract and what is not. The operations, input parameters, and return types are all the responsibility of the developer.

Another benefit of using custom services is the ability to use shared data contracts as parameters for your operations. Think of a company-wide software solution that involves the use of Microsoft Dynamics AX 2012 together with SharePoint and .NET applications that are all linked through BizTalk. You could opt to share data contracts to make sure that entities are the same for all of the components in the architecture.

In that scenario, you're able to create a data contract in managed code and reference it in Microsoft Dynamics AX 2012. Then you can use that .NET data contract in your service operations as a parameter.

There will probably be more factors that you will take into consideration to choose between the service types, but we can come to the following conclusion about when to use which type of service:

- **Custom services**: These should be used when exposing entities that have a low complexity or data contracts that need to be shared between other applications. They are also ideal when custom logic needs to be exposed that may have nothing to do with data structures within Microsoft Dynamics AX.

- **Document services**: These should be used when exposing entities that have high complexity and when validation of the data and structure would require a lot of work for developers to implement on their own.

- **Query service**: This should be used only when read operations are needed and there is no need for updates, inserts, or delete actions. It can be used when writing .NET Framework applications that leverage the data from Microsoft Dynamics AX and are returned as an ADO.NET DataSet.

- **Metadata service**: This service should be used when metadata information about objects in the AOT is required.

- **User session service**: This should be used when user-session-related information is required.

- **OData query service**: The OData query service can be used when you want to expose data from AX over HTTP using the OData protocol. This allows for compatibility with other applications that support OData, such as the PowerPivot add-in for Microsoft Excel.

Summary

In this first chapter, we went through the major changes that Microsoft Dynamics AX 2012 brings for services architecturally and saw that a lot has changed because of the WCF support.

Looking at the new features that were added, it is clear that Microsoft has provided us with a lot of new tools and methods for integration. A lot of work has been done to enable developers to expose business logic in a more intuitive way using attributes. The setup is simplified, and the system services allow you to build entire applications without the need for development in X++.

There are a lot of options to choose from, so it is not always easy to choose the right approach for your implementation. In this book, you will get to know all of the features to help you to make the best choice.

In the next chapter, we will look at the service architecture in more detail and review the many options that are available when deploying services.

2
Service Architecture and Deployment

There is always more than one solution to a problem. This is certainly true when designing solutions for your integration scenarios with Microsoft Dynamics AX 2012. As we learned in the previous chapter, there are a lot of options to choose from, both for deployment and development of services. In this chapter, we will focus on the options that are available when deploying services.

The following topics are covered in this chapter:

- **WCF**: Windows Communication Foundation provides the basis for building, configuring, and deploying services with Microsoft Dynamics AX 2012, so we will discuss the key concepts that are related to WCF.

- **Service deployment**: Deployment of services is enabled by integration ports. You will learn how to create, configure, and deploy these integration ports.

- **Service generation**: There is a lot going on when services are deployed. We will explore the artifacts that are generated and learn about Common Intermediate Language.

Introducing WCF

Windows Communication Foundation (WCF) was introduced with the release of .NET Framework 3.0. This release of the .NET framework was in essence Version 2.0 along with four additional components:

- Windows Presentation Foundation (UI graphical platform)
- Windows CardSpace (identity management platform)

- Windows Workflow Foundation (workflow platform)
- Windows Communication Foundation (communication platform)

Existing technologies

WCF is meant to provide a unified programming model to build, configure, and deploy services on distributed networks. It combines well-known technologies that have been around for some time, such as .NET remoting, **Web Services Enhancements** (**WSE**), MSMQ, ASMX, and message-oriented programming.

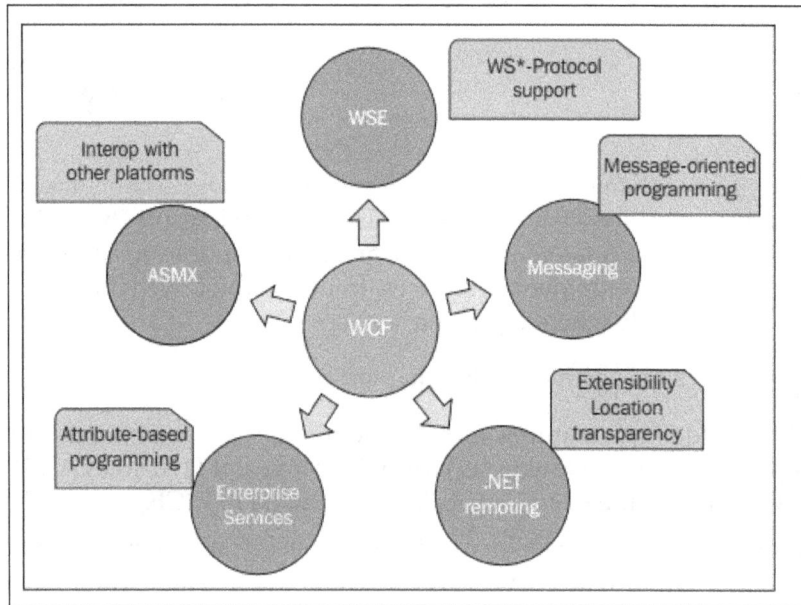

[The preceding diagram is provided courtesy of wcftutorial.net. If our introduction to WCF makes you curious about WCF and its technologies, this website does a great job of explaining it in detail.]

The ABC of WCF

An elaborate explanation of all of the features that WCF has to offer is not in the scope of this book because it would take us too long to cover them all. However, one of the important concepts to review is the **ABC of WCF**. Each service has endpoints through which communication is possible, and an endpoint has the following properties:

- **Address**: The endpoint address can be used to tell consumers where the service can be found. It consists of a **Unified Resource Identifier** (**URI**).

- **Binding**: The binding actually defines how communication is done. It defines the protocol, security, and encoding required for services and clients to be able to communicate with each other.

- **Contract**: Contracts are used to define what can be communicated. The following are the three types of contracts:

  ○ **Service contracts**: These describe the service functionality that is exposed to external systems

  ○ **Operation contracts**: These define the actual operations that will be available on the service

  ○ **Data contracts**: These are used to shape the data that will be exchanged by the operations of the service

The following diagram sums it up. On one side, you have the client, and on the other, a service. This service has one or more endpoints that each consist of an address, a binding, and a contract. After adding a reference to the endpoint on the client side, the client becomes aware of the ABC, and messages can be exchanged.

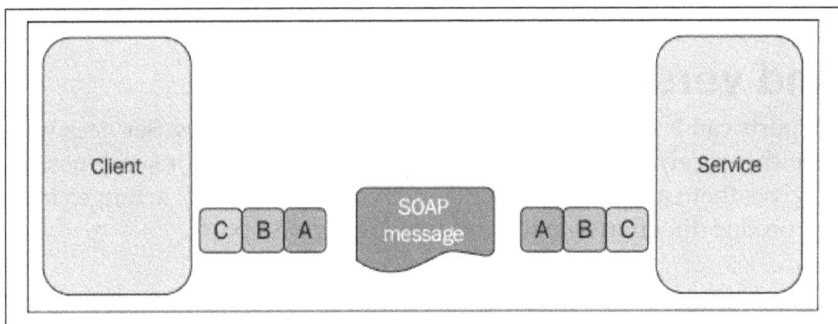

Service deployment

Microsoft Dynamics AX 2012 does a lot to simplify service deployment; not so much by reducing the number of concepts, but by gradually presenting these concepts to users when needed. This is immediately obvious when you look at the setup menu for services and AIF. When you navigate to **System administration | Setup | Services and Application Integration Framework**, you only see four options. The first two are the most important: inbound ports and outbound ports. These two types of ports are known as integration ports.

Integration ports provide a way to group services and manage them together. They have at least the following properties:

- One or more service operations
- A direction that is inbound or outbound
- A category that is either basic or enhanced
- An adapter
- The address of the port

We will discuss these properties and others in detail.

Service operations

An integration port contains one or more service operations. These must be operations from services that all have the same type. This means that you shouldn't mix operations from document services and custom services because this can cause problems with the WSDL generation.

Inbound versus outbound ports

Integration ports can be thought of as destinations for messages. Services within these ports either receive messages from external applications or send messages to them. This gives them a direction. Microsoft Dynamics AX 2012 arranges integration ports based on this direction into inbound and outbound ports.

Inbound ports

Inbound ports are identified as integration ports that receive messages that originate outside of Microsoft Dynamics AX 2012. In other words, the destination for the message is Microsoft Dynamics AX 2012. One example of when to use an inbound port (discussed later in this book) is when we create a WCF service and consume it in a .NET application.

Outbound ports

An outbound port is a destination for a message that originates from inside Microsoft Dynamics AX. In other words, it is used when you want to send a message to an external application based on an action in Microsoft Dynamics AX 2012. You can use outbound ports with asynchronous adapters such as the MSMQ and filesystem adapter.

Basic versus enhanced ports

Integration ports can exist in two categories: **basic** and **enhanced**. Outbound ports are always enhanced ports. Inbound ports can be either basic or enhanced.

Basic ports

Basic ports can only be created by developers because they are linked to a service group. They are created in the **Service Groups** node in the **Application Object Tree (AOT)**. Services are added to the group, and after the service group has been deployed, a basic integration port is created, which exposes all of the service operations from the group. All basic ports are inbound ports that are hosted on the AOS and use the NetTcp adapter. The WCF configuration editor allows you to change the WCF options; but apart from that, there are few options you can set up. Although this makes basic ports somewhat limited in their functionality, it has the advantage of getting your services up and running in no time.

There are a number of services that come with Microsoft Dynamics AX 2012 that are deployed by default. You can find these in the **Inbound Ports** form.

Creating a basic port

If you were to press the **New** button in the **Inbound Ports** form, you would not create a basic port, but an enhanced port. To create a basic port, we will have to open a developer workspace and perform the following steps:

1. Open the AOT.
2. Go to the **Service Groups** node, right-click on it, and click on **New Service Group**.
3. A new service group will be created. Right-click on it and select **Properties**.
4. In the **Properties** screen, change the name to SRVTestBasicServiceGroup.
5. In the **Description** property, you can specify a meaningful label. This won't show up anywhere, so this is not mandatory.
6. Next, right-click on the service group and then click on **New Service Node Reference**.
7. In the **Properties** screen, click on the **Service** property and select a service you want to deploy from the list.
8. Click on **Save All** in the AOT to save your changes.
9. To deploy the service group, right-click on the service group and then click on **Deploy Service Group**.

After a few moments, you will see an Infolog message letting you know that all service artifacts have been generated and that your service group is deployed and activated. Your service is now visible in the **Inbound ports** form and is ready to be consumed.

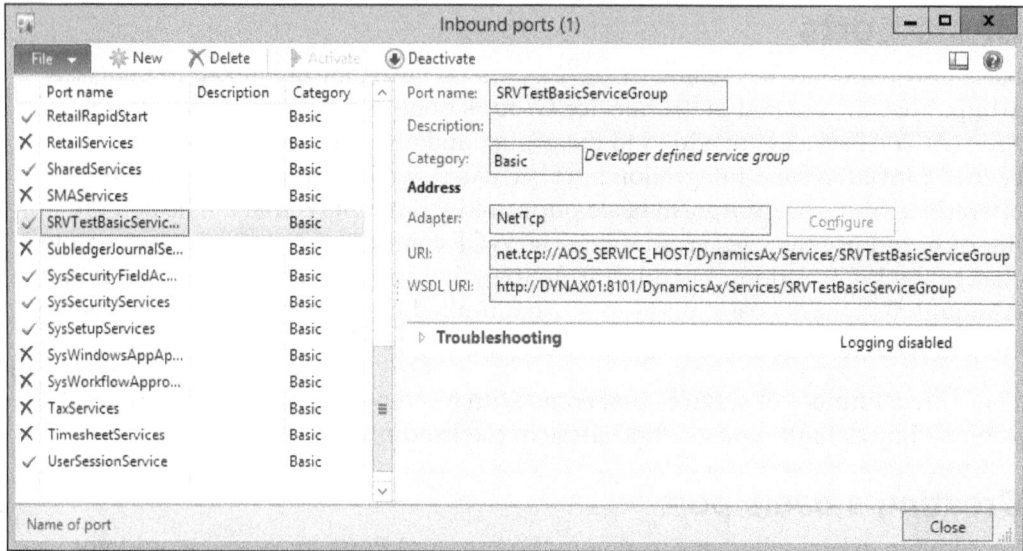

> An interesting property on the service group node is the **AutoDeploy** property. Setting this to **Yes** will automatically deploy and activate the port when the AOS is started.

Enhanced ports

As the name suggests, enhanced ports provide more options than basic ports. Unlike basic ports, they are not tied to service groups, but can be created in the **Inbound Ports** and **Outbound Ports** forms. Before we take a look at the options that are available on enhanced ports, let us first create an enhanced port.

Creating an enhanced port

Almost all options that are available on outbound ports are available on inbound ports too. Inbound ports have more options, so for this demonstration, we will create an inbound port.

Before we create the port, we need to ensure that all services are registered within the system. Registering services will insert a record in the `AifService` table for each service and insert a record in the `AifAction` table for each service operation. These records are then used to populate lookups and lists on the forms while setting up services.

To register services, perform the following steps:

1. Navigate to **System administration | Setup | Checklists | Initialization checklist**.
2. Expand the **Initialize system** section.
3. Click on **Set up Application Integration Framework** to register services and adapters.

You should register services if you are using AIF for the first time or if you've added new services or service operations in the AOT. This process will also register all adapters and basic ports.

Now, to create an enhanced inbound port, let's perform the following steps:

1. Navigate to **System administration | Setup | Services and Application Integration Framework | Inbound ports**.
2. Click on the **New** button or press *Ctrl + N* to create a new enhanced port.
3. In the **Port name** field, enter `SRVTestEnhancedInboundPort`.
4. Enter a description in the **Description** field so that you can easily identify the port later.
5. On the **Service contract customizations** FastTab, click on **Service operations**. The **Select service operations** form opens.
6. From the **Remaining service operations** list, select the **DocumentHandlingService.create** operation and click on the arrow pointing to the left to add this operation to the **Selected service operations** list.
7. Close the form.
8. Click on the **Activate** button to deploy the port.

Your enhanced port is now successfully created and activated. You cannot modify the configuration of activated ports. To modify the configuration, first deactivate the port by clicking on the **Deactivate** button.

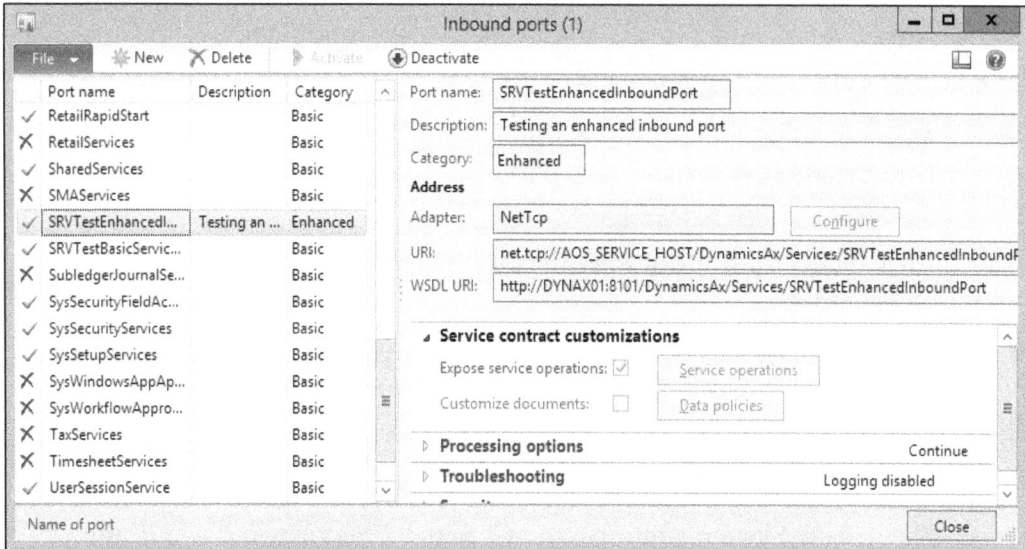

Now that we've created an enhanced port, let's look at the options that are available on the form.

Adapters

While basic ports only support the NetTcp adapter, enhanced ports allow you to specify which adapter you want to use. There are three WCF adapters to choose from: the NetTcp, HTTP, and MSMQ adapters. To exchange messages using filesystem directories, the filesystem adapter is also available. We will go into more detail about these adapters later in this chapter.

Service operations

With enhanced ports, you can manually select which service operations are to be exposed. This is unlike basic ports, where all service operations of the services within the service group are exposed.

Data policies

For custom services, the developer defines the parameters that are exposed in the data contract. This is reflected in WSDL when the data contract is used to generate the XSD schema for the type definition. The only way to change this schema is by changing the data contract in the code.

While exposing document services, you can change the schema that is generated using data policies. Enabling or disabling fields in the data policies will add or remove fields in the schema, allowing you to manage which fields are exposed or not. It is also possible to mark fields as required.

Transforms

Transforms allow you to transform inbound and outbound messages that are exchanged asynchronously. This transformation applies to the complete message, including the headers. For inbound exchanges, the transforms are applied before the message is stored in the gateway queue. For outbound exchanges, transforms are applied after the message has been fetched from the gateway queue. The following are the two types of transforms that are available:

- **XSL**: You can use **Extensible Stylesheet Language Transformations (XSLT)** to transform any XML-based document to an XML document that uses the AIF schema or vice versa.

- **.NET assembly**: When a document is not based on XML, for example, a text file with **comma-separated values (CSV)**, you can use a .NET assembly to convert the file into an XML message that complies with the AIF schema. This assembly is a DLL that contains a class that implements the `ITransform` interface and contains the code that transforms the message.

Pipelines

Pipelines are a lot like transforms, but there are a few differences. They allow you to transform contents of the message instead of the full message and can be used for both synchronous and asynchronous exchanges. They are also run before or after the transforms, depending on the direction. The following table explains the difference between transforms and pipelines:

Property	Transforms	Pipelines
What it processes	The full message including header and body	Only the body of the message
Runs for inbound	Before a message is stored in the gateway queue and before pipelines	After a message is retrieved from the gateway queue and after transforms
Runs for outbound	After a message is retrieved from the gateway queue and after pipelines	Before a message is stored in the gateway queue and before transforms
Mode supported	Asynchronous	Synchronous and asynchronous

There are two types of pipelines available; these are as follows:

- **XSL**: This is similar to transforms that use XSL, except that the XSL is only applied to the body of the message.

- **Value substitution**: The value substitution pipeline component allows you to replace one value with another based on a simple lookup table. For example, when messages are sent to a vendor, you can replace your currency code with the currency code of your vendor; for example, EUR versus EURO. When the direction is inbound, you can substitute in the opposite manner. The value substitution is based on **Extended Data Types (EDTs)**. A value substitution map must be created, which contains a mapping between the internal and external value for a specific EDT. These maps are set up in the following form: **System administration | Setup | Services and Application Integration Framework | Value substitution maps**.

You can easily create your own pipeline components by creating an X++ class that implements the `AifPipelineComponentInterface` interface.

Value mapping

Value mapping is similar to the value substitution pipelines, but it differs by allowing you to substitute values based on business rules. For example, you can replace your item ID with the item number that is used by a vendor.

Document filters

Document filters can be used to filter the keys that are returned while calling the service operations `getKeys` and `getChangedKeys` based on the query you provide. These filters will only be applied when change tracking is activated. There's more about this when we create a document service.

Troubleshooting

On the troubleshooting FastTab, you can enable logging for messages. When activated, the following three options are available:

- **Original document**: When selected, only the original document before modification by pipeline components is stored

- **All document versions**: When selected, a version of the document is stored every time a document is modified by a pipeline component

- **Message header only**: When selected, only the headers of the documents are stored

To consult the log, navigate to **System administration | Periodic | Services and Application Integration Framework | History**.

There is also the option to provide more information about exceptions in AIF faults and the ability to send error messages for asynchronous requests.

Security

On the security FastTab, you can limit integration ports to only process requests for specific companies instead of for all companies. Access can also be configured to allow access only for certain users and user groups. For added security, be sure to set these options as strict as possible.

Bindings

When a client and service communicate, there are several aspects to the communication.

- **Synchronous/asynchronous**: Messages can be used in a request/response pattern or they can be used in asynchronous communication depending on whether the client waits for the response or not.

- **Transport protocol**: The protocol used for transporting the messages can vary depending on the needs. Protocols such as HTTP, **Transmission Control Protocol (TCP)**, **Microsoft Message Queuing (MSMQ)**, and **Inter-process communication (IPC)** can be used.

- **Encoding**: You have a choice on how to encode the messages. You can choose to use plain text if you want maximum interoperability. Alternatively, you can use binary encoding to speed up performance, or using the **Message Transport Optimization Mechanism (MTOM)** to handle larger payloads.

- **Security**: There are also some options that can be used to handle security and authentication. Security can be implemented at the transport level, at the message level, or can be skipped altogether.

As you can imagine, keeping track of all of the options can be a little difficult, and making the right choice on how to configure the different settings is not easy. To solve this, WCF introduces bindings. A **binding** is merely a grouping of choices that deal with each aspect of the communication that we just discussed.

WCF supports several bindings out of the box. If these do not suffice, there is always the alternative of creating a custom binding of your own. The following are the most commonly used bindings:

- `NetTcpBinding`: This uses the TCP protocol and is mainly used for cross-machine communication over an intranet. It is WCF-optimized and thus requires both the client and the server to use WCF.

- `BasicHttpBinding`: This binding is used to expose a service as an ASMX web service so that older clients that comply with WS-I Basic Profile 1.1 are supported.

- `WsHttpBinding`: This binding is used for communication over the Internet. It uses the HTTP and HTTPS protocols and complies with `ws-*` standards. So, any party that supports the `ws-*` standards is able to communicate with the service.

- `NetMsmqBinding`: This type of binding will be used when support is needed for MSMQ queues. The `NetMsmqBinding` binding is actually a compact binding that does not provide all of the possible options to configure MSMQ. There are other bindings that provide more options.

Now that we have elaborated on some of the out-of-the-box bindings, you are probably asking yourself, how can I make sure I'm using the appropriate binding for my scenario? Well, the following flowchart may help you with this choice:

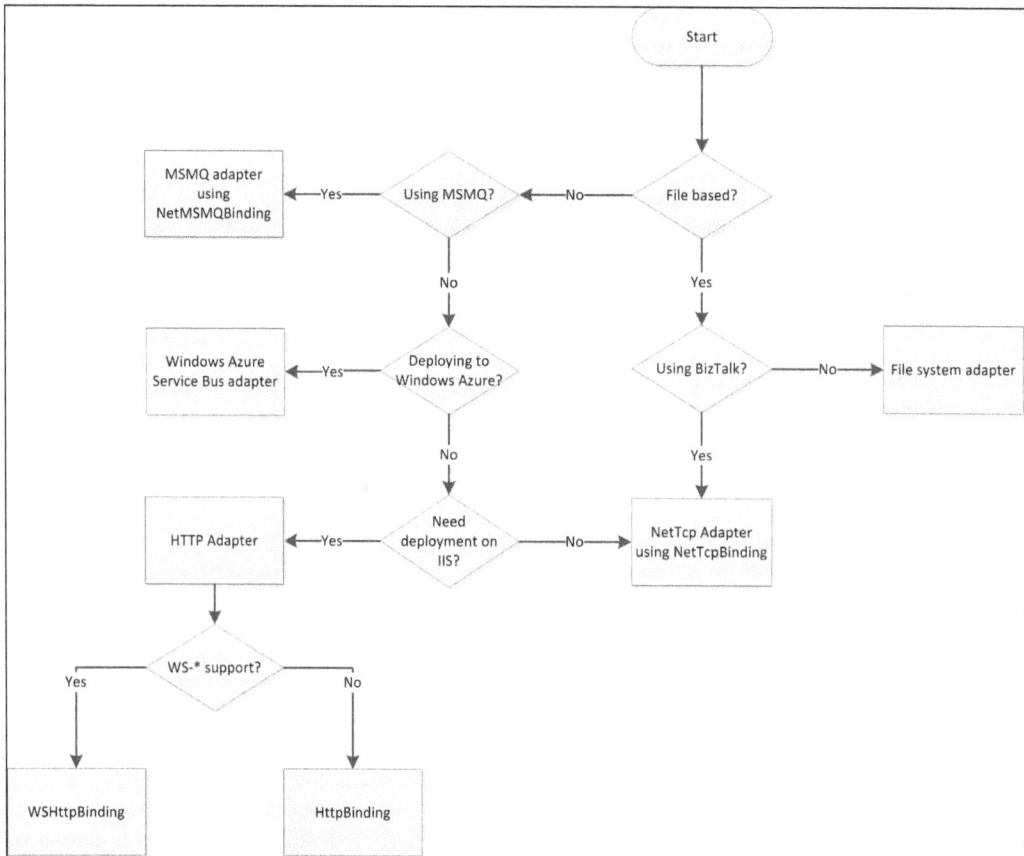

Adapters

Microsoft Dynamics AX 2012 allows you to exchange messages using various transport protocols. This is enabled by the use of adapters. An adapter has an adapter type that determines if it can be used on an inbound port, an outbound port, or both. The standard adapter types that are used are **send and receive**, **receive or send**, and **receive and respond**. The naming of these types is rather confusing, but the following table shows how this translates to inbound or outbound ports:

Adapter name	Adapter type	Inbound	Outbound	Mode
NetTcp	Send and receive	Yes	No	Synchronous
HTTP	Send and receive	Yes	No	Synchronous
Windows Azure Service Bus	Receive and respond	Yes	No	Synchronous/Asynchronous
Filesystem adapter	Receive or send	Yes	Yes	Asynchronous
MSMQ	Receive or send	Yes	Yes	Asynchronous

Adapters also have an address property. This address is a URI that refers to the destination or source location of the port. Depending on the adapter, this is a URL, a filesystem path, or a message queue format name.

The NetTcp adapter

The NetTcp adapter is the only adapter that can be used on basic ports. On enhanced ports, the NetTcp adapter is only supported for inbound ports. This adapter type corresponds to the WCF `NetTcpBinding` and provides synchronous message exchanges by using `WS-*` standards over the TCP.

The NetTcp adapter is used for communication with other WCF applications hosted on an intranet.

The HTTP adapter

The HTTP adapter supports synchronous message exchanges over HTTP. When an integration port that uses this adapter is activated, a WCF routing service is deployed on IIS. This routing service routes all requests to the WCF services that are hosted on the AOS.

The HTTP adapter can be used for synchronous communication when the NetTcp adapter is not an option because of interoperability issues or because the services have to be available on the Internet.

The filesystem adapter

The filesystem adapter is used for the asynchronous exchange of messages using files that are stored on the filesystem. The exchange is asynchronous because it uses the AIF gateway queue to store both incoming and outgoing messages. A batch job is needed to process this queue. Files are then read from or written to a directory on the filesystem.

The filesystem adapter can be used when there is a need to import or export files. The filesystem adapter supports non-XML files by using transformations. This adapter can also be used to decrease the load on the system, improving performance. Instead of handling requests synchronously during working hours by using the NetTcp or HTTP adapter, messages can be processed asynchronously in batches during the nights or over the weekends.

The MSMQ adapter

The MSMQ adapter provides support for message queuing using MSMQ. This adapter is actually a WCF adapter that uses `NetMsmqBinding`. Like the filesystem adapter, this adapter exchanges messages asynchronously and can therefore be used to decrease the load during working hours.

The Windows Azure Service Bus adapter

A new addition to Microsoft Dynamics AX 2012 R2 CU7, **Service Bus** is a messaging service that is provided by the Windows Azure platform. It provides a secure way to create cloud applications that connect over public networks to Microsoft Dynamics AX. When a service is deployed using this adapter, it is exposed on IIS using the WCF routing service, as is the case with the HTTP adapter. This service then listens to Service Bus for messages sent by clients, forwards these messages to the services hosted on the AOS, and sends a response back to Service Bus. Security is provided by tokens that are handed out by an identity provider such as **Active Directory Federation Services (AD FS)**.

Custom adapters

Having all of these features available, it's hard to imagine that you would need another adapter. When you do have a scenario that cannot be covered with the standard adapters, consider bringing Microsoft BizTalk Server into the picture. Among many other things, BizTalk can act as an intermediary between Microsoft Dynamics AX 2012 and an external application using any of the adapters that we just described. When this still doesn't fit your needs, you can always create your own adapter. You can do this by implementing the `AIFIntegrationAdapter` interface.

Service generation - under the hood

While services are being deployed when activating integration ports, there is more going on than meets the eye. A service generator written in X++ kicks in and creates the artifacts needed by the AOS to host the WCF services. These artifacts are files containing managed code (C#) and contain the service implementation, message contracts, and a WCF configuration. To explain this, we will take a closer look at one of the out-of-the-box integration ports: the `DocumentHandling` port.

Generated artifacts

When you take a look at the `DocumentHandlingService` service node in the AOT, you will find that this service has one method called `Create()`. So, when we deploy this service, we expect the following generated artifacts to be able to host the WCF service:

- A service contract that contains the service's interface
- An operation contract for the `Create` service operation
- Request and response message contracts for each operation used for implementing the `Create` operation
- A DLL file containing all of the previous artifacts

All of these generated artifacts can be found in the filesystem directory under `%ProgramFiles%\Microsoft Dynamics AX\60\Server\<Server Name>\bin\XppIL\AppShare\ServiceGeneration\<Integration Port Name>`.

Service contract and implementation

The service contract definition and implementation can be found in the
DocumentHandlingService.cs file. The service contract is a reflection of the
DocumentHandlingService class that can be found in the AOT. The following
code shows the part of the source file that defines the interface:

```
[ServiceKnownType("GetKnownTypes", typeof(ServiceHelper))]
[ServiceContract(Name = "DocumentHandlingService", Namespace="http://
schemas.microsoft.com/dynamics/2011/01/services")]
public interface DocumentHandlingService
{

    [OperationContract(Name="create")]
    [FaultContract(typeof(AifFault))]
    DocumentHandlingServiceCreateResponse Create(
DocumentHandlingServiceCreateRequest createRequest);

}
```

Let's take a closer look at the code of the service interface:

```
[ServiceContract(Name = "DocumentHandlingService", Namespace="http://
schemas.microsoft.com/dynamics/2011/01/services")]
```

The previous line of code states that the interface that follows this attribute is the
service's contract. The name of the contract and the namespace in the WSDL are also
defined as follows:

```
[OperationContract(Name="create")]
[FaultContract(typeof(AifFault))]
DocumentHandlingServiceCreateResponse Create(
DocumentHandlingServiceCreateRequest createRequest);
```

By using the OperationContract attribute, the previous statement defines that
the Create() method is a service operation. It also attributes the type of WCF
FaultContract that will be thrown if exceptions occur when this operation
is called. For Microsoft Dynamics AX WCF services, this will always be the
AifFault fault contract.

As for the `Create` operation itself, the `Create()` method has been generated to make use of a `DocumentHandlingServiceCreateRequest` message contract as the input parameter. The return type of the operation is also a message contract of the type `DocumentHandlingServiceCreateResponse`. Whether this return contract is actually used in the WCF client depends on whether the service reference is configured to generate message contract types on the client side.

A bit further in the file, we find the actual implementation of the `DocumentHandlingService` service interface as shown in the following code snippet:

```
public partial class DocumentHandling : ServiceGroup,
DocumentHandlingService
{
    DocumentHandlingServiceCreateResponse DocumentHandlingService.Crea
te(DocumentHandlingServiceCreateRequest createRequest)
    {
        // Implementation code omitted
    }
}
```

The previous code shows the class implementing the `DocumentHandlingService` interface and the actual implementation of the `Create()` method.

Message contracts

WCF uses SOAP messages to communicate. SOAP is a protocol that sends XML messages. It uses an envelope to define what will be put in a message and how to process it. The SOAP envelope contains a header and a body.

In WCF, message contracts are used to provide more control to the developer over the structure of the SOAP message. Although Microsoft Dynamics AX 2012 does not allow developers to create message contracts, they are generated by the service generator. This is important because a call context is included in the message contract that allows clients to pass contextual information specific to Microsoft Dynamics AX, such as the message ID, the calling user, the company, and the language in which the messages are displayed.

Message contracts should not be confused with data contracts. While message contracts determine the structure of the SOAP message by providing a mapping between the types and the SOAP message, data contracts are used to serialize the types that are used within the message contract.

The `MessageHeader` attribute is used to specify that a member is part of the SOAP header. In the following example, this is the case for the call context member. For the rest of the members, the `MessageBodyMember` attribute is used as follows to specify that the member will be part of the body of the SOAP message:

```
[MessageContract]
public class DocumentHandlingServiceCreateRequest
{
    [MessageHeader(Name = "CallContext", Namespace = "http://schemas.
microsoft.com/dynamics/2010/01/datacontracts")]
    public Microsoft.Dynamics.Ax.Services.CallContext context;

    [MessageBodyMember(Order=1)]
    public DocumentFileList _documentFileList;

    [MessageBodyMember(Order=2)]
    public DocuValueType _docuValueType;

    [MessageBodyMember(Order=3)]
    public Boolean _submitToWorkflow;
}
```

WCF configuration storage

WCF services can be configured by using configuration files. The advantage of using configuration files is that they can be configured at the time of deployment instead of at the time of designing.

The configuration is done in XML by providing elements that configure details such as the bindings, behaviors, and endpoint addresses that are used to communicate with the service. You can also use a configuration file to specify diagnostics elements to enable tracing and logging.

Microsoft Dynamics AX also creates a configuration file to accompany the deployed service. Developers can modify the contents of this configuration file by using the WCF configuration tool, which can be started by clicking on the **Configure** button on the integration port form, as shown in the following screenshot. The scope of the WCF configuration tool will not be discussed in this book as it would be far too detailed.

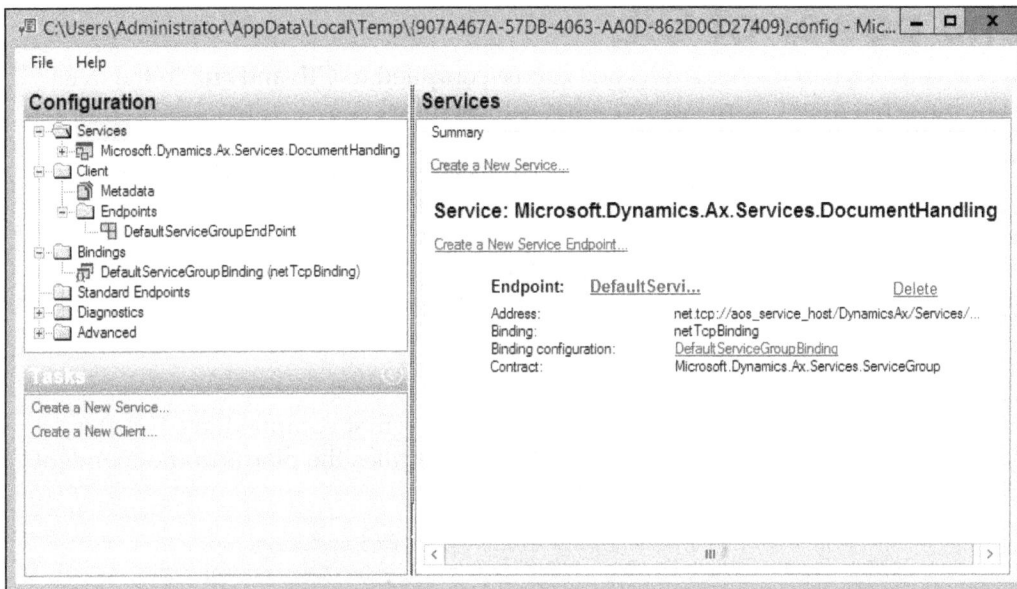

Once the configuration is saved, Microsoft Dynamics AX will save the XML contents of the file in the `AifWcfConfiguration` table in the AOT. When the **Configure** button is used the next time, this content will be opened by the configuration tool.

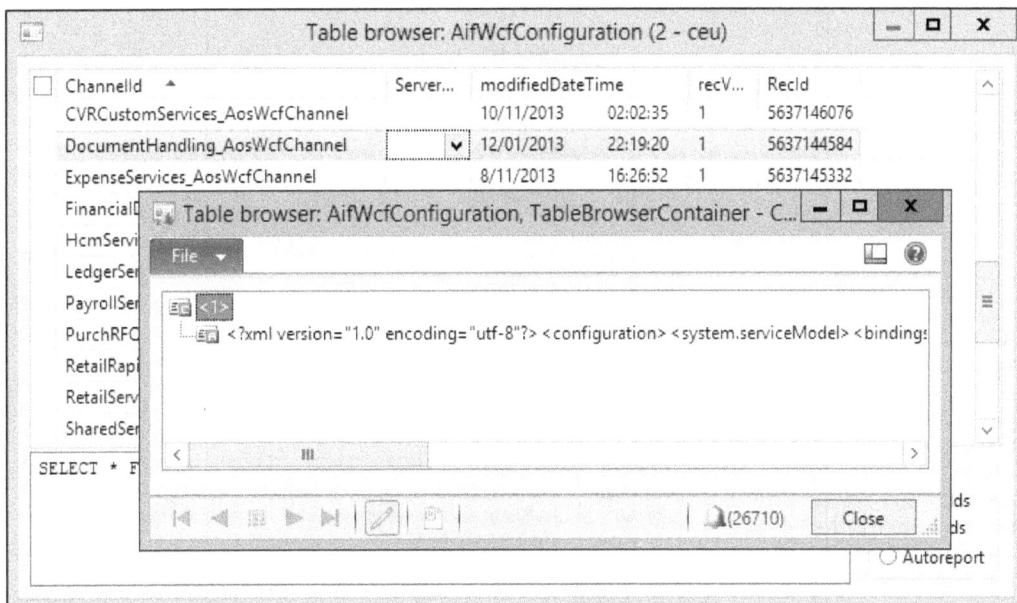

The power of CIL

In Microsoft Dynamics AX 2012, code can be compiled to CIL and run in the .NET CLR. But what does CIL mean and what is it used for?

Common Intermediate Language (**CIL**) is in essence an object-oriented assembly language. It complies with the **Common Language Infrastructure** (**CLI**), which is a specification that was developed by Microsoft to describe a set of rules that programming languages need to comply with when they are targeting the CLI. One of the most important aspects of the CIL is that it is a platform- and CPU-independent instruction set. This enables the code to be executed on different environments as long as they comply with the CLI specification.

The following diagram shows that the languages are first compiled in CIL, after which the **Common Language Runtime** (**CLR**) compiles the platform-independent CIL code into machine-readable code:

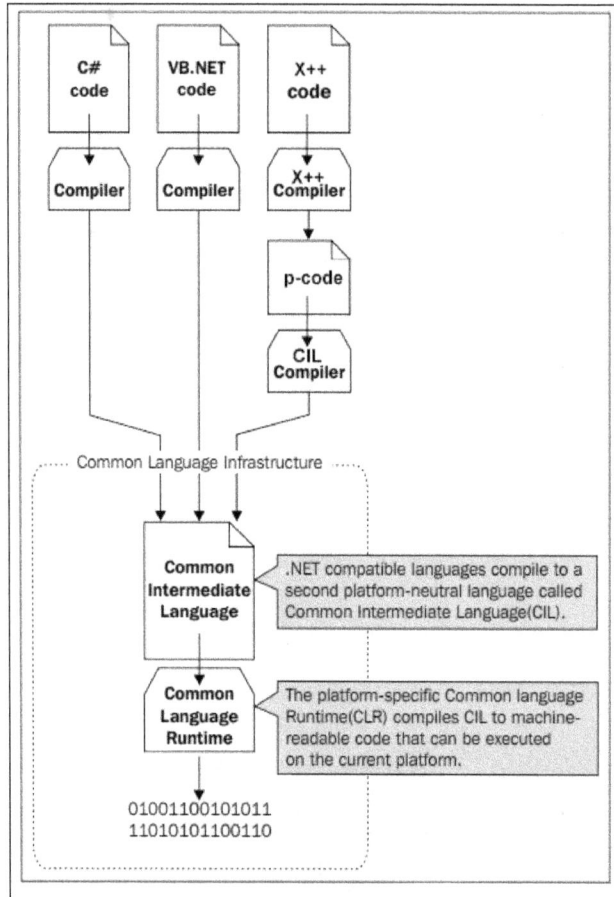

As you can see, Microsoft Dynamics AX 2012 does not compile the X++ code directly to CIL. It is compiled to p-code, which can be interpreted by the kernel first, and this p-code is then compiled to CIL. This is quite a step forward because CIL is much faster than X++. We also need to keep CIL in mind when developing services later on. Code that runs on the server, such as batch jobs and services, will run in CIL, and therefore the X++ code needs to be compiled to CIL.

As compilation into CIL takes a long time, it is not done automatically when the X++ code is compiled. We need to do this manually when code has been modified by using the new CIL compilation buttons in the developer workspace, as shown in the following screenshot:

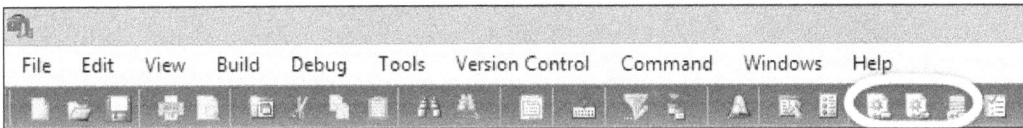

You can either start a full CIL generation or an incremental one. The main difference between the two is that incremental generation only regenerates the objects that were modified since the previous generation, while full generation completely regenerates all objects. As you can imagine, the incremental process is much faster than the full process, but do keep in mind that incremental generation will not always be enough. Sometimes, you will have no option than to completely regenerate CIL, for example, when you have removed a method from a class. No matter how you look at it, compiling CIL is not optional; without CIL, your services cannot run!

CIL output

So, now the CIL generation is done, but what has changed and where can we find the results of the process? The answers to these questions can be found in the server's `bin` directory. By default, the filesystem folder is `%ProgramFiles%\Microsoft Dynamics AX\60\Server\<Server Name>\bin\XppIL\`. In this folder, you can find the resulting `Dynamics.Ax.Application.dll` assembly file along with a list of NetModule files.

NetModule files differ from .NET assemblies as they do not contain an assembly manifest. They only contain type metadata and compiled code. Next to the files containing the CIL code, this folder may also contain a subfolder named `source`. In this folder, we can find files with the `.xpp` extension. These files contain the X++ source code, and they can be used while debugging the CIL code in Visual Studio so that the editor and debugger can show the actual source code.

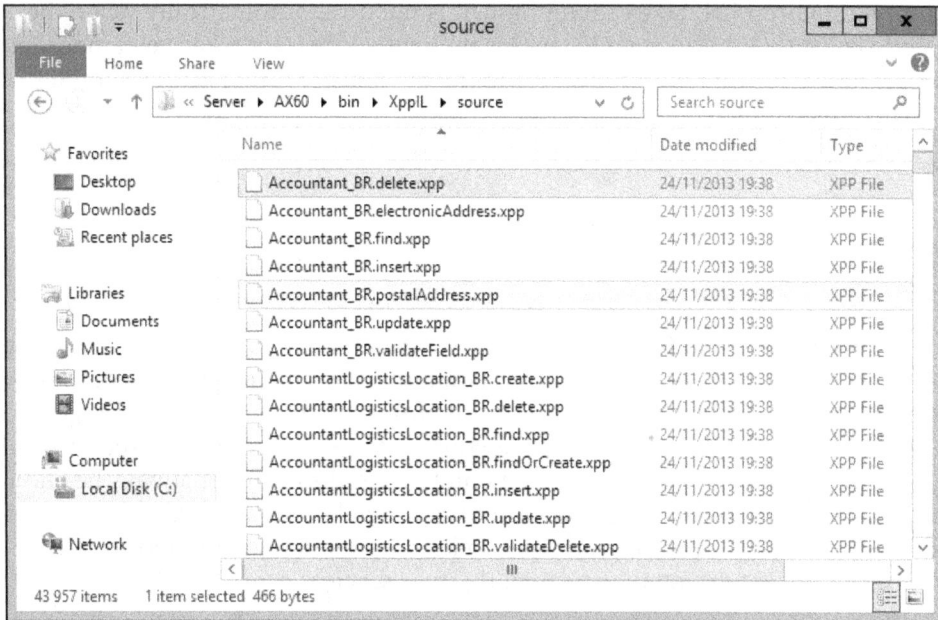

Note that the existence of the `source` subfolder depends on the server configuration. When the options are set to enable debugging on the server, the `source` folder will be generated at the AOS startup. Without the options enabled, you cannot debug, and so the `source` folder will not be generated as it is not needed. The following screenshot illustrates this:

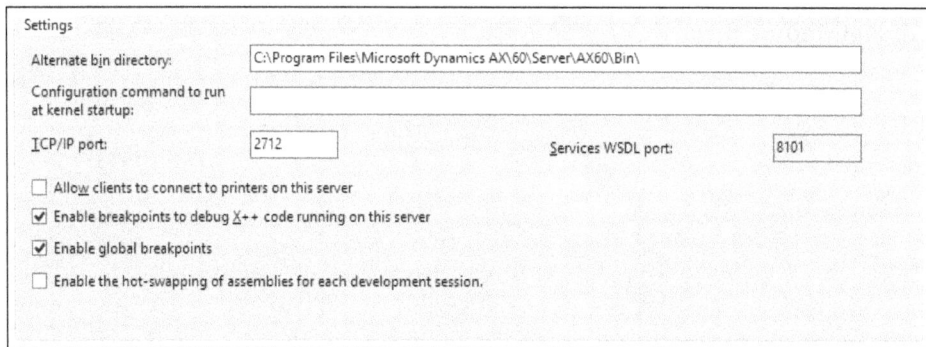

Summary

In this chapter, we familiarized ourselves with the service architecture. We clearly saw that Microsoft has put a lot of effort into providing us with a simplified administration process for services by introducing integration ports. Because a large part of the architecture is built on WCF, at least a basic understanding of the technologies that are used in WCF is needed.

To enable all of these technologies in combination with Microsoft Dynamics AX 2012, compilation into CIL was introduced. This allows the X++ code to be compiled into CIL and benefit from all of the advantages CIL has to offer.

In the next chapter, we will start digging deeper into the AIF services and get some hands-on time by creating our own AIF services.

3
AIF Document Services

When we think of services, we typically think about exposing business logic or consuming it. In many cases, though, it is business data that needs to be exchanged. With Microsoft Dynamics AX 2012, the preferred method to exchange business entities is using document services.

In this chapter, we will discuss the AIF document services and learn about the components that make up a document service. By the end of this chapter, you will be able to create, deploy, and consume such a service.

The following topics are covered in this chapter:

- **Document services**: We start by explaining why you would need document services in Microsoft Dynamics AX 2012.

- **Key components**: There are some components that are specific to document services. It's important to know what these components are and what their role in the concept of services is, so we will discuss their functions in detail.

- **Creating a document service**: You will learn how to create a document service and how to configure and deploy the service using an enhanced integration port.

- **Consuming a document service**: After we have deployed a document service, we will consume it using a .NET WCF application and look at how change tracking can help us in some scenarios.

Introducing document services

If you've worked with Microsoft Dynamics AX for a while, you will know that it contains many tables with a lot of data. These tables can be related to each other to form logical entities such as sales orders. Tables not only contain fields, indexes, and relations, but they also contain code that handles business logic such as initialization, validation, and manipulation of data. When you send data from Microsoft Dynamics AX, especially when you receive data from external systems, you want to make sure that all of the business logic contained in the tables and entities is executed so that the data is consistent. It would be troublesome to have to code all of this yourself when creating a service. Fortunately, AIF solves this problem by providing a framework and the tools to create these services.

So what are these tools and components? This is exactly what we will discuss next.

Key components

We will start by looking at the framework and its components. The key components of a document service are as follows:

- A **query** that is used in the AIF Document Service Wizard to create the document service
- A **document** class that represents a business entity and contains the business logic for this entity
- One or more **AxBC** classes that encapsulate a table and are used by the document class to create, modify, and delete data in tables
- A **service** class that contains the service's operations

Of course, there's more to these components than the few words we've used here to describe them. We will now look at these components one by one, starting with the query.

The document query

Each document service is based on a query defined in the AOT. Using the AIF Document Service Wizard, a document class is generated and XML schema definitions that are used for the XML serialization are derived from the corresponding query. Therefore, the XML message will have a correlation to the query object. In the following screenshot, we can see the query for the InventItemService document service:

```
Axdltem(sys) [Foundation]
  Methods
  Data Sources
    InventTable(InventTable)
      Fields
      Sorting
      Ranges
      Data Sources
        Sales(InventTableModule)
        Purch(InventTableModule)
        Invent(InventTableModule)
        InventTableDocuRef(DocuRef)
        InventItemSalesSetup(InventItemSalesSetup)
        InventItemPurchSetup(InventItemPurchSetup)
        InventItemInventSetup(InventItemInventSetup)
        StorageDimensionGroup(EcoResStorageDimensionGroupItem)
        TrackingDimensionGroup(EcoResTrackingDimensionGroupItem)
        InventItemGroupItem(InventItemGroupItem)
        InventModelGroupItem(InventModelGroupItem)
        PdsCatchWeightItem(PdsCatchWeightItem)
      Group By
      Having
      Order By
    Dependent Objects
    Composite Query
```

If we look at an actual XML message, we can clearly see that it matches the structure of the query object. The following screenshot shows us the XML content after the serialization of the item's business object:

```xml
<Item xmlns="http://schemas.microsoft.com/dynamics/2008/01/documents/Item">
  <DocPurpose>Original</DocPurpose>
  <SenderId>ceu</SenderId>
  <InventTable class="entity">
    <_DocumentHash>902fc7c1e95536276c0d60a4d9d0a192</_DocumentHash>
    <ItemId>1001</ItemId>
    <!-- Omitted fields -->
    <Sales class="entity">...</Sales>
    <Purch class="entity">...</Purch>
    <Invent class="entity">...</Invent>
    <InventItemSalesSetup class="entity">...</InventItemSalesSetup>
    <InventItemSalesSetup class="entity">...</InventItemSalesSetup>
    <InventItemSalesSetup class="entity">...</InventItemSalesSetup>
    <InventItemSalesSetup class="entity">...</InventItemSalesSetup>
    <InventItemPurchSetup class="entity">...</InventItemPurchSetup>
    <InventItemPurchSetup class="entity">...</InventItemPurchSetup>
    <InventItemPurchSetup class="entity">...</InventItemPurchSetup>
    <InventItemPurchSetup class="entity">...</InventItemPurchSetup>
    <InventItemInventSetup class="entity">...</InventItemInventSetup>
    <InventItemInventSetup class="entity">...</InventItemInventSetup>
    <InventItemInventSetup class="entity">...</InventItemInventSetup>
    <InventItemInventSetup class="entity">...</InventItemInventSetup>
    <StorageDimensionGroup class="entity">...</StorageDimensionGroup>
    <TrackingDimensionGroup class="entity">...</TrackingDimensionGroup>
    <InventItemGroupItem class="entity">...</InventItemGroupItem>
    <InventModelGroupItem class="entity">...</InventModelGroupItem>
  </InventTable>
</Item>
```

The document class

Document classes extend the AxdBase class and represent a business document, for example, a sales order. They contain the business logic across all of the tables that correspond with the document. Hence, the details about the underlying tables are hidden from the consumer.

A document class also handles the generation of **XML Schema Definition** (**XSD**). The XSD schema defines the document structure and the business rules that are to be followed. Along with the generation of XSD, the document class also contains logic to serialize the table entity's classes into XML and deserialize them from XML.

Responsibilities of a document class

Document classes have a number of responsibilities, and among them, we have the following:

- Generating an XSD schema.
- Serializing and deserializing classes to and from XML.
- Guaranteeing the document life cycle by making sure that operations do not violate business rules that correspond with the document.
- Containing business logic that applies to data across tables.
- Providing a means to define the document-level properties. For example, whether a document is an original or a duplicate.
- Handling consolidation of table-level errors and returning them as a single list to the calling code.

Let's look at an example document class and analyze it to see how some of these responsibilities are actually handled. In this example, we will take a closer look at the sales order document class, AxdSalesTable.

XSD generation

XSD is generated in the getSchema() and getSchemaInternal() methods of the AxdBase class. The AxdBaseGenerationXSD class is called to generate XSD based on this document class and its underlying table classes, as shown in the following code snippet:

```
private AifDocumentSchemaXml getSchemaInternal(Boolean _includeLabels,
container _languageIds)
{
    AxdBaseGenerateXSD genXsd;
    str documentClass ;
```

```
AifDocumentSchemaXml schemaXml;
genXsd = AxdBaseGenerateXSD::construct();
genXsd.parmIncludeLabels(_includeLabels);
genXsd.parmLanguageIds(_languageIds);
documentClass = new SysDictClass(classIdGet(this)).name() ;

genXsd.setSharedTypesSchema(sharedTypesSchema);
schemaXml = genXsd.generate(documentClass,this.getName(),
this.getQuery());
sharedTypesSchema = genXsd.getSharedTypesSchema();

return schemaXml;
}
```

XML serialization and deserialization

XML serialization and deserialization is performed in several places depending on the operation that is being executed. Either the axdBaseRead, axdBaseUpdate, or axdBaseCreate class is used to service the consumer's call. For example, take a look at the axdBaseRead class that is used when performing a read operation. Here, you can find the serializeDocument() method that is used to serialize the document into XML, as shown in the following code snippet.

```
protected AifDocumentXml serializeDocument(AifConstraintListCollection
_constraintListCollection, boolean _calledFromRead)
{
    ClassName documentName;
    Map propertyInfoMap;
    this.init();

    this.setDocumentNameSpace();

    documentName = axdBase.getName();
    propertyInfoMap = this.getMethodInfoMap(classIdGet(axdBase));

    axdXmlWriter.writeStartDocument(documentName);

    this.serializeClass(propertyInfoMap, axdBase);

    // Omitted code

    axdXmlWriter.writeEndDocument();
    return axdXmlWriter.getXML();
}
```

In the preceding code, the following methods are used:

- `getMethodInfoMap()` fetches all of the fields for the document class
- `writeStartDocument()` writes the XML document's begin tag
- `serializeClass()` takes care of serializing all of the properties into XML
- `writeEndDocument()` writes the XML document's end tag

Cross-table business logic

The `AxdSalesOrder` document class contains logic to handle cross-table dependencies. The `prepareForSave()` method is an example of this. This method is called for every record that is saved. Let's take a look at a small piece of the code that is used for the sales document and see how it handles logic across the `SalesLine` and `InventDim` tables:

```
case classNum(AxInventDim) :
    axInventDim = _axdStack.top();
    axSalesLine = axInventDim.parentAxBC();
    axSalesLine.axInventDim().resetInternalValues();

    if (createRecord)
    {
        axSalesLine.salesLine().unLinkAgreementLine();
    }
    else
    {
        //InventDimId marked as touched in update scenarios and we need
        //new InventDimId
        axSalesLine.clearField(fieldNum(SalesLine,InventDimId),false);
    }

    axInventDim.moveAxInventDim(axSalesLine.axInventDim());
    axSalesLine.setInventDimIdDirtySaved(false);

    return true;
```

In the code, we can see the following:

- In the case of an insert, the link with any possible agreement lines is removed
- In the case of an update, the current `InventDimId` field is blanked out so a new `InventDimId` can be filled in
- Lastly, the values of the `InventDim` table class are copied to the `SalesLine` table class, and the `InventDim` field of `SalesLine` is marked as dirty to be saved

Validation and business rule enforcement

The document class is also responsible for validating the business document and making sure that the business rules are enforced. An example of this can be found in the `checkSalesLine()` method. This method is called from within the `prepareForSave()` method to ensure that the `SalesLine` record does not contain any values that conflict with the business rules. The following code snippet shows us how two of the business rules are validated:

```
salesLineOrig = _axSalesLine.salesLine().orig();
if (salesLineOrig.LineDeliveryType == LineDeliveryType::DeliveryLine)
{
    if (_axSalesLine.parmSalesQty() != salesLineOrig.SalesQty)
    {
        // It is not allowed to change quantity on delivery schedule
        // order lines.
        error("@SYS133823");
    }
    if (_axSalesLine.parmSalesUnit() != salesLineOrig.SalesUnit)
    {
        // It is not allowed to change sales unit on delivery schedule
        // order lines.
        error("@SYS133824");
    }
}
```

The code checks the `SalesQty` and `SalesUnit` fields when `LineDeliveryType` is `DeliveryLine`. If these fields do not match, an error is written to the Infolog.

AxBC classes

AxBC classes can be seen as wrapper classes for tables as they provide an object interface to the underlying table. They manage data access from and to the underlying table and contain business logic that is otherwise contained on forms. They also provide a means to specify default values for fields. Another name for AxBC classes is **Ax<Table>** classes.

AxBC classes are optional. It is possible to have a document service in which the underlying tables have no corresponding AxBC classes. If so, the framework will use the `AxCommon` class to perform read and write operations to the table. In this case, you will have to place your code in the `Axd<Document>` class in the `prepareForSave()` and `prepareForSaveExtended()` methods.

One example that shows how AxBC classes are optional is **value mapping**. Value mapping can be set up in the processing options of an integration port. When this type of value mapping suffices, it is not necessary to create an AxBC class for value mapping purposes. In this case, an AxBC class becomes necessary only if you want to perform more elaborate value mapping than the standard setup allows you to.

Therefore, depending on what your needs are, you can choose not to create AxBC classes for the tables in your document service, or you can create them using the AIF Document Service Wizard. The wizard creates the AxBC classes only if the **Generate AxBC classes** option is selected.

Responsibilities of an AxBC class

The following are the responsibilities of an AxBC class:

- **Performing validation**: AxBC classes make sure that all of the rules and logic contained in the underlying table are adhered to. Things such as data integrity and business rules defined on the field level are also maintained.

- **Providing field sequencing**: Using AxBC classes, you can specify the order in which fields are processed. This is particularly useful when the value of one field depends upon the value of another.

- **Performing value mapping**: Values can be mapped between external systems and Microsoft Dynamics AX 2012. Value mapping can be performed at the AxBC level if the possibilities provided by value mapping at the integration port are insufficient.

- **Enabling value defaulting for fields**: Fields that are not set by the calling code and do not receive a default value in the initValue() method of the table can be defaulted in the AxBC class.

Performing validation

In the AxSalesLine class, we can see that there is validation logic in the validateWrite() method, as shown in the following code snippet:

```
protected void validateWrite()
{
    if (this.validateInput())
    {
        if (!salesLine.validateWrite(true))
        {
            if (continueOnError)
            {
                error("@SYS98197");
            }
```

```
        else
        {
            throw error("@SYS23020");
        }
    }
  }
}
```

The code shows us that the `AxSalesLine` class also calls the `validateWrite()` method on the underlying table. This is done to make sure that the validation rules on the table are adhered to.

Providing field sequencing

In almost all AxBC classes, you will find a method called `setTableFields()`. In the `AxSalesLine` class, this method calls all of the setter methods present for the fields of the `SalesLine` table, as shown in the following code snippet:

```
protected void setTableFields()
{
    //<GMX>
    #ISOCountryRegionCodes
    /</GMX>
    super();
    useMapPolicy = false;
    this.setAddressRefTableId();
    [...]
    this.setCustAccount();
    this.setCustGroup();
    [...]
```

When you want to define the order in which the fields are set, you can modify the code and rearrange the setter methods into the sequence that you want. In the preceding code, you can see that the `CustAccount` field is set first and then the `CustGroup` field is set. This is because determining the `CustGroup` field depends on the value of the `CustAccount` field.

Performing value mapping

If we look at the `valueMapDependingFields()` method, we will see an example of how value mapping can be performed, as shown in the following code snippet:

```
protected void valueMapDependingFields()
{
    ItemId valueMapedItemId;
```

```
    InventDim valueMapedInventDim;

    if (this.valueMappingInbound())
    {
        if (salesLine.CustAccount && item)
        {
            [valueMapedItemId,valueMapedInventDim] = this.
axSalesItemId(salesLine.CustAccount,item);
            this.parmItemId(valueMapedItemId);
                if (!InventDim::isInventDimEqualProductDim(EcoResProductDimGr
oupSetup::newItemId(salesLine.ItemId), valueMapedInventDim,InventDim::
find(InventDim::inventDimIdBlank())))
                {
                    axInventDim.productDimensions(valueMapedInventDim);
                    this.parmInventDimId(InventDim::
findOrCreate(axInventDim.inventDim()).InventDimId);
                }
        }
    }
}
```

The exact implementation of the previous code is unimportant, but you can clearly see that the axSalesItemId() method performs the value mapping to determine the item's number. Then, the mapped item number is used on the SalesLine record. Apart from the value mapping of the item number, a mapping for the inventory dimensions of the corresponding InventDim record is also performed.

Setting default values

AxBC classes can also contain logic that sets default values on fields. An example of this is found in the setLineNum() method, as shown in the following code snippet:

```
protected void setLineNum()
{
    if (this.isMethodExecuted(funcName(), fieldNum(SalesLine,
    LineNum)))
    {
        return;
    }
    this.setSalesId();

    if (this.isFieldSet(fieldNum(SalesLine, SalesId)))
    {
```

```
            if (!lineNum)
            {
                lineNum = SalesLine::lastLineNum(this.parmSalesId());
            }
            lineNum += 1;

            this.parmLineNum(lineNum);
        }
    }
```

In the previous code, we can see the following:

- Firstly, the framework checks whether this method has already been executed
- The `setSalesId()` method makes sure that the sales order number's value is set
- If no line number is provided, the `lastLineNum()` method is used to determine the highest line number used at the time
- Lastly, the line number is incremented and set in the `SalesLine` record

The service class

Service classes are classes that contain the operations used in the integration port of that document service. Only the operations needed by the business are available. All service classes extend the `AifDocumentService` class and delegate their operations to the `AifDocumentService` class. For example, when the `Read` operation is available on a service class, the implementation of the operation will call the `ReadList()` method on the `AifDocumentService` parent class.

The following operations are available:

- `Create`: This operation receives a document class and creates records as and when required. The return value is an `AifEntityKeyList` object that contains a list of key/value pairs that reference a record.
- `Delete`: This operation is used to delete records from the database. The IDs of the records to be deleted are passed as a parameter.
- `Find`: This operation takes an `AifQueryCriteria` parameter and queries the database. The return value is a document class that contains the resulting records.

- `Findkeys`: This operation does the same thing as the find operation but returns an `AifEntityKeyList` object, which contains only the IDs of the resulting records instead of all of the data.

- `Read`: This operation takes an `AifEntityKeyList` object as a parameter, reads the records from the database, and returns them in a document. This operation is typically used in combination with the `FindKeys` operation that first returns the values that are needed as an input for the `Read` operation.

- `Update`: This operation takes an `AifEntityKeyList` object that contains the IDs of the records to be updated. The second parameter is the document that contains the updated records.

- `GetKeys`: This operation uses a document filter and returns the resulting document keys in an `AifEntityKeyList` object.

- `GetChangedKeys`: This operation also uses a document filter along with a `DateTime` parameter to return the document keys of the documents that have changed.

The service node

For our service operations to be available in the inbound and outbound port forms, a service class alone is not enough. The services framework requires that you create a service node in the AOT for the service and its service operations that you want to expose. This is true for document services but applies equally to custom services.

A service node allows you to create service contracts based on service classes in a flexible and customizable way. If you wish, you can create multiple service nodes for one service class, each with a different external name and a different set of service operations that are exposed. You can even specify the namespace for the service and change the names of the service operations.

Creating a document service

As you've read previously, there are a lot of components that need to be created when developing a document service. This may lead you might think that creating a document service is a daunting task but fortunately, that is not the case.

Microsoft has provided us with the AIF Document Service Wizard. This wizard allows you to create a document service fairly quickly based on a query you provide. In the next few pages, we will walk through all of the steps needed to create a document service using this wizard.

> **Downloading the example code**
>
> You can download the example code files for all Packt books you have purchased from your account at http://www.packtpub.com. If you purchased this book elsewhere, you can visit http://www.packtpub.com/support and register to have the files e-mailed directly to you.
>
> For information on how to install and run the code, please refer to *Appendix, Installing the Demo Application*

The document service that we will build in this chapter will allow us to demonstrate all of the service operations that are available on a document service. We will need an entity from the demo application for this purpose and for that, we will use titles that are stored in the CVRTitle table. At the end of this chapter, we will have built a fully functional document service that can create, read, and modify the title information.

Setting the compiler level

Before we start, let's make sure that the compiler is set up correctly. When developing for Microsoft Dynamics AX 2012, it is important to adhere to the best practices that Microsoft has defined. Many of these best practices are checked by the compiler. Depending on the compiler level, a smaller or larger set of best practices will be checked during compilation.

We recommend that you set the compiler level to **4**, the maximum, so all best practice errors are shown to us when compiling. We also recommend setting the compiler to check the best practices, at least on the **Error** level. When setting the best practice parameters, also make sure that the layer setting is set to **Check all nodes**.

The layer setting is important when creating document services because it helps you make sure that the AxBC classes that are in the lower layers are checked when new fields are added to the corresponding tables. You will receive recommendations about what methods should be created. This is important so that the AxBC classes are up to date.

> **Best practices for Microsoft Dynamics AX development**
>
> It is worth reading through the best practices that are formulated by Microsoft for development in Microsoft Dynamics AX 2012. This is available on MSDN at `http://msdn.microsoft.com/en-us/library/aa658028.aspx`.

Creating the query

As every document service is based on a query, we will start by creating the query. Create a new query in the AOT, name it `AxdCVRTitle`, and add the `CVRTitle` table to the data sources. When you're done, it will look similar to the following screenshot:

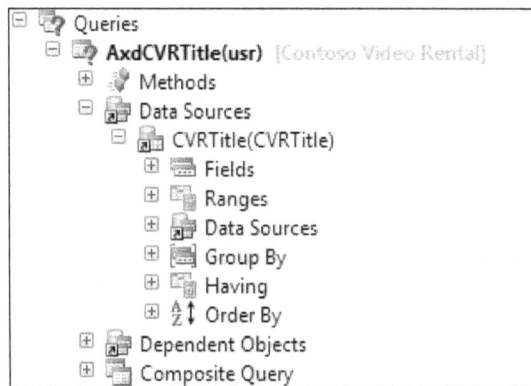

You now have the basis for the query. However, you should see a compiler error that says that you should specify the dynamic property on the data source. To set the property, select the **Fields** node of the data source, and in the properties form, set **Dynamic** to **No**.

Setting the property to **No** allows you to specify the fields on the data sources yourself. You should do this for all document queries. If you had set this property to **Yes**, the number of fields in the document would change when fields are added to the table, and that's not desirable.

For this demonstration, we will add all of the fields from the table to the data source. The easiest way to do this is by setting the **Dynamic** property to **Yes**, saving the query, and then setting it to **No** again.

In a real-life scenario, you should only expose fields that are really needed. If you are unsure, you can still add the field and use data policies to disable it.

To finish up, set the **Update** property to **Yes** on the data source. This will enable us to perform the `update` operation on the document service using the previously created query.

Running the AIF Document Service Wizard

Now that the query has been created, we can use it to run the AIF Document Service Wizard. This wizard will guide you through a series of steps that will generate the necessary artifacts.

There are three ways to start the AIF Document Service Wizard:

- In the Development Workspace, navigate to **Tools | Wizards | AIF Document Service Wizard**.
- The same wizard can also be started by navigating to **Tools | Application Integration Framework | Create document service**.
- You can also start the wizard by right-clicking on a query and then navigating to **Add-Ins | AIF Document Service Wizard**. This last option takes you immediately to the second screen of the wizard with the parameters filled in, depending on the query that you selected.

The first screen of the wizard is the **Welcome** screen. It informs you that this wizard will help you generate document services. Click on **Next** and the **Select document parameters** screen will be displayed.

Selecting document parameters

In the **Select document parameters** screen, you can select the query and specify the document name. Select the **AxdCVRTitle** query from the drop-down list. The **Document name** field is automatically filled in. Accept the name that was generated. In the **Document label** field, enter Titles. We will create a label for this text later on in the chapter. Now, click on **Next**:

Selecting code generation parameters

On the **Select code generation parameters** screen, you can specify the class names and the service operations that need to be generated. You can also generate AxBC classes for tables if they don't exist yet, or update the existing AxBC classes.

In the **Class names** section, you should accept all the class names that are proposed by the wizard. The following list shows us how the class names are generated:

- The service class's name is the name of the query with the Service suffix added and the Axd prefix removed
- The document object's class name is based on the name of the query without the Axd prefix
- The Axd class name is the same as the query name

Sometimes, class names can conflict with the names of existing objects. In our case, the CVRTitle class name will conflict with the CVRTitle table name. So, we will have to add Document to the document object class name to fix this. In this example, we also add Document to the service class name, so we can differentiate between it and another service for the titles that we will create in the next chapter.

In the **Service operations** section, you can specify the service operation(s) that you want to generate for the document service. For this demonstration, we will select all of the service operations.

In the **AxBC generation** section, select the **Generate AxBC classes** option. This will ensure that the AxBC classes are generated for the tables that we use in the data sources of our query. Do not select **Regenerate existing AxBC classes**, as this may overwrite the customizations that you've made to existing AxBC classes. Now, click on **Next**:

AIF Document Service Wizard   — ▫ ✕

Select code generation parameters
Select class names, service operations, and AxBC generation parameters.

Class names

Service class name:	CVRTitleDocumentService
Document object class name:	CVRTitleDocument
Axd class name:	AxdCVRTitle

Service operations

create:	✔	find:	✔
read:	✔	findKeys:	✔
update:	✔	getKeys:	✔
delete:	✔	getChangedKeys:	✔

AxBC generation

Generate AxBC classes:	✔
Regenerate existing AxBC classes:	☐

< Back   Next >   Cancel

Generating code

You are now presented with a list of artifacts that will be created. Review this list to check for any mistakes you might have made. You can always return to the previous screens using the **Back** button:

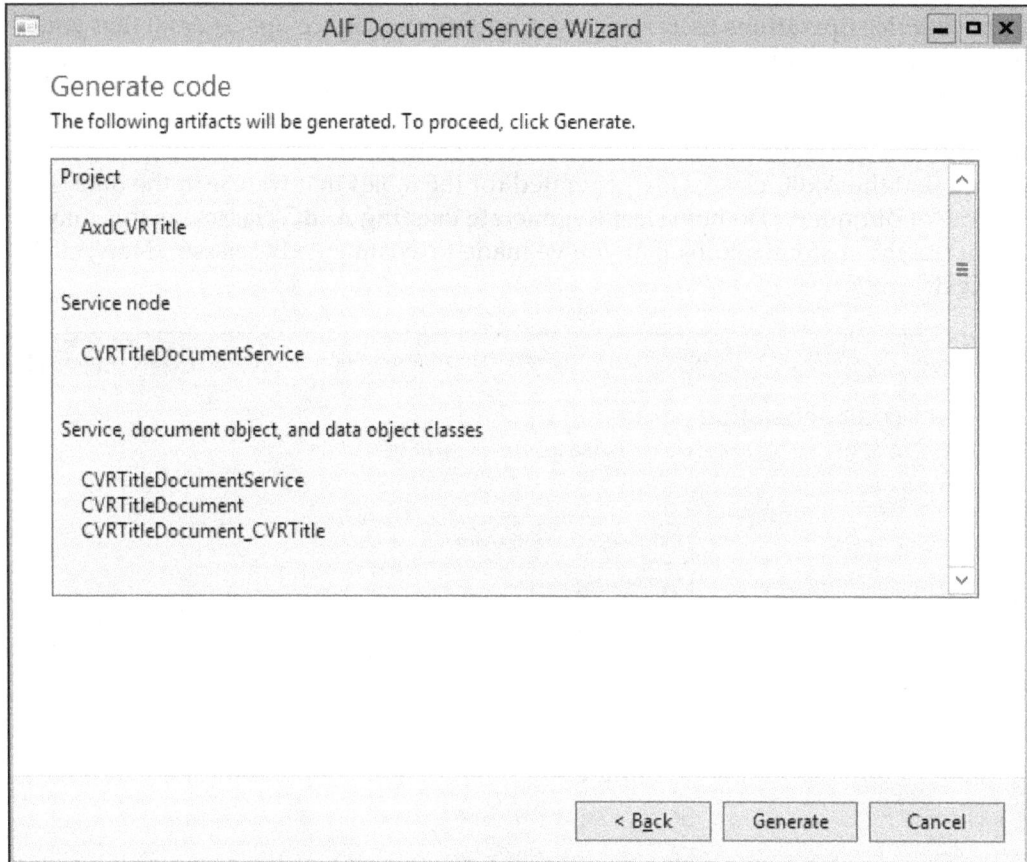

Click on **Generate** to continue. The wizard will generate all of the artifacts, and when this is done, a screen titled **Completed** will appear, informing you about the artifacts that have been generated. Click on **Finish** to close the form.

Finishing up

The output of the AIF Document Service Wizard is stored in a private project that has the same name as the query that the service is based on. You have to compile this project because it will contain compiler errors that need fixing and the tasks that you need to perform, as shown in the following screenshot:

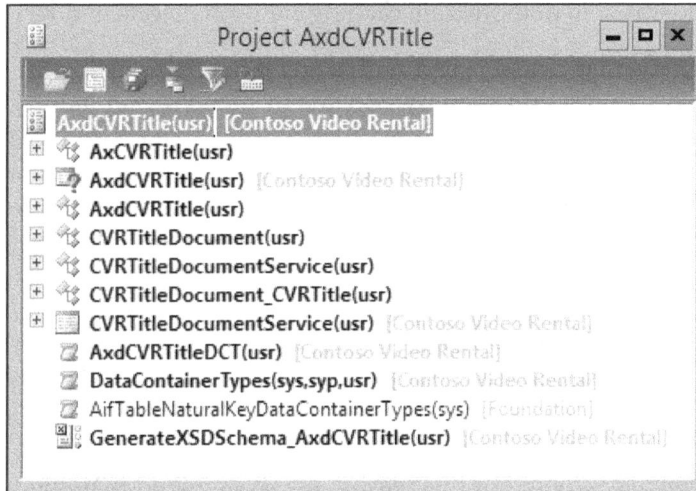

Fixing compiler errors

If you have followed all of the previous steps, you should see two compiler errors for the AxBC class that was generated. This is because two template methods that enable caching are generated for an AxBC class: `cacheObject` and `cacheRecordRecord`.

Caching is used to speed up the performance when defaulting values for inbound messages. Without caching, multiple methods would have to construct the same object or select the same record multiple times, thereby decreasing the performance.

When you don't want to use object or record caching, you can simply delete these methods to fix the compiler errors. When you delete the methods, remember to remove the declaration of the `cacheRecordIdx` and `cacheObjectIdx` variables from `classDeclaration` as well. We don't want to use caching in this example, so we will do just that.

When you do want to use object or record caching, you should refactor the methods to fit your needs. The explanation given in the following sections should enable you to do that.

ClassDeclaration

Object and record caching use map variables that are declared in the `AxInternalBase` class to store objects or records. As you probably know, a map allows you to associate a key with a value. In our case, the value is either a class or a record. As a map can only contain values of one type, we need two maps: one to cache objects and one to cache records. This is also the reason why two cache methods are generated to demonstrate caching for both objects and records.

As each value in the map is associated with a key that allows us to access the value, we need some way to store that key. We do this by declaring an index for each object or record that we want to cache. So, there's a variable for each cache method we write. By default, `cacheRecordIdx` and `cacheObjectIdx` are generated. You should rename them appropriately to the corresponding value. When you cache the `SalesTable` records, name the variable `salesTableIdx`, and when you cache `axSalesTable` objects, name the variable `axSalesTableIdx`.

The cacheObject() method

You can use the `cacheObject()` method as a guide when you want to cache objects. Unfortunately, the code that is automatically generated is flawed. Instead of using the `classCacheInsert()` method, it uses the the `tableCacheInsert()` method at one point, which is wrong. For this reason, we recommend that you use the `AxSalesLine.axSalesTable()` method to guide you. You can copy the code in this method, replace the variables with your own, and you're all set.

The cacheRecordRecord() method

The `cacheRecordRecord()` method can be used as a guide when caching for records is required. It uses the `tableCacheInsert()` method instead of the `classCacheInsert()` method to add records to the cache. The flow is the same as the `cacheObject()` method.

An example of a method that uses caching is the `setCustAccount()` method of the `AxSalesLine` class. It uses both object and record caching using the `axSalesTable()` and `projTableRecord()` methods to default the `custAccount` field.

Fixing tasks

When you are done with the compiler errors, you will still have a lot of tasks left to perform. This is exactly what we will discuss next.

Labels

When you plan on creating a document service, be ready to make some labels. For this small example, over 10 labels have to be created. Fortunately, they are all marked with a TODO notation in code, which makes it easy to find them in the compiler output window. Create all labels using the label editor and remove the TODO notations when you're done.

Generating an XSD schema

The AIF Document Service Wizard automatically generates a job that allows you to save the document schema to a file. This schema can be used by external applications so that they know how to generate a valid document. You can change the location of where the XML should be saved in the job.

However, you will most likely change the schema of the document using data policies. In that case, you will have to generate a schema for each integration port on which the document is used. The schema can be generated from the data policies form by clicking on the **View schema** button. This schema will contain only the fields that are enabled instead of all the fields that are generated by the job.

There is no real need to generate the XSD schema when using an adapter that supports WCF. This is because the schema for WCF services is contained in the WSDL document that is exposed by the integration port. We will use this WSDL document when we add a reference to the service that we've created.

Constraints

In the document class, the getConstraintList() method is generated, which contains three tasks to be performed. This method must be implemented because it is abstract in the parent class, AxdBase. However, constraints are a deprecated feature because there is no way to set up constraints for endpoints anymore. Microsoft Dynamics AX 2012 does offer a similar feature called **legal values** that you can specify when setting up data policies.

To get rid of the tasks, just remove them along with all the other code in the method that is commented out. This will make sure that no constraints are applied to the document.

Validation

Two tasks that deal with validation are added in the prepareForSaveExtended() method of the document class. The prepareForSaveExtended() method is the perfect location to place the validation for the entity as a whole, so add the validation to it, if applicable.

Our example is pretty simple, so there is no need to add an extra validation. When you do need the validation of your entity, the `prepareForSaveExtended()` method of the `AxdSalesOrder` class is a good example.

Updating the service contract

A very important component that is generated by the AIF Document Service Wizard is the service node. However, you may want to update the namespace of this service. To do this, perform the following steps:

1. Open the AOT by pressing *Ctrl + D*.

2. Go to the **Services** node and locate the **CVRTitleDocumentService** service.

3. Change the **Namespace** property to `http://schemas.contoso.com/ServiceContracts`.

4. Click on the **Save All** button to save the changes.

Finally, after all of the objects have been created, you might have to register the new service and its operations in one of the following ways:

- Navigate to **System administration | Setup | Checklists | Initialization checklist | Initialize system | Set up Application Integration Framework**. This is what we did in *Chapter 2, Service Architecture and Deployment*, when we created an integration port.

- Or, you can right-click on the service, navigate to **Add-Ins | Register service**, and then click on the **Refresh** button.

Fixing best practice errors

The project will contain the best practice errors. To check for errors, right-click on the project, click on **Add-Ins**, and finally, click on **Check best practices**. The output will be displayed in the **Compiler output** window.

Privileges

The Application Integration Framework uses the role-based security framework. This means that whoever uses the service operation has to have a role that allows them to invoke that service operation.

You will have to create a privilege for each service operation of the service. To create a privilege for the `update` operation, perform the following steps:

1. Open the AOT by pressing *Ctrl + D*.

2. Expand the **Security** node, right-click on the **Privileges** node, and then click on **New Privilege**.

3. Rename the privilege using the `<NameOfService><ServiceOperation>` format. For example, `CVRTitleDocumentServiceUpdate`.

4. Right-click on the privilege and click on **Properties**. In the **Properties** tab, enter a label in the **label** field.

5. Expand the **CVRTitleDocumentServiceUpdate** node. This will expose the **Entry Points** and **Permissions** nodes.

6. Drag-and-drop the **Update** service operation node to the **Entry Points** node of the **CVRTitleDocumentServiceUpdate** privilege.

7. Click on the **Save All** button to save the changes.

Repeat these steps for all of the service operations. When all privileges have been created, perform the following steps to add them to the **ServiceOperations** duty:

1. Open the AOT by pressing *Ctrl + D*.

2. Expand the **Security** and **Duties** nodes and locate the **ServiceOperations** duty.

3. Expand the node and drag-and-drop all of the new privileges to the **Privileges** node.

4. Click on the **Save All** button to save the changes.

The **ServiceOperations** duty contains privileges for all of the service operations in the system. This ensures that the system administrators have access to these service operations. When other roles need access to a specific service operation, you should add that privilege to an appropriate duty for that role.

Setting mandatory fields

The `Id` field of the `CVRtitle` table is mandatory, but we want the service to use the number sequence that is defined for the field. The `initValue()` method of the table automatically generates an ID for each record, so there is no need to set the field as mandatory in our service.

To achieve this, we will override the `initMandatoryFieldsExemptionList()` method of the `AxCVRTitle` class so it looks like the following code:

```
protected void initMandatoryFieldsExemptionList()
{
    super();
    // Set the Id field as not mandatory since we are going to use a
    // number sequence for the Id
    this.setParmMethodAsNotMandatory(methodstr(AxCVRTitle, ParmId));
}
```

If you ever want to set a field as mandatory in your document that isn't mandatory in the table, you can override the initMandatoryFieldsMap() method in the document class of your service.

Updating an existing document service

In some cases, you will want to update an existing document service. For example, when you have added a data source to an existing document query, or when you want to add a service operation to an existing document service. To assist you with this, you can use the **Update document service** form.

To open this form, open the Development Workspace and navigate to **Tools | Application Integration Framework | Update document service**, as shown in the following screenshot:

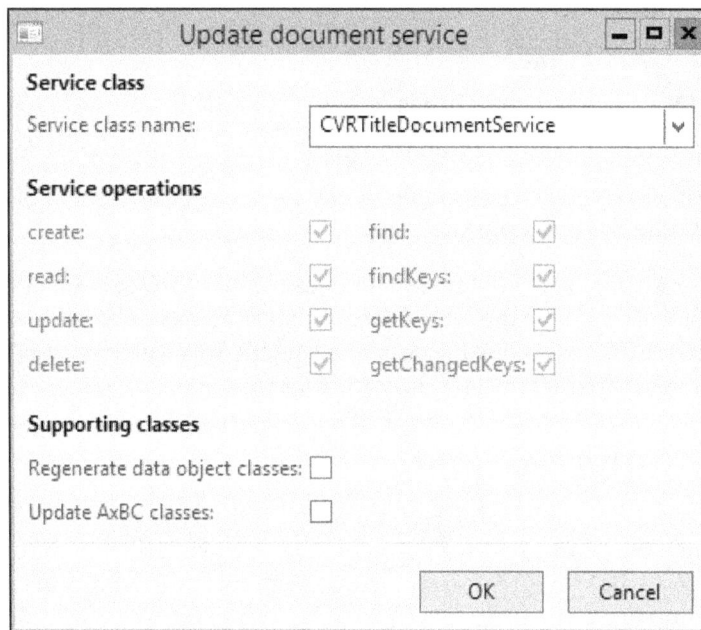

	Update document service	— □ ✕
Service class		
Service class name:	CVRTitleDocumentService	⌄
Service operations		
create: ☑	find: ☑	
read: ☑	findKeys: ☑	
update: ☑	getKeys: ☑	
delete: ☑	getChangedKeys: ☑	
Supporting classes		
Regenerate data object classes: ☐		
Update AxBC classes: ☐		
	OK	Cancel

Adding service operations

As you can see in the previous screenshot, you can select new operations to add to the document service. Click on **OK** to add the selected service operations to the document service. This will update the document and service classes so that the new operations are supported.

The only thing left for the developer to do is to manually add the service operation to the service node. To do this, go to the **Services** node in the AOT, expand the node of the service that was updated, right-click on the **Operations** node, and click on **Add operation** to add the new operations.

Updating supporting classes

When fields or data sources have been added to the query of an existing document service, the supporting classes will have to be created or regenerated. In this case, select the **Regenerate data object classes** and **Update AxBC classes** options.

When a field has been removed, the parm() and set() methods will not be automatically deleted from the AxBC classes, so you'll have to do this manually before you update the document service.

As always, after changing the services, it's a good idea to register them again.

Deploying a document service

The development phase of the document service is complete, so now it is ready to be deployed. We need an enhanced integration port for this service because we will demonstrate how to use the getKeys and getChangedKeys operations. These operations require that the document filters are enabled—a feature that is only available in enhanced ports.

The steps that need to be performed to create an enhanced port have already been described in *Chapter 2, Service Architecture and Deployment*. Take a look at the section on enhanced ports and follow the steps in it to create one. Make sure that the **Port name** field is set to CVRDocumentServicesEnhanced and that all of the service operations of the **CVRTitleDocumentService** service are added to the exposed service operations.

Consuming a document service

Let's head to Visual Studio and start consuming the document service that we created. You can open the Visual Studio project for this chapter, included in the code files for the book, to see the service in action.

If you are a more experienced Visual Studio user, you can create a project yourself by performing the following steps:

1. In Visual Studio, create a project for a console application by navigating to **File | New | Project...**.

2. In the **Installed Templates** section, navigate to **Visual C# | Windows**.

3. Choose a project of type **Console Application**, insert a name and location for the project, and click on **OK**.

To add the service reference, perform the following steps:

1. In **Solution Explorer**, right-click on the name of your project and click on **Add Service Reference...**.

2. Enter the WSDL location in the **Address** field and click on **Go**. Of course, you'll need to replace DYNAX01:8101 with the server and port of your installation. You should see a form that looks similar to the following screenshot:

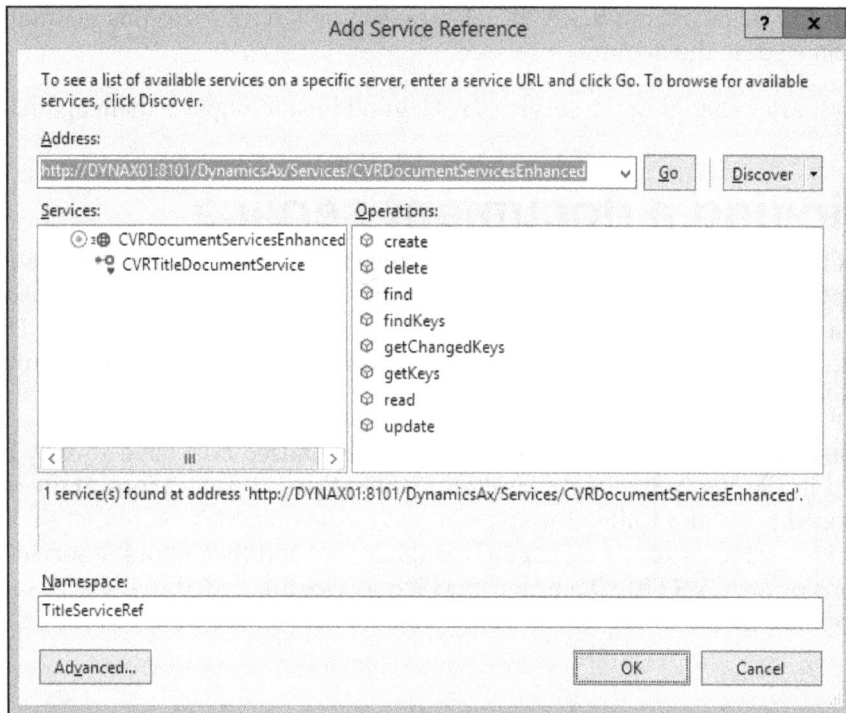

3. Enter TitleServiceRef in the **Namespace** field and click on **OK**.

In the following sections, we will go through all of the operations that are available in the service by using a console application. The console application prompts the user to select the action that needs to be executed. We will look only at the methods that consume the service. For the complete sample application, download and install the sample project for this chapter, which is included in the code files of the book. Be sure to read *Appendix*, *Installing the Demo Application*, for information on how to install and run the code.

Create

The first service operation lets us insert records into Microsoft Dynamics AX. The flow for using the `Create` operation is as follows:

1. Create a new record entity and fill in the field information.
2. Create a new document instance and put in the table entity array that contains the entities that you want to insert.
3. Invoke the `Create` operation that returns the entity keys of the inserted records.

The following code reads an XML file that contains some sample titles to be inserted:

```
static void createTitles()
{
    List<MovieTitle> sampleTitles;
    int i = 0;

    // Read the XML file containing the sample data into a list
    using (var reader = new StreamReader(@"C:\Temp\TitleDemoData.
xml"))
    {
        XmlSerializer deserializer = new XmlSerializer(typeof(List<Mo
vieTitle>));
        sampleTitles = (List<MovieTitle>) deserializer.
Deserialize(reader);
    }

    // For all of the titles, create a title in the Ax database
    foreach (MovieTitle title in sampleTitles)
    {
        i++;

        // Create a title entity
        AxdEntity_CVRTitle titleEntity = new AxdEntity_CVRTitle();

        // Fill in all the fields
        titleEntity.Name = title.Name;
        titleEntity.Description = title.Description;
        titleEntity.LengthInMinutes = Convert.ToInt32(title.Length);

        // For int and real values, you must flag them as fill in
        // This is to tell Dynamics that they are not null, but the
        // default value
        titleEntity.LengthInMinutesSpecified = true;

        // Create a title document instance
```

```
AxdCVRTitle titleDocument = new AxdCVRTitle();

// Initialize the list of title entities in the document
// CVRTitle is a list of title entities
titleDocument.CVRTitle = new AxdEntity_CVRTitle[1] {
titleEntity };

// Create an instance of the document service client
using (CVRTitleDocumentServiceClient client = new
CVRTitleDocumentServiceClient())
{
    // Insert the title in Ax
    EntityKey[] entityKeys = client.create(null,
    titleDocument);

    // Report progress to the user
    Console.WriteLine(String.Format("Title {0} created",
    titleEntity.Name));
    }
    }
}
```

After executing the previous code, we can see the titles within Microsoft Dynamics AX:

Find

The Find operation uses a QueryCriteria object that contains the criteria to be filtered and returns a document that contains the record entities. The flow for using the Find operation is as follows:

1. Create a QueryCriteria object that contains the criteria's elements.

2. Invoke the Find operation to retrieve a document instance that contains the resulting records.

Creating query criteria

For some operations, including the Find operation, you are required to pass a QueryCriteria object. Based on this QueryCriteria object, records are queried in Microsoft Dynamics AX. To facilitate the creation of QueryCriteria instances, a method was created, which is shown as follows:

```
static QueryCriteria createSingleCriteria(string dataSource
                                        , string fieldName
                                        , Operator op
                                        , string value1
                                        , string value2)
{
    // Prepare a queryCriteria instance
    QueryCriteria criteria = new QueryCriteria();

    // Create a criteria element that represents a query range
    CriteriaElement criteriaElement = new CriteriaElement();

    criteriaElement.DataSourceName = dataSource;
    criteriaElement.FieldName = fieldName;
    criteriaElement.Operator = op;
    criteriaElement.Value1 = value1;
    criteriaElement.Value2 = value2;

    // Put the criteria element in the QueryCriteria instance
    criteria.CriteriaElement = new CriteriaElement[1]
                                {
                                        criteriaElement
                                };

    return criteria;
}
```

Using Find

Now that we have a way to create the query criteria that is needed for the `Find` operation, we can go ahead and use the `Find` operation to get the data from Microsoft Dynamics AX, as demonstrated in the following code snippet:

```
static void getTitles_Find()
{
    // Variable to hold the title document
    AxdCVRTitle titleDocument = new AxdCVRTitle();

    // Create a criteria element that selects titles that run over 110
    // minutes
    QueryCriteria criteria = Program.createSingleCriteria("CVRTitle" ,
"LengthInMinutes", Operator.Greater, "110", null);

    // Create a client for as long as we need to
    using (CVRTitleDocumentServiceClient client = new
CVRTitleDocumentServiceClient())
    {
        // Find the titles that match the criteria
        titleDocument = client.find(null, criteria);

        // Loop all the titles
        foreach (AxdEntity_CVRTitle title in titleDocument.CVRTitle)
        {
            // Report the results to the console window
            Console.WriteLine(title.Id + ' ' + title.Name + ' ' +
title.LengthInMinutes);
        }
    }
}
```

A part of the result looks as follows:

```
T000000006 Schindler's List 114
T000000007 The Dark Knight 119
T000000008 The Lord of the Rings: The Return of the King 112
T000000011 Fight Club 115
```

Read

The Read operation sounds like the Find operation, but there is a difference. Find uses the query criteria as input and returns the title document immediately with all of the resulting rows. Read returns the same document but does not take the query criteria as a parameter. Instead, Read uses a set of Entitykey objects as input. As a result, the Read operation returns only one record for each entity key in the set, because the entity keys correspond to the primary key of the record.

You could be asking yourself why you would want to use Read instead of Find if the latter gives you the same result in one operation. Well, the answer is twofold.

The first scenario is one where you have already cached the entity keys in your application. In other words, you already know the unique key of the records that you want to retrieve. Then you can just construct an array of entity keys and invoke the Read operation.

The flow for using the Read operation with the custom entity keys is as follows:

1. Create an array of the Entitykey objects that contain the keys of the records that you want to find.
2. Invoke the Read operation to return a document that contains the related records.

The following is the code implementation:

```
static void getTitle_ReadWithEntityKey()
{
    // Let the user enter an Id in the console window
    Console.WriteLine("Enter a title Id to look for :");
    string titleId = Console.ReadLine();

    // Create an instance of the keyfield containing the title id to
    // search for
    KeyField keyField = new KeyField() { Field = "Id", Value = titleId
};

    // Create an entity key instance and put in the key field data
    EntityKey entityKey = new EntityKey();
```

```
        entityKey.KeyData    = new KeyField[1] { keyField };

    // Create an array of entity keys and put in the previously
created key
    EntityKey[] entityKeys = new EntityKey[1] { entityKey };

    AxdCVRTitle titleDocument = new AxdCVRTitle();

    // Create a client for as long as we need to
    using (CVRTitleDocumentServiceClient client = new
    CVRTitleDocumentServiceClient())
    {
        // Use the keys to read all of the titles
        titleDocument = client.read(null, entityKeys);
    }

    // Loop all the titles to report to the console window
    foreach (AxdEntity_CVRTitle title in titleDocument.CVRTitle)
    {
        Program.printSingleTitle(title);
    }
}
```

If we execute the previous code for title ID T000000007, the following result is printed to the console window:

```
Title : T000000007
Name : The Dark Knight
Length in minutes : 119
Description : When Batman, [...]
```

FindKeys

The second scenario, in which you can use the Read operation, is used in combination with the FindKeys operation. This can enhance the performance. Let's say that you have a .NET application that queries Microsoft Dynamics AX. It's possible that your query will return a large number of records but you want to use paging so that you don't have to load all of the data at once. So, you can use the FindKeys operation to return only the keys of the records instead of all of the fields. Once you have the keys, you can implement paging in your application and call the Read operation with the subset of keys that are actually needed.

The flow for using the `Read` operation with `FindKeys` is as follows:

1. Create a `QueryCriteria` instance that contains the criteria for finding the records.

2. Invoke the `FindKeys` operation to retrieve the keys that match the query.

3. Using the keys, invoke the `Read` operation to return a document that contains the related records.

The following is the code implementation:

```
static void getAllTitles_ReadWithFindKeys()
{
    // Variable to hold the title document
    AxdCVRTitle titleDocument = new AxdCVRTitle();

    // Create a criteria element that selects titles that run over 110
    // minutes
    QueryCriteria criteria = Program.createSingleCriteria("CVRTitle" ,
"LengthInMinutes", Operator.Greater, "110", null);

    // Create a client for as long as we need to
    using (CVRTitleDocumentServiceClient client = new
CVRTitleDocumentServiceClient())
    {
        // Call the findKeys operation to fetch all of the keys that
        // match the query criteria
        EntityKey[] entityKeys = client.findKeys(null, criteria);

        // Check if we had matching titles
        if (entityKeys.Length > 0)
        {
            // Use the keys to read all of the title records
            titleDocument = client.read(null, entityKeys);
        }
    }

    if (titleDocument != null)
    {
        // Loop all the titles to report to the user
        foreach (AxdEntity_CVRTitle title in titleDocument.CVRTitle)
        {
            Console.WriteLine(title.Id + ' ' + title.Name + ' ' +
            title.LengthInMinutes);
        }
    }
}
```

As we are using the same query criteria, we should see the same result as the Find operation. A part of the result looks as follows:

```
T000000006 Schindler's List 114
T000000007 The Dark Knight 119
T000000008 The Lord of the Rings: The Return of the King 112
T000000011 Fight Club 115
```

Update

To update records in the Microsoft Dynamics AX database, the Update operation can be used. First, you need to use the Read operation to get the records that you want to update. For this, you need to specify the entity keys. Once you have the document that contains the records that you want to update, you can edit the fields and then call the Update operation. The basic flow for updating the records is as follows:

1. Create an array of Entitykey objects.
2. Invoke the Read operation to retrieve the data from Microsoft Dynamics AX.
3. Update the fields that you want to change.
4. Change the action property on the changed records to be updated.
5. Invoke the Update operation.

The following is the code implementation:

```
static void updateTitle()
{
    Console.WriteLine("Enter a title Id to look for :");
    string titleId = Console.ReadLine();

    // Create an instance of the keyfield containing a record id to
    // search for
    KeyField keyField = new KeyField() { Field = "Id", Value = titleId
};

    // Create an entity key instance and put in the key field data
    EntityKey entityKey = new EntityKey();
    entityKey.KeyData = new KeyField[1] { keyField };

    // Call the findKeys operation to fetch all of the keys that match
    // the query criteria
    EntityKey[] entityKeys = new EntityKey[1] { entityKey };

    // Create a client for as long as we need to
```

```
using (CVRTitleDocumentServiceClient client = new
CVRTitleDocumentServiceClient())
{
    // Use the keys to read all of the titles
    AxdCVRTitle titleDocument = client.read(null, entityKeys);

    // Get the CVRTitle record entity
    AxdEntity_CVRTitle title = titleDocument.CVRTitle.First();

    title.Description = "Updated Description";
    title.action = AxdEnum_AxdEntityAction.update;
    title.actionSpecified = true;

    // Invoke the update operation
    client.update(null, entityKeys, titleDocument);
}
}
```

Delete

As you might have guessed already, the Delete operation will delete records from Microsoft Dynamics AX. The flow for using the Delete operation is as follows:

1. Create an array of EntityKey objects.

2. Invoke the Delete operation to delete the data from Microsoft Dynamics AX.

The following code will prompt the user to enter a title ID and then delete that title from Microsoft Dynamics AX:

```
static void deleteTitle()
{
    // Let the user enter an Id in the console window
    Console.WriteLine("Enter a title Id to delete :");
    string titleId = Console.ReadLine();

    // Create an instance of the keyfield containing the title id to
    // search for
    KeyField keyField = new KeyField() { Field - "Id", Value - titleId
};

    // Create an entity key instance and put in the key field data
    EntityKey entityKey = new EntityKey();
```

```
        entityKey.KeyData = new KeyField[1] { keyField };

        // Create an array of entity keys and put in the previously
        // created key
        EntityKey[] entityKeys = new EntityKey[1] { entityKey };

        using (CVRTitleDocumentServiceClient client = new
        CVRTitleDocumentServiceClient())
        {
            client.delete(null, entityKeys);
        }
    }
}
```

GetKeys

The GetKeys operation will return the keys for records that match the document filter that is configured on the integration port. Document filters are only available on enhanced integration ports.

Document filter

For the sake of this demonstration, we assume that a document filter is added on the port used by the **CVRTitleDocumentService** service, as shown in the following screenshot:

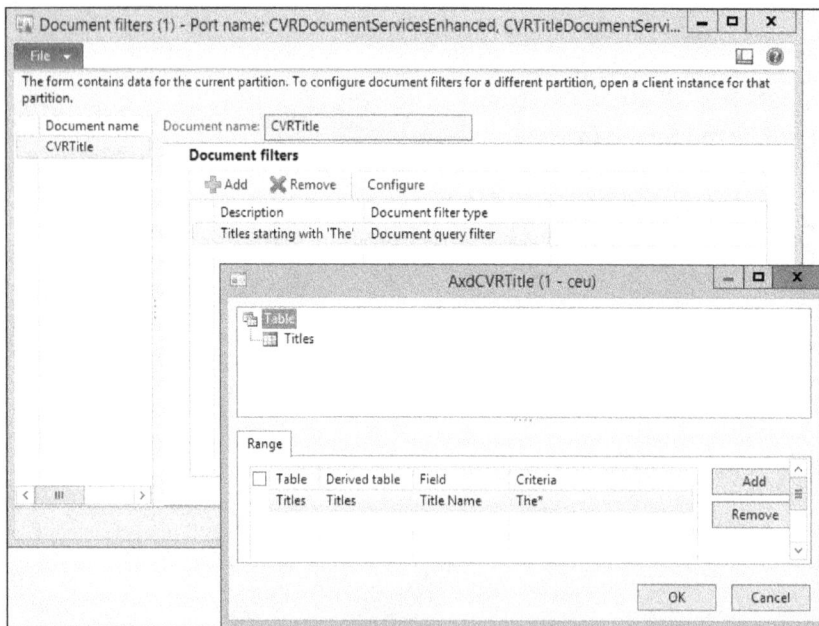

Using GetKeys

The flow for using the GetKeys operation is as follows:

1. Create a DocumentPaging object that contains the number of keys to be returned (optional).
2. Invoke the getKeys operation that returns the entity keys that match the document filter.
3. Use the Read operation to retrieve the data of the related records when needed.

The following code uses GetKeysoperation to fetch the records from Microsoft Dynamics AX that match the document filter that we just discussed:

```
static void getKeys()
{
    AxdCVRTitle titleDocument = new AxdCVRTitle();

    // Create a client for as long as we need to
    using (CVRTitleDocumentServiceClient client = new
    CVRTitleDocumentServiceClient())
    {
        // Call the findKeys operation to fetch all of the keys that
        // match the document filter
        EntityKeyPage keyPage = client.getKeys(null, null);

        // Fetch the entity key list from the page
        EntityKey[] entityKeys = keyPage.EntityKeyList;

        // Check if we had matching titles
        if (entityKeys.Length >= 0)
        {
            // Use the keys to read all of the titles
            titleDocument = client.read(null, entityKeys);
        }
    }

    // Loop all the titles to report to the console
    foreach (AxdEntity_CVRTitle title in titleDocument.CVRTitle)
    {
        Console.WriteLine(title.Id + ' ' + title.Name + ' ' + title.
        LengthInMinutes);
    }
}
```

Based on the document filter that selects titles starting with `The`, a part of the resulting titles looks as follows:

```
T000000001 The Godfather 102

T000000002 The Godfather: Part II 102

T000000004 The Good, the Bad and the Ugly 97

T000000007 The Dark Knight 119

T000000008 The Lord of the Rings: The Return of the King 112

T000000009 The Dark Knight Rises 103
```

GetChangedKeys

The `GetChangedKeys` operation also fetches the keys of records from Microsoft Dynamics AX that match the document filter. In addition to this, it also restricts the returned keys to records that have changed since a given date and time.

> **Change tracking**
>
> To be able to use `getChangedKeys`, SQL Server Change Tracking has to be configured. Once change tracking has been configured, the integration ports will need to be reactivated.
>
> Information about change tracking can be found at the following links:
>
> - **Configuring AIF for change tracking**: `http://msdn.microsoft.com/en-us/library/hh433529.aspx`
> - **Enabling/disabling change tracking for SQL Server**: `http://technet.microsoft.com/en-us/library/bb964713.aspx`
> - **Enabling/disabling change data capturing**: `http://technet.microsoft.com/en-us/library/cc627369`

The flow for using the `GetChangedKeys` operation is the same as the one for using the `getKeys` operation. The difference is that you can retrieve only the records that have changed since a given date instead of all the records that the document filter applies to. The following code shows us the use of the same document filter. It also illustrates the use of change tracking to further narrow down the list to only the records that were changed. This assumes that we have updated the records with change tracking enabled:

```
static void getChangedKeys()
{
    AxdCVRTitle titleDocument = new AxdCVRTitle();

    // Create a client for as long as we need to
```

```
using (CVRTitleDocumentServiceClient client = new
CVRTitleDocumentServiceClient())
{
    // Call the getChangedKeys operation to fetch all of the keys
    // that were changed
    // The change date used here was 2013/12/01 15:30
    EntityKeyPage keyPage = client.getChangedKeys(null, null, new
    DateTime(2013, 12, 01, 15, 30, 00));
    // Fetch the entity key list from the page
    EntityKey[] entityKeys = keyPage.EntityKeyList;

    // Check if we had matching titles
    if (keyPage.PageStatus == EntityKeyPageStatus.Success &&
    entityKeys.Length > 0)
    {
        // Use the keys to read all of the titles
        titleDocument = client.read(null, entityKeys);
    }
}

// Loop all the titles to report to the console
foreach (AxdEntity_CVRTitle title in titleDocument.CVRTitle)
{
    Console.WriteLine(title.Id + ' ' + title.Name + ' ' +
    title.LengthInMinutes + ' ' + title.Description);
}
}
```

As we updated one record for this sample, the following is the result:

```
T000000007 The Dark Knight 119 Updated Description for the dark knight
```

Asynchronous communication

So far, we have focused on synchronous communication using the NetTcp adapter. The filesystem adapter and the MSMQ adapter work asynchronously and differently from synchronous adapters.

Asynchronous adapters use the following two tables to store messages:

- `AifGatewayQueue`: The `AifGatewayQueue` table is used in the asynchronous processing of both inbound and outbound messages. Inbound messages are stored in this table after they are retrieved by the gateway receive service. Outbound messages are stored in this table after they are processed by the outbound processing service.

- **AifOutboundProcessingQueue**: The `AifOutboundProcessingQueue` table is used by the send service framework to store requests for outbound messages. These requests are then processed by the outbound processing service that stores a message in the `AifGatewayQueue` table.

The following flowchart displays the relationship between the tables and the classes that are used for asynchronous communication:

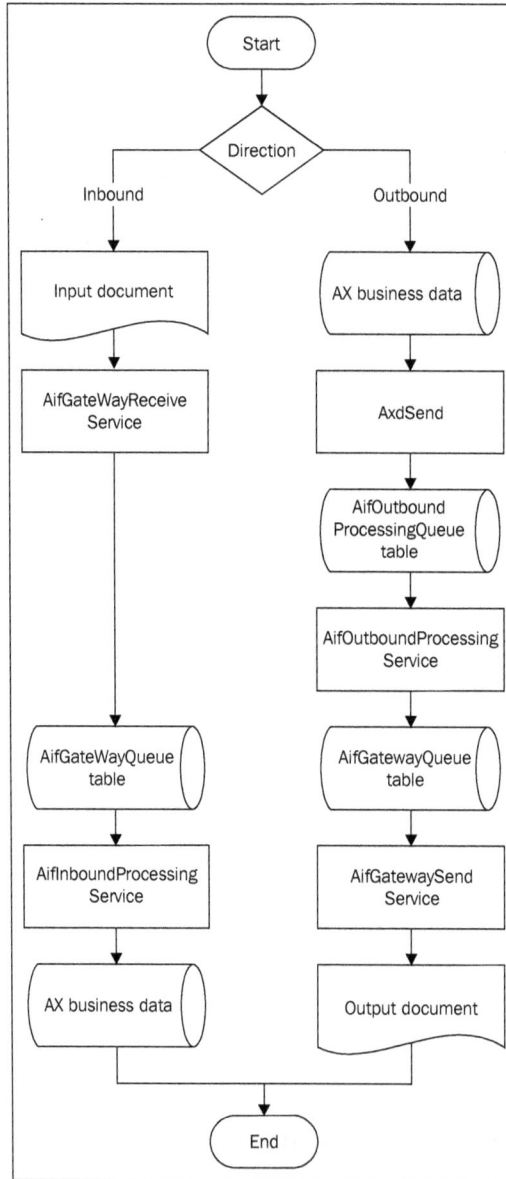

The send service framework

You can use the send service framework when you want to send outbound messages to asynchronous adapters. The following job demonstrates how you can send documents that contain titles to an outbound port:

```
static void CVRAxdSendTitles(Args _args)
{
    AxdSend axdSend = new AxdSend();
    AifConstraintList aifConstraintList = new AifConstraintList();
    AifConstraint aifConstraint = new AifConstraint();

    aifConstraint.parmType(AifConstraintType::NoConstraint);
    aifConstraintList.addConstraint(aifConstraint);

    axdSend.sendMultipleDocuments(classNum(CVRTitleDocument), classNum(
    CVRTitleDocumentService), AifSendMode::Async, aifConstraintList);
}
```

When you run the job, the following dialog will appear:

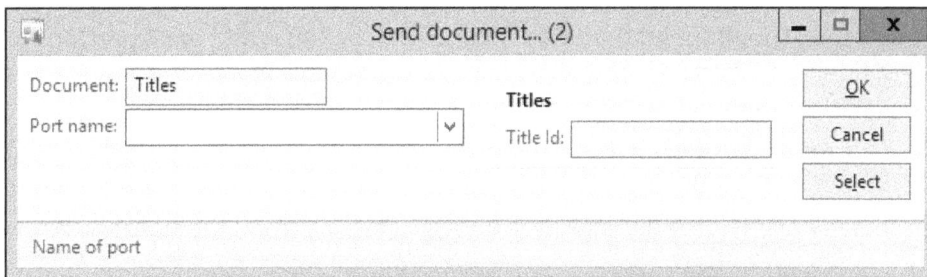

In this dialog, you can select an outbound port in the **Port name** field. In order for this to work, you should create an outbound port and add the CVRTitleDocumentService.find operation to the service operations that are exposed by the port. The Find operation is the default operation used by the AxdSend.sendMultipleDocuments() method as this method uses a query. You can change this query by clicking on the **Select** button.

In a real-life scenario, you should create a new class that extends the AxdSend class instead of creating a job. This will allow you to customize the behavior of the AxdSend class.

When you click on **OK**, a record will be inserted in the AifOutboundProcessingQueue table. To process this record, we will need to set up batch processing, which is what we will discuss next.

Batch processing

When you use an asynchronous adapter such as the filesystem adapter or the MSMQ adapter, you will have to schedule batch tasks to process the messages that are exchanged.

To enable batch processing for asynchronous communication, perform the following steps:

1. Navigate to **System Administration | Inquiries | Batch jobs | Batch jobs**.

2. Press *Ctrl + N* to create a new batch job and enter a description; for example, **AIF asynchronous processing**.

3. Select the new batch job and click on **View tasks**.

4. Press *Ctrl + N* and enter `AifGateWayReceiveService` in the **Class name** field. Also, select the appropriate company account and save the record.

5. Repeat the previous step for the `AifInboundProcessingService`, `AifOutboundProcessingService`, and `AifGatewaySendService` classes. Be sure to add them in that sequence.

6. On all but the first task, add a record in the **Has conditions** grid. The **Task ID** field should point to the task that comes before it and the **Expected status** field should be set to **Ended**. This will help you make sure that the tasks are executed in the correct order.

7. Exit the screen and click on **Recurrence**. Enter a recurrence pattern that fits your scenario and click on **OK**.

8. Finally, navigate to **Functions | Change status** and set the status to **Waiting**.

When developing, waiting for a batch to start is not very efficient. The following job processes the asynchronous messages just as the batches do but saves you time because it can be run manually:

```
static void CVRRunAsycManually(Args _args)
{
    // read the messages
    new AifGateWayReceiveService().run();

    // process inbound messages in queue
    new AifInboundProcessingService().run();

    // process outbound messages in queue
    new AifOutboundProcessingService().run();

    // send messages
```

```
    new AifGateWaySendService().run();

    info('done');
}
```

Summary

In this chapter, we created our first document service in Microsoft Dynamics AX 2012. Document services distinguish themselves from other types of services because they can be created using a wizard. This wizard creates components that are specific to document services and uses them in AIF.

In doing this, the AIF Document Service Wizard allows developers to create services that are capable of the **Create, Read, Update, and Delete (CRUD)** operations on complex documents. The advantage of using document services operations over other solutions such as creating data using SQL statements is that the business logic that is contained in all of the components that make up the service are also executed, such as defaulting and validation of values.

Document services are great for exposing documents, but not so much for exposing pure business logic. In the next chapter, we will discuss a type of service that is ideal for this purpose – custom services.

4
Custom Services

The ability to develop custom services in Microsoft Dynamics AX is not new, but the way it is done in Microsoft Dynamics AX 2012 is. Developers can now create a WCF service in a way that is similar to how they would develop a WCF service in a language like C#. Using attributes to create data and service contracts, development is simplified because you don't have to worry about the technical details of serialization and deserialization. These things are all handled by WCF, which allows you to quickly create powerful services.

By the end of this chapter, you will have learned how to use attributes to create data and service contracts and how to use them to create custom services. You will also be able to deploy services and consume them using a WCF client application.

The following topics will be covered in this chapter:

- **Key components**: Just as some components are specific to document services, there are also components that are specific to custom services. Most of these components use attributes, so we'll see what that is all about too.

- **Creating custom services**: We will create a custom service step-by-step and deploy it. This service will focus on retrieving data from Microsoft Dynamics AX 2012 and exposing it. In another service, we will focus on a more complex scenario. That scenario will expose business logic that allows you to create data in Microsoft Dynamics AX 2012.

- **Consuming a custom service**: Finally, you will learn how to consume a custom service in a .NET WCF application. This is similar to how a document service is consumed.

Key components

In the previous chapter, we discussed the key components of document services. When developing custom services, there are also a few concepts you should be familiar with, starting with attributes.

Attributes

Attributes are classes that contain data just like normal classes, but the purpose of this data is different. Attributes contain metadata that describes targets. **Targets** can be of different types such as classes, interfaces, methods, events, and so on.

Attributes can either be intrinsic or custom. **Intrinsic attributes** are part of **Common Language Runtime (CLR)** and are contained in the .NET framework. **Custom attributes** are attributes that you can create yourself.

Because attributes contain metadata, they are useful only when reflection is used. An example of this is the `DataContract` attribute. The service generation process uses reflection on the classes that the service class uses to determine which of these classes are data contracts.

The following code shows the usage of another attribute called `SysObsoleteAttribute`. It tells the compiler to generate warnings or errors, suggesting that the class has become obsolete and should therefore not be used anymore:

```
[SysObsoleteAttribute("You should be using the SysOperation framework
now instead RunBase", false)]
class RunBase
{
}
```

Custom services attributes

When you create custom services, you will certainly encounter some attributes in X++ that provide metadata to the service generation process. The following table shows you the most commonly used attributes:

Attribute	Description
SysEntryPointAttribute	This is a mandatory attribute in methods that are exposed as a service operation. It indicates that the method is a service operation. Not using this attribute will result in a service group deployment failure.
	An optional parameter specifies whether the AOSAuthorization setting on the tables will be checked when this method is executed on the server.

Attribute	Description
DataContractAttribute	This attribute defines that the attributed class is used as a data contract for a service.
DataMemberAttribute	This attribute indicates that a parameter method is a data member in a data contract for a service.
AifCollectionTypeAttribute	This attribute specifies the type that is used in a collection. It contains the name of the parameter that is targeted and the types of the objects that are contained in the collection.

Data contracts

Because a service and client don't necessarily use the same types internally, they must agree on the type that they will use to exchange data. This agreement, or contract if you will, is called a **data contract**, and is used to describe these datatypes. The data contract is then used to serialize and deserialize the type.

Services use data contracts to describe the parameters and return types for their service operations. However, there are some types that can be serialized without using data contracts. The following types serve as implicit data contracts:

- Primitive types (such as str, int, int64, real, guid, utcdatetime, and date)
- Extended datatypes
- Base enums
- Collections in which all elements are the same type and are of a type that is a valid data contract
- Tables and views

One noticeable exception is the X++ AnyType type, which cannot be used in data contracts. On the other hand, any .NET type that can be serialized by WCF can be used as a data contract, which more than makes up for that.

If you need types other than the ones that are described in the preceding table, you can always create your own data contract in X++. A data contract can be created in the AOT by creating a new class and by adding the DataContractAttribute attribute to the class declaration. You will do this a lot when developing custom services.

Of course, a class without properties cannot hold any data; so, to complete the data contract, you must add data members in the form of methods. You can use the `DataMemberAttribute` attribute to specify that a method is a data member. The data members themselves can use data contracts or any of the types described previously as return types and parameters.

Service contracts

When we talked about the WCF, we saw that a service contract describes the functionality that is exposed. In Microsoft Dynamics AX 2012, you can create a service contract by creating a class in the AOT. This class is called a **service class**. A service class does not need an attribute to specify that it is a service contract, although it is required that this class have the `RunOn` property set to `Server`.

However, when you create such a class, all you have is just a regular class that runs on the server when it is executed. What makes a class a true service class is having methods that are service operations. These methods must have the `SysEntryPointAttribute` attribute to indicate that they are service operations.

Collection types

X++ does not support strongly typed collections, so when we want to return or receive a collection of data contracts, we have to use the `AifCollectionTypeAttribute` class. This attribute is used to specify the type of the collection, both for parameters and return types.

It's possible to specify the following five parameters when using the attribute:

Parameter	Description
Parameter name	This specifies the parameter that the attribute applies to. This is either the name of the parameter or `return` for return values.
Item type	This is the base type of the collection or the key value when the collection is a map.
Extended type name	When the type is `Class`, `Enum`, or `UserType`, this specifies the name of the type.
Value type	When the collection type is a map, this is the type of the value in the map.
Value extended type name	When the collection type is a map and the type is `Class`, `Enum`, or `UserType`, this specifies the name of the type.

Creating custom services

In this section, we will discuss two custom services. One service focuses on exposing data from Microsoft Dynamics AX 2012 while the other focuses on exposing business logic.

The Title service

We will use the `CVRTitleService` service as an example to demonstrate how to create a simple yet powerful service. This service will allow an external program to do the following two things:

- Retrieve the details of a title based on its ID
- Retrieve a list of all titles

Creating the Title data contract

Let's start by creating a new class for the data contract that will contain the data for one title. Create a new class and name it `CVRTitleContract`. In the class declaration, add `DataContractAttribute` to specify that the class is a data contract. Also, declare the variable's ID, name, and description, as shown in the following code snippet:

```
[DataContractAttribute('Title')]
public class CVRTitleDataContract
{
    CVRTitleId      id;
    CVRTitleName    name;
    Description     description;
}
```

Next, add three parameter methods, one for each of the properties of the data contract. Use `DataMemberAttribute` to indicate that the methods are data contract members, as shown in the following code snippet:

```
[DataMemberAttribute('Description')]
public Description parmDescription(Description _description =
description)
{
    description - _description;
    return description;
}


[DataMemberAttribute('Id')]
```

```
public CVRTitleId parmId(CVRTitleId _id = id)
{
    id = _id;
    return id;
}

[DataMemberAttribute('Name')]
public CVRTitleName parmName(CVRTitleName _name = name)
{
    name = _name;
    return name;
}
```

As you can see in the preceding code, we construct the attributes using an optional string parameter. This parameter is the name. Because we do that, a client application can get the value of a member using code such as title.Description. If we don't pass a name, the client application would have to use CVRTitleDataContract. parmDescription instead, which doesn't look as neat. It's better to not expose the prefixes and other naming conventions that are specific to Microsoft Dynamics AX such as the DataContract suffix and parm prefix.

Essentially, you now have a functional data contract. However, there are a few tweaks that we can still perform when constructing the data contract. Because our contract is tied to a record of the CVRTitle type, we can create a static new() method that creates an instance of the data contract based on a record of this type. Note that these steps are optional, but performing them has the following main advantages:

- In Microsoft Dynamics AX 2012, it is impossible to create an instance of the contract in a way other than the one used by the developer who created the intended contract, because both the new() and construct() methods are not publicly available. This way, a developer who creates an instance of the contract is less likely to make mistakes.

- When creating an instance of the data contract, you will have less coding to do because the contract is filled in the static new() method. This will make your code cleaner and easier to understand.

Start by overriding the new() method and set it as protected so only the CVRTitleDataContract class or one of its subclasses can call the method, shown as follows:

```
protected void new()
{
}
```

Always create a `construct()` method for your classes, but if it doesn't return a valid instance, set it as `private`. A valid instance means that when constructed, all of the variables needed for execution have to be initialized. Creating an instance of the data contract using the `construct()` method isn't valid in this case because the properties `id`, `name`, and `description` are not set:

```
private static CVRTitleDataContract construct()
{
    return new CVRTitleDataContract();
}
```

Finally, create a static `new()` method that takes a `CVRTitle` record as a parameter, uses it to construct an instance of the `CVRTitleDataContract` class, and returns it:

```
public static CVRTitleDataContract newFromTableRecord(CVRTitle
_title)
{
    CVRTitleDataContract    contract = CVRTitleDataContract::
    construct();

    contract.parmId(_title.Id);
    contract.parmName(_title.Name);
    contract.parmDescription(_title.Description);

    return contract;
}
```

> **Best practices**
> These recommendations are based on the best practices defined by Microsoft at `http://msdn.microsoft.com/en-us/library/aa854210.aspx`.

So there you go, you have created your first data contract. That wasn't too hard, was it? Now, let's see how we can create a list data contract, which is a little more complex.

Creating the Title list data contract

We will create a list data contract using the data contract that we just created by performing the following steps:

1. Start by creating a new class and name it `CVRTitleListDataContract`. Add the `DataContractAttribute` attribute to it to declare that the class is a data contract and add a list variable that will store a list of titles, shown as follows:

    ```
    [DataContractAttribute]
    public class CVRTitleListDataContract
    {
        List titleList;
    }
    ```

2. Next, we add the usual constructers, `new()` and `construct()`. Also, don't forget to initialize the list object, shown as follows:

    ```
    protected void new()
    {
        titleList = new List(Types::Class);
    }

    public static CVRTitleListDataContract construct()
    {
        return new CVRTitleListDataContract();
    }
    ```

3. Next, we have to provide you with a way to add titles to the list. Add a method that takes a title data contract and adds it to the end of the list, as shown in the following code snippet:

    ```
    public void addTitleToList(CVRTitleDataContract
    _titleDataContract)
    {
        titleList.addEnd(_titleDataContract);
    }
    ```

4. Finally, we add the data member method that will return a list of titles. Add the `DataMemberAttribute` attribute as you would for every other data member, but also add two more attributes of the type `AifCollectionTypeAttribute`, as shown in the following code snippet:

    ```
    [DataMemberAttribute
    ,AifCollectionTypeAttribute('return', Types::Class,
    classstr(CVRTitleDataContract))
    ```

```
,AifCollectionTypeAttribute('_titleList', Types::Class,
classstr(CVRTitleDataContract))]
public List parmTitleList(List _titleList = titleList)
{
    titleList = _titleList;
    return titleList;
}
```

As we've discussed previously, the `AifCollectionTypeAttribute` attribute is used to specify the type of the list, because X++ does not support strongly typed lists. In this case, `AifCollectionTypeAttribute` takes the following three parameters:

- The name of the parameter; in this example, `_titleList`. For the return value, the name is `return`.
- The base type of the type, which is `Class` in this example.
- The name of the type; in our case, the class name is `CVRTitleDataContract`.

This concludes the creation of the two contracts that we will need for our service. Now let's see how we can use them.

Creating the Title service class

We will create a service class that has the following two service operations:

- An operation that returns the details of a title based on its ID
- An operation that returns all of the titles

First, we create a service class. Create a new class and name it `CVRTitleService`, as shown in the following code snippet. We do not need to add anything more to the class declaration because a service class declaration does not need an attribute:

```
public class CVRTitleService
{
}
```

One thing we have to make sure is that this class runs on the server when it is executed. To do this, right-click on the class, click on **Properties**, and then set the **RunOn** property to **Server**.

Creating the Title service operation

OK, let's create a service operation that retrieves the details of a title based on its ID. Start by creating a new method. You can see the source code of this method in the following snippet. As you can see, we add the `SysEntryPointAttribute` attribute to specify that the method is a service operation. We add `true` between brackets when constructing the attribute to specify that the AOS authorization has to be performed when the code runs on the server. This will help you make sure that the user who calls the service operations has the necessary permissions on the tables that the method uses:

```
[SysEntryPointAttribute(true)]
public CVRTitleDataContract getTitle(CVRTitleId _titleId)
{
    CVRTitleDataContract contract;

    contract = CVRTitleDataContract::newFromTableRecord(CVRTitle::
    find(_titleId));

    return contract;
}
```

As you can see, further in the method, we use the `_titleId` parameter to find the record in the database and construct a new data contract with it. Then, we return the data contract.

Creating the Title list service operation

This service operation will use the list data contract to return a list of all the titles. As you can see in the following code, all titles in the `CVRTitle` table are traversed. Then, a data contract is constructed and added to the list contract. Finally, a list contract that contains the details of all of the titles is returned:

```
[SysEntryPointAttribute(true)]
public CVRTitleListDataContract getAllTitles()
{
    CVRTitleListDataContract titleListDataContract =
    CVRTitleListDataContract::construct();
    CVRTitleDataContract      titleContract;
    CVRTitle                  titleRecord;

    while select titleRecord
    {
```

```
        // Convert the record to a data contract
        titleContract = CVRTitleDataContract::newFromTableRecord(
        titleRecord);

        // Add the title data contract to the list of data contracts
        titleListDataContract.addTitleToList(titleContract);
    }

    return titleListDataContract;
}
```

Creating the Title service contract

The final thing we have to do before we can deploy our service is define the service contract. To create the service contract, perform the following steps:

1. Open the AOT by pressing *Ctrl* + *D*.
2. Right-click on the **Services** node and then click on **New Service**.
3. Right-click on the newly created service and then click on **Properties**.
4. Change the value of the **Name** and **Class** properties to CVRTitleService.
5. Change the value of the **Namespace** property to http://schemas.contoso.com/ServiceContracts.
6. Expand the **CVRTitleService** node, right-click on **Operations**, and click on **Add Operation**.
7. The **Add service operations** form pops up. Select the **Add** field for the **getAllTitles** and **getTitle** methods and then click on **OK**.
8. Click on the **Save All** button to save the changes.

Deploying services

To deploy our custom services, we will use a basic port. For this reason, we need to add the services that we want to deploy to a service group. We will add all of them to one service group: **CVRCustomServices**. Let's deploy our custom services using the following steps:

1. Open the AOT by pressing *Ctrl* + *D*.
2. Right-click on the **Service Groups** node and then click on **New Service Group**.
3. Right-click on the newly created service group and then click on **Properties**.
4. Change the value of the **Name** property to CVRCustomServices.
5. Right-click on the service group and select **New Service Node Reference**.

6. Select the service node reference that was added and change the value of the **Service** property to CVRTitleService.

7. Finally, right-click on the service group and click on **Deploy Service Group** to deploy the service.

Now that you have completed these steps, navigate to **System administration | Setup | Services and Application Integration Framework | Inbound ports**. The **CVRCustomServices** inbound port is available there as a basic inbound port and is now ready to be consumed.

The rental service

The contracts and service operations that we have created to retrieve titles are pretty simple. They might be all you need in a real-life application. However, it is more likely that you will need data contracts that are more complex. To demonstrate this, we've added the rental service to the demo application. The rental service allows external applications to retrieve rental information or create rentals. Creating this service with all data contracts step-by-step would take too long, so we will discuss the artifacts only at a high level, starting with the database schema of the tables that we will use.

Rental header and line tables

The following is a simple schema of the tables that we will use. A rental header contains information about the rental, such as the store and the transaction date. A rental header is related to one or more lines that contain the details of the rental, such as the item that was rented:

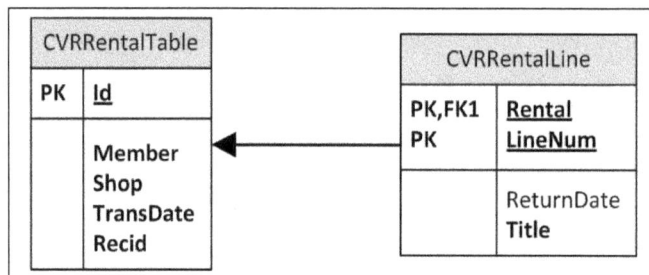

Rental service operations

There are three service operations available in the rental service:

- CreateRental: This service operation takes a parameter of type CVRRentalDocumentDataContract and uses it to register a rental in the CVRRentalTable and CVRRentalLine tables

- GetAllRentals: This service operation returns a list of CVRRentalDocumentDataContract data contracts by using the CVRRentalDocumentListDataContract data contract

- GetAllRentalsForMember: This service operation does the same as the GetAllRentals operation but returns rentals only for a specific member

Rental data contracts

There are a total of five data contracts that the rental service uses. The relationships between these data contracts and the service operations are explained in the following diagram:

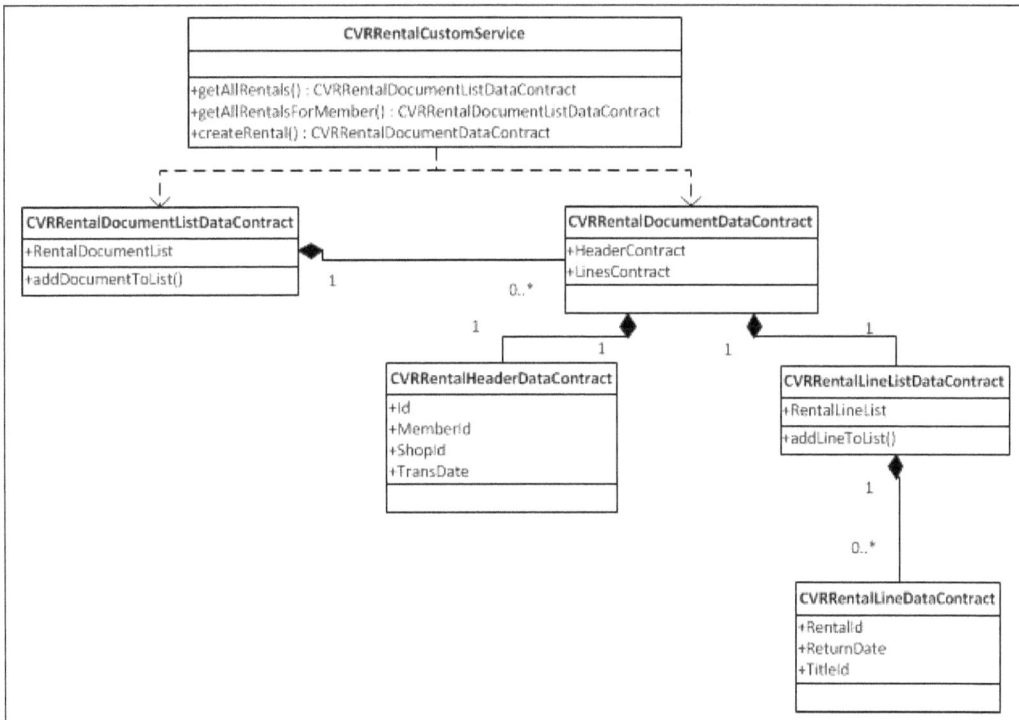

From the bottom up, the following are the contracts and their functions:

- CVRRentalLineDataContract: This data contract contains the properties of a rental line, including the title and the return date.

- CVRRentalLineListDataContract: This data contract contains a list of lines. It uses AifCollectionTypeAttribute to describe that the list contains items of the CVRRentalLineDataContract type.

- CVRRentalHeaderDataContract: This data contract contains the header information about a rental, including the member ID and the transaction date.

- CVRRentalDocumentDataContract: This data contract represents a rental document. It contains a header and a list of lines, respectively using the CVRRentalHeaderDataContract and CVRRentalLineListDataContract types.

- CVRRentalDocumentListDataContract: This data contract contains a list of rental documents and is used in the getAllRentals and getAllRentalsForMember service operations.

This demonstrates that you can use data contracts within data contracts to make logical entities. Although it might seem complex at first glance, each class has its own responsibilities, which makes them reusable and easier to maintain.

The createRental service operation

The following is the createRental service operation. It uses the rental document data contract to register a rental in the database:

```
[SysEntryPointAttribute(true)]
public CVRRentalRefRecId createRental(CVRRentalDocumentDataContract
_rentalDocument)
{
    CVRRentalTable rentalTable;
    CVRRentalLine   rentalLine;

    CVRRentalLineDataContract      lineDataContract;
    CVRRentalLineListDataContract  lineListDataContract;

    ListEnumerator   enumerator;

    // Insert the rental header
```

```
    rentalTable.clear();
    rentalTable.Id = _rentalDocument.parmHeaderContract().parmId();
    rentalTable.Member = CVRMember::find(_rentalDocument.
parmHeaderContract().parmMemberId()).RecId;
    rentalTable.Shop = CVRShop::find(_rentalDocument.
parmHeaderContract().parmShopId()).RecId;
    rentalTable.TransDate  = _rentalDocument.parmHeaderContract()
    .parmTransDate();
    rentalTable.insert();

    // Get the list of rental lines
    lineListDataContract = _rentalDocument.parmLinesContract();

    // Initialize an enumerator to loop the lines
    enumerator = lineListDataContract.parmRentalLineList()
    .getEnumerator();

    // As long as we have lines
    while(enumerator.moveNext())
    {
        // Get the current line
        lineDataContract = enumerator.current();

        rentalLine.clear();
        rentalLine.Rental = rentalTable.RecId;
        rentalLine.Title = CVRTitle::find(lineDataContract.
parmTitleId()).RecId;
        rentalLine.ReturnDate  = lineDataContract.parmReturnDate();
        rentalLine.insert();
    }

    return rentalTable.RecId;
}
```

Now, let's see how we can consume the services that we have created using a .NET WCF application.

Consuming services

Now that we have created and exposed our custom services, they can be consumed by other applications. To demonstrate this, we will use Visual Studio and write two code samples.

Example 1 – retrieving titles

The first example of consuming a service deals with the retrieval of a title list. We want to be able to write a list of titles to the console window.

Adding the service reference

To add the service reference, perform the following steps:

1. In Visual Studio, create a console application just like we did in the previous chapter when testing the document service.

2. Right-click on the project node and select **Add Service Reference...**. The **Add Service Reference** window opens.

3. In the **Address** drop-down box, specify `http://DYNAX01:8101/DynamicsAx/Services/CVRCustomServices` as the address for the service and then click on **Go**. Of course, replace `DYNAX:8101` with the server and WSDL port of your installation. The address is queried and the services and operations that are available are listed.

4. In the **Namespace** box, specify the namespace that you want to use: `AxCustomServicesRef`.

After performing these steps, the **Add Service Reference** window should look similar to the one shown in the following screenshot. On the left-hand side of the window, the services that were found are listed. In our case, we see that **CVRCustomServices**, along with three other services, are contained in the service group. On the right-hand side of the window, we see the operations that are available for the selected service:

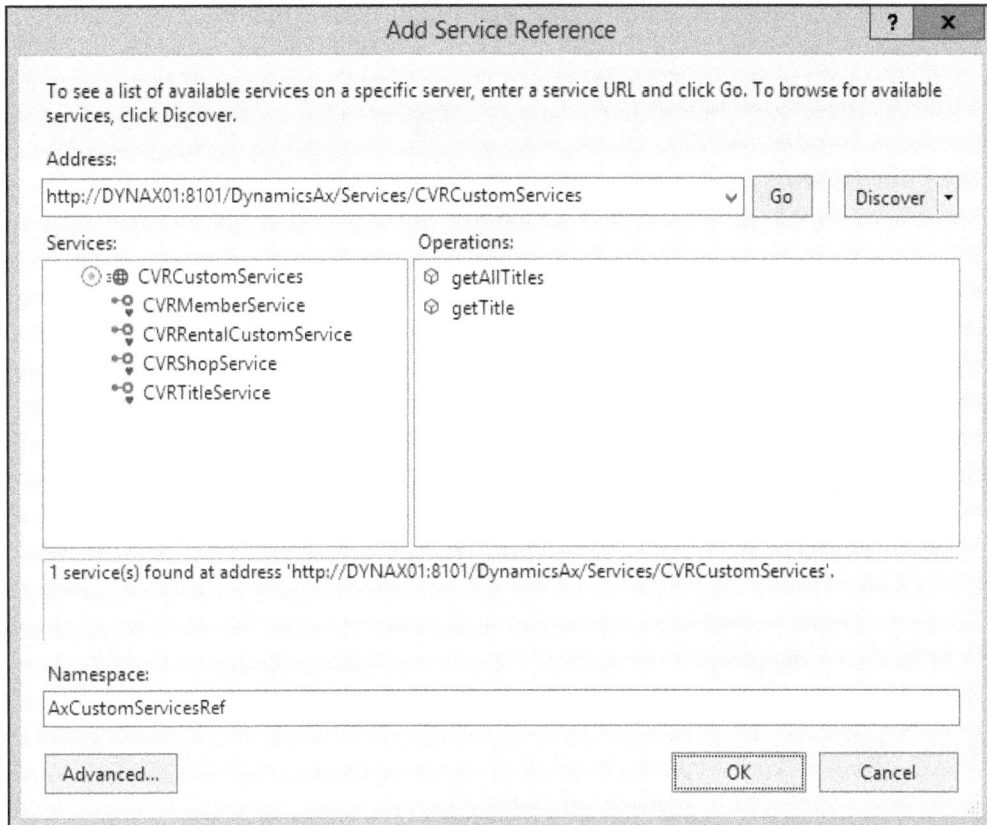

When you click on **OK**, **ServiceModel Metadata Utility** (SvcUtil.exe) creates a client proxy and types according to the metadata found in the service WSDL. You can view the types by opening the **Object Browser** menu.

Consuming the service

To consume the service in the console application and retrieve a list of titles, you can use the following code:

```
static void Main(string[] args)
{
    // Create an instance of the proxy client
```

```
CVRTitleServiceClient theClient = new CVRTitleServiceClient();

// Create the call context
CallContext theContext = new CallContext();
theContext.Company = "CEU";
theContext.Language = "EN-US";
theContext.LogonAsUser = "UserName";

// Invoke the getAllTitles service operation
CVRTitleListDataContract theListContract =
theClient.getAllTitles(theContext);

// Loop all of the returned titles
foreach (Title title in theListContract.parmTitleList)
{
    Console.WriteLine(String.Format("{0} - {1} - {2}", title.Id,
    title.Name, title.Description));
}

// Wait for the user to press a key
Console.Read();
}
```

The output should be a title list shown as follows:

```
T000000001 - Memento - Memento weird movie
T000000002 - Lord of the rings - Lord of the rings long movie
```

Example 2 – registering a rental

In this second example, we will consume a service that enables us to register a rental. We will again take a look at creating the service reference but focus a little more on some advanced options available to us when creating the service reference.

Creating the service reference – advanced

We added a service reference in the previous example, so first delete it. This allows us to recreate the service reference for this example and look at it in more detail.

To create the service reference again, perform the following steps:

1. In the **Solution Explorer** panel in Visual Studio, right-click on the project node and click on **Add Service Reference....** The **Add Service Reference** window opens.

2. In the **Address** drop-down box, specify `http://DYNAX01:8101/`
   `DynamicsAx/Services/CVRCustomServices` as the address for the service
   and then click on **Go**. The address is queried and the services and operations
   that are available are listed.

3. In the **Namespace** box, specify the namespace that you want to use:
   `AxCustomServicesRef`.

4. Click on the **Advanced** button available on this screen. The **Service
   Reference Settings** window opens.

Let's pause here and look at two options (as shown in the following screenshot)
that are of particular interest to us: **Always generate message contracts** and
Collection type:

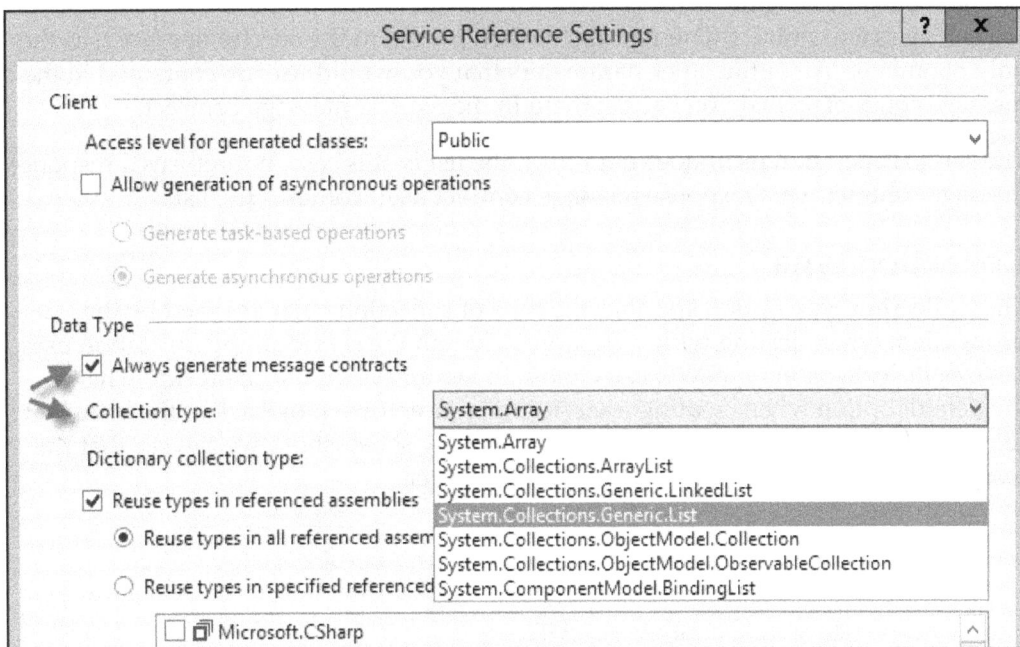

Always generate message contracts

The **Always generate message contracts** option determines if the message contracts
will be generated for the client. When you do not use this, the client has service
operations that contain the same number of parameters as provided on the service
operation. When this option is checked, the message contracts are used on the service
operations instead of the parameter list. The parameters that would normally be passed
to the service operation are then wrapped in a message contract. This can be useful
when you want to make sure that all of the service operations take only one parameter.

If we look back at the previous sample code, it could also be modified to work with the message contracts that were generated, as demonstrated in the following code:

```
// Create the request message contract
CVRTitleServiceGetAllTitlesRequest theRequest = new
CVRTitleServiceGetAllTitlesRequest(theContext);

// Invoke the getAllTitles service operation
CVRTitleServiceGetAllTitlesResponse theResponse = theClient.
getAllTitles(theRequest);

// Retrieve the list of titles
CVRTitleListDataContract theListContract = theResponse.response;
```

Instead of just passing the context to the service operation, we need to create a request message contract. This contract is then passed to the service operation as the only parameter. All of the other parameters that you would use are contained in the message contract so that you can set them in the request message contract.

The service operation itself does not return the list in this case, but returns a response message contract. This response message contract itself contains the list.

Collection type

The **Collection type** option specifies the type of collections that are used by the proxy client when dealing with collections. Though the service implementation uses `List` as the collection type, you can choose to use arrays on the client side. This is the default option when creating a service reference. If we look back at the code that retrieves the list of titles (as shown in the following screenshot), we can see that the resulting collection type is an array of `Title` objects:

```
// Invoke the getAllTitles service operation
CVRTitleListDataContract theListContract = theClient.getAllTitles(theContext);

// Loop all of the returned titles
foreach (Title title in theListContract.parmTitleList)
{
    Console.WriteLine(String.Format("{0}   Title[] CVRTitleListDataContract.parmTitleList   itle.Description));
}
```

If we choose a different type, for example, `System.Collections.Generic.List`, we can see that the return type is now a generic list of `Title` objects instead of an array, as shown in the following screenshot:

```
// Invoke the getAllTitles service operation
CVRTitleListDataContract theListContract = theClient.getAllTitles(theContext);

// Loop all of the returned titles
foreach (Title title in theListContract.parmTitleList)
{
    Console.WriteLine(String.Format("{0}  List<Title> CVRTitleListDataContract.parmTitleList  .Description));
}
```

Consuming the service

The following code uses the rental service and creates a rental with two titles. First, start by adding the `using` statement so that the types in the service reference are available to you. Use the following code to do this:

```
using DynamicsAxServices.Chapter4.Rentals.AxCustomServiceRef;
```

Then, you can add the following code to consume the rental service:

```
CVRRentalCustomServiceClient client = new
CVRRentalCustomServiceClient();

// Create the rental header information
RentalHeader header = new RentalHeader();
header.MemberId = "M00001";
header.RentalId = "R00001";
header.ShopId = "S00002";
header.TransDate = DateTime.UtcNow;

// Create a rental line
RentalLine line = new RentalLine();
line.RentalId = "R00001";
line.Title = "T00001";
line.ReturnDate = DateTime.UtcNow;

// Create a second rental line
RentalLine secondLine = new RentalLine();
secondLine.RentalId = "R00001";
secondLine.Title = "T00003";
secondLine.ReturnDate = DateTime.UtcNow;

// Add it to the lines for the Rental
RentalLines lines = new RentalLines();
```

```
lines.LinesList = new List<RentalLine>();
lines.LinesList.Add(line);
lines.LinesList.Add(secondLine);

// Compose the Rental document
Rental Rental = new Rental();
Rental.RentalHeader = header;
Rental.RentalLines = lines;

// Invoke the creation of the Rental
long rentalRecId = client.createRental(null, Rental);

Console.WriteLine(String.Format("Rental created with record id {0}",
Convert.ToString(rentalRecId)));
Console.ReadLine();
```

To explain how this works, we will go through the code one block at a time. The following is the first line of code:

```
CVRRentalCustomServiceClient client = new
CVRRentalCustomServiceClient();
```

Just as in the previous samples, the first thing to do is to create an instance of the proxy client. When we have instantiated the client, we can start building the document that is required by the service operation that we are going to call. First up is the rental header, shown as follows:

```
RentalHeader header = new RentalHeader();
header.MemberId = "M00001 ";
header.RentalId = "R00001";
header.ShopId = "S00002";
header.TransDate = DateTime.UtcNow;
```

The header is created by creating an instance of the RentalHeader contract. Note that this is a data contract that is generated by the SvcUtil tool and corresponds with CVRRentalHeaderDataContract. The name RentalHeader comes from the DataMemberAttribute attribute that we defined in X++. The following block of code creates a rental line:

```
RentalLine line = new RentalLine();
line.RentalId = "R00001";
line.Title = "T00001";
line.ReturnDate = DateTime.UtcNow;
```

In this sample, we are adding two of those lines. As with `RentalHeader`, the same remark applies for the `RentalLine` type. This is the `CVRRentalLineDataContract` contract that has been generated at the client side with the name that was specified in the `DataMemberAttribute` attribute:

```
RentalLines lines = new RentalLines();
lines.LinesList = new List<RentalLine>();
lines.LinesList.Add(line);
lines.LinesList.Add(secondLine);
```

Next, the lines that we previously created need to be added to a list data contract. We do this by creating an instance of the `CVRRentalLineListDataContract` contract. In this contract, we add a list that contains the two lines that we have created:

```
Rental Rental = new Rental();
Rental.RentalHeader = header;
Rental.RentalLines = lines;
```

We have created the header, two lines, and a list that contains these lines. At this point, we can glue these together and obtain a rental document object to pass to the service operation. The `Rental` type matches the `CVRRentalDocumentDataContract` contract and gets its name from the `DataMemberAttribute` attribute in X++.

Last but not least, we invoke the `createRental` service operation and pass the document to it. The result is `RecId` of the created `CVRRentalHeader` record.

```
long rentalRecId = client.createRental(null, Rental);

Console.WriteLine(String.Format("Rental created with record id {0}",
Convert.ToString(rentalRecId)));
```

Summary

It should be clear that custom services provide a fast and powerful way to expose data and business logic. Custom services are capable of exposing both simple and complex entities. This makes them an alternative to document services. An aspect that custom services are far superior in is the aspect of exposing business logic. This will probably make custom services the preferred method of integration in many of your implementations.

In the next chapter, we will see how we can use custom services and data contracts in the SysOperation framework.

5
The SysOperation Framework

The SysOperation framework is new in Microsoft Dynamics AX 2012 and is the preferred way to create batch jobs. It replaces the RunBase and RunBaseBatch frameworks, which remain available for backward compatibility. When Microsoft Dynamics AX 2012 was released, the SysOperation framework was known as the **Business Operation Framework (BOF)**.

The SysOperation framework provides all of the functionality of the RunBaseBatch framework and more. In this chapter, we will discuss the differences between these frameworks and point out the benefits of the SysOperation framework.

The following topics are covered in this chapter:

- **SysOperation versus RunBaseBatch**: In the previous versions of Microsoft Dynamics AX, the RunBaseBatch framework was the preferred way to create business logic that should run in batches. By comparing RunBaseBatch and SysOperation, we will show you that using SysOperation is the way to go in Microsoft Dynamics AX 2012.

- **Creating a SysOperation service**: We will demonstrate how to create a SysOperation service. Much of this will already be familiar to you as we will be using services and data contracts. Some new elements will be introduced, including attributes.

- **Running a SysOperation service**: The RunBaseBatch framework can only run logic in two modes: synchronously on the client side or asynchronously in the batch. The SysOperation framework has four modes; these modes are called execution modes. This section will help you in picking the best mode for your situation.

- **Custom controllers**: Some batches stand alone but others are started in a specific context, for example, a form. In many cases, you want to act on the arguments that this form passes to the SysOperation framework, such as the record that was selected. Creating custom controllers allows you to do so, and that's exactly what we will do.

- **Custom UI Builders**: When you want to modify the user interface of a SysOperation service, UI Builder classes are the way to go. In this part, we will create a UI Builder class and look at the various ways through which we can change the behavior of the user interface.

- **Multithreading**: The SysOperation framework leverages the batch framework for better performance. It uses multiple threads that run in parallel to achieve a larger throughput.

At the end of this chapter, you will be able to create a SysOperation service, use controllers, and customize the user interface of a SysOperation service. You will also have learned how to improve the performance of your code using execution modes and runtime tasks.

SysOperation versus RunBaseBatch

Before going into the details of using the new SysOperation framework, let's put it next to the RunBaseBatch framework to find out what the main differences between the two of them are.

The first difference is that the SysOperation framework uses WCF services to run the processes and handle communication between the client and server. One of the advantages of this is that the client/server communication is less chatty, so the connection doesn't need to be kept alive as opposed to the RPC communication of the RunBaseBatch framework.

The second big difference between the two is the way they implement the **Model-View-Controller (MVC)** pattern. The RunBaseBatch framework uses one class that extends from the `RunBaseBatch` class. All of the components contained in the MVC pattern are contained within the same class, described as follows:

- The **model** is identified by the **class members**.
- The **view** is handled by the `dialog()`, `putToDialog()`, and `getFromDialog()` methods. These methods present a dialog to the user and help you put data on and get data from the dialog.
- The **controller** is the `run()` method as this is the place where you implement the business logic.

Thus, the biggest disadvantage of the RunBaseBatch framework is clear: everything is contained in the same class.

The SysOperation framework makes better use of the MVC pattern than the RunBaseBatch framework. All of the MVC components are separated. This is demonstrated as follows:

- The **model** is handled by a class that defines the **data contract**.
- The **view** is a dialog that is now automatically generated by the **UI Builder**. This UI Builder uses the data contract to determine the contents of the dialog.
- The **controller** is being taken care of by the service controller class.

The implementation of the MVC pattern for both the frameworks is visualized in the following diagram:

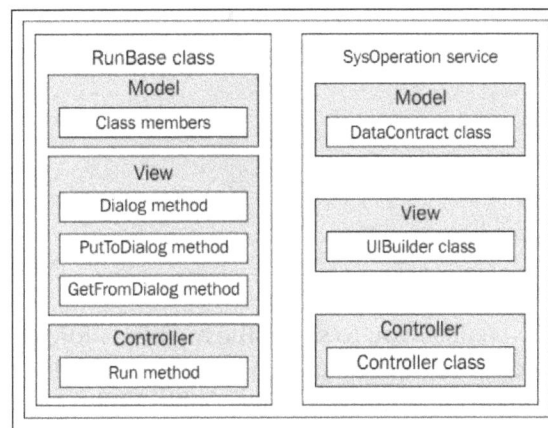

A third notable advantage is that it is fairly easy to expose SysOperation framework services to external consumers. The only thing that you need to do for this is add the SysOperation framework service to a service group and deploy this using an integration port.

So, the advantages of the SysOperation framework can be summarized as follows:

- It makes use of services
- The SysOperation framework makes correct use of the MVC pattern
- It has more efficient client/server communication
- The UI is automatically generated based on data contracts
- It involves less extra effort to externally expose the services
- It's a way to build service-oriented applications in Microsoft Dynamics AX

Creating a SysOperation service

In this demonstration, we will create a SysOperation service that detects members with overdue rentals. These members will get the blocked status by setting a checkbox on the member in the database.

The dialog for the service will look like the following screenshot:

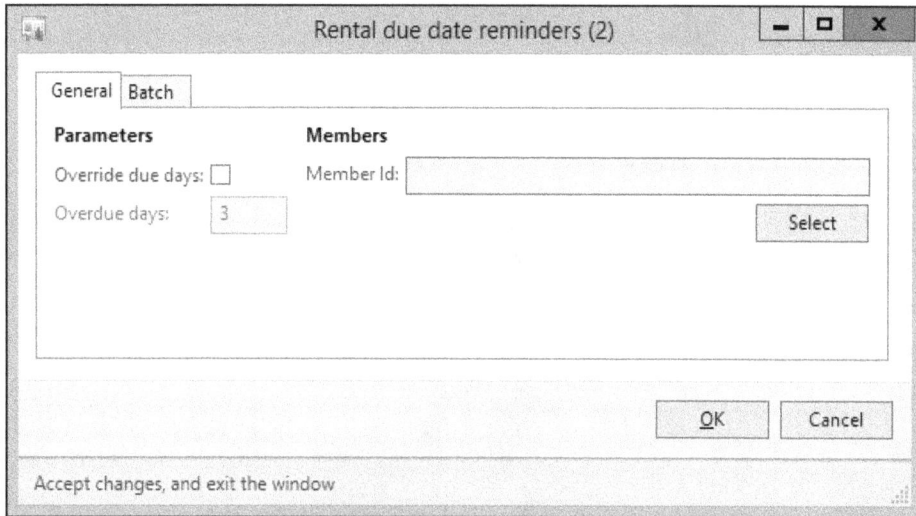

Rental due date reminders (2)			— □ X
General Batch			
Parameters		**Members**	
Override due days: ☐		Member Id:	
Overdue days: 3			Select
		OK	Cancel
Accept changes, and exit the window			

As you can see, a query enables you to select the members for which the rentals should be checked. By enabling the checkbox, you can override the number of overdue days that are allowed before a member is blocked.

The SysOperation framework uses services to execute business logic; you have already learned most of the skills needed in *Chapter 4*, *Custom Services*.

The data contract

We will now create a new data contract, but as we have already demonstrated the creation of a data contract in the earlier chapters, we can be briefer here. The data contract that we'll make will have the following three members:

- parmNumberOfOverdueDays: This holds the value for the number of overdue days that are allowed.

- parmOverrideNumOfDays: This is a Boolean value that indicates that we want to override the number of overdue days that are allowed. We will use this later to demonstrate how to override the modifiedField() method.

- parmQuery: This holds the query as a string.

Declaration and members

To start, create a new class and name it `CVRRentalDueDateReminderContract`. Set the new method to `protected` and add a construct method in the same way as the earlier examples. The rest of the class and its members look like the following code:

```
[DataContractAttribute]
public class CVRRentalDueDateReminderContract
{
    CVRNumberOverdueDays              numberOverdueDays;
    CVROverrideNumberOfOverdueDays    overrideNumOfDays;
    str                               packedQuery;
}

[DataMemberAttribute('OverdueDays')
,SysOperationDisplayOrderAttribute('2')]
public CVRNumberOverdueDays parmNumberOverdueDays(CVRNumberOverdueDays
_numberOverdueDays = numberOverdueDays)
{
    numberOverdueDays = _numberOverdueDays;
    return numberOverdueDays;
}

[DataMemberAttribute('OverrideNumOfDays')
,SysOperationDisplayOrderAttribute('1')]
public CVROverrideNumberOfOverdueDays parmOverrideNumOfDays(CVROverrid
eNumberOfOverdueDays _overrideNumOfDays = overrideNumOfDays)
{
    overrideNumOfDays = _overrideNumOfDays;
    return overrideNumOfDays;
}

[DataMemberAttribute
,AifQueryTypeAttribute('_packedQuery', querystr(CVRMember))]
public str parmQuery(str _packedQuery = packedQuery)
{
    packedQuery = _packedQuery;
    return packedQuery;
}
```

As you can see, the data contract uses a number of new attributes. The `SysOperationDisplayOrderAttribute` attribute is used to specify the order in which the fields are displayed on the dialog. The `AifQueryTypeAttribute` attribute specifies that a member is a query. Adding this attribute will add a **Select** button and query values on the dialog.

Query helper methods

When we want to use a query on a SysOperation service, we have to declare it using a string variable in our data contract. You can clearly see this in the data contract that we have described previously. The data member must have the string type to make sure that the data contract can be serialized.

To make working with the data contract easier, we will add two helper methods to the data contract. One method will set the query based on a query object; the other will return a query object based on the string value in the data contract, shown as follows:

```
public void setQuery(Query _query)
{
    packedQuery = SysOperationHelper::base64Encode(_query.pack());
}

public Query getQuery()
{
    return new Query(SysOperationHelper::base64Decode(packedQuery));
}
```

These methods are optional, but they create cleaner code for other methods such as the service operation.

Service and service operation

A SysOperation service needs a service and a service operation. This operation will be executed when the **OK** button is clicked on the dialog or when the job executes in the batch. Logically, this is where the business logic goes.

To create the service, add a new class to the AOT and name it CVRRentalDueDateReminderService:

```
public class CVRRentalDueDateReminderService
{
}
```

Next, add a new method. This method is the service operation and contains the business logic for the SysOperation service. The operation contains the following code:

```
[SysEntryPointAttribute(true)]
public void checkDueDates(CVRRentalDueDateReminderContract
  _dueDateReminderContract)
{
    QueryRun    queryRun;
```

```
CVRMember    cvrMember;

// Get the query from the data contract
queryRun = new QueryRun(_dueDateReminderContract.getQuery());

// Loop all the members in the query
while (queryRun.next())
{
    // Get the current member record
    cvrMember = queryRun.get(tableNum(CVRMember));

    // Check if the member is already blocked
    if(!cvrMember.BlockedForRental &&
        this.doesMemberHaveOverdueRentals(cvrMember.RecId,
        _dueDateReminderContract.parmNumberOverdueDays()))
    {
        ttsBegin;
        cvrMember.selectForUpdate(true);
        cvrMember.BlockedForRental = NoYes::Yes;
        cvrMember.update();
        ttsCommit;
    }
}
}
```

As you can see, a new `QueryRun` instance is created based on the query of the data contract. We use the helper method that we added previously to retrieve the query object. Next, we use the `queryRun` object to loop all members and check if the member has rentals that are overdue. If so, we set the `BlockedForRental` field to `true` on the member record.

The `doesMemberHaveOverdueRentals()` method contains the logic that checks if the member has rentals that are overdue:

```
private boolean doesMemberHaveOverdueRentals(    CVRMemberRefRecId
_memberRecId

                                            ,    CVRNumberOverdueDays
_overDueDays )
{
    CVRRentalTable   rentalTable;
    CVRRentalLine    rentalLine;
    TransDate        dateLimit = systemDateGet() - _overDueDays;

    // Check if there is a rental line that is not returned yet,
    // overdue and for the current member
```

```
select firstOnly RecId from rentalLine
    join    RecId, Member from    rentalTable
    where   rentalTable.RecId    == rentalLine.Rental
    &&      rentalTable.Member   == _memberRecId
    &&      !rentalLine.ReturnDate
    &&      dateLimit > rentalLine.DueDate;

    return rentalLine.RecId;
}
```

Menu item

The SysOperation framework is menu-item-driven. To start a SysOperation service from the user interface, you click on a menu item. This menu item contains a few properties that are related to the SysOperation framework. We will discuss these properties in further detail later, but for now, let's just create a menu item in the most basic way. To create the menu item, perform the following steps:

1. In the developer workspace, open the AOT.

2. Expand the **Menu Items** node, right-click on **Action**, and then click on **New Menu Item**.

3. Rename the menu item to CVRRentalDueDateReminderService.

4. Right-click on the menu item and then click on **Properties**.

5. Set the label property to **Rental due date reminders**.

6. Set the **ObjectType** to **Class** and enter SysOperationServiceController in the **Object** property.

7. In the **Parameters** field, enter CVRRentalDueDateReminderService. checkDueDates. This corresponds to the service class and service operation that we want to use, separated by a period.

8. Set the **EnumTypeParameter** property to **SysOperationExecutionMode** and the **EnumParameter** property to **Synchronous**.

9. Set the **RunOn** property to **Client**.

10. Right-click on the menu item and then click on **Save**.

Testing

Before testing, remember to compile CIL by clicking on the **Generate Incremental CIL** button or by pressing *Ctrl + Shift + F7*. When the compilation is successfully completed, you can run the SysOperation service. Just right-click on the **CVRRentalDueDateReminderService** menu item and click on **Open**. The following dialog will appear:

When the **OK** button is clicked on, the service operation is executed using the parameters that appear on the screen. You can open the CVRMember table to check that members with overdue rentals are blocked after the service has run.

Validation

When you create a SysOperation service, it is likely that you will need to validate the values that the user inputs. In our example, it would not make sense to allow the number of days to be an amount that is smaller than one because in that case, the rental would not be overdue.

The SysOperation framework allows you to put validation code on the data contract. To enable this, the data contract should implement the SysOperationValidatable interface. The following is what the updated data contract looks like:

```
[DataContractAttribute]
public class CVRRentalDueDateReminderContract implements
SysOperationValidatable
{
```

```
    CVRNumberOverdueDays              numberOverdueDays;
    CVROverrideNumberOfOverdueDays    overrideNumOfDays;
    str                               packedQuery;
}
```

When you compile the data contract now, you should see one or more errors that inform you that the class should implement the `validate()` method. This is because we now implement an interface that has this method. So, add the following method:

```
public boolean validate()
{
    boolean ret = true;

    if(numberOverdueDays <= 0)
    {
        ret = checkFailed("The number of days overdue cannot be 0 or
        less");
    }

    return ret;
}
```

The method checks if the number of overdue days is smaller than or equal to 0, and if so, it returns `false` to indicate that the validation has failed.

Generate Incremental CIL and then run the service again. Enter 0 or less in the **Number of Overdue days** field; then, click on **OK** and you will see the following **Infolog**:

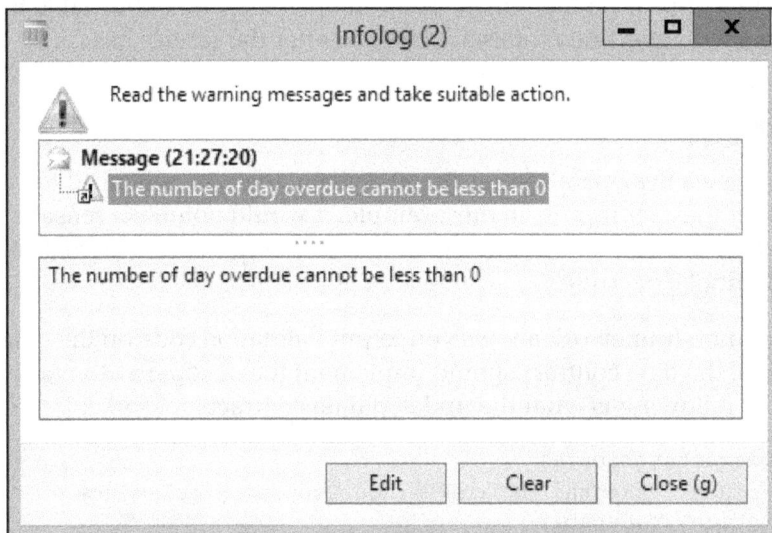

Defaulting

In our example, we also want the number of overdue days to get a default value that differs from 0, for example, 3. The best way to do this is to implement the defaulting logic on the data contract. The data contract should implement the `SysOperationInitializable` interface to enable the defaulting of values:

```
[DataContractAttribute]
public class CVRRentalDueDateReminderContract implements
SysOperationValidatable, SysOperationInitializable
{
    CVRNumberOverdueDays                numberOverdueDays;
    CVROverrideNumberOfOverdueDays  overrideNumOfDays;
    str                                 packedQuery;
}
```

Then, add the `initialize()` method and put the initialization code in it:

```
public void initialize()
{
    // default the number of overdue days to 3
    this.parmNumberOverdueDays(3);
}
```

Initialization will only occur the first time you open the dialog; from then on, usage data will be used. If you clear the usage data for the dialog, the `initialize()` method will be executed again; so, remove your usage data before you test this. After this, generate Incremental CIL and then run the service again. You should see that the number of overdue days is defaulted to 3:

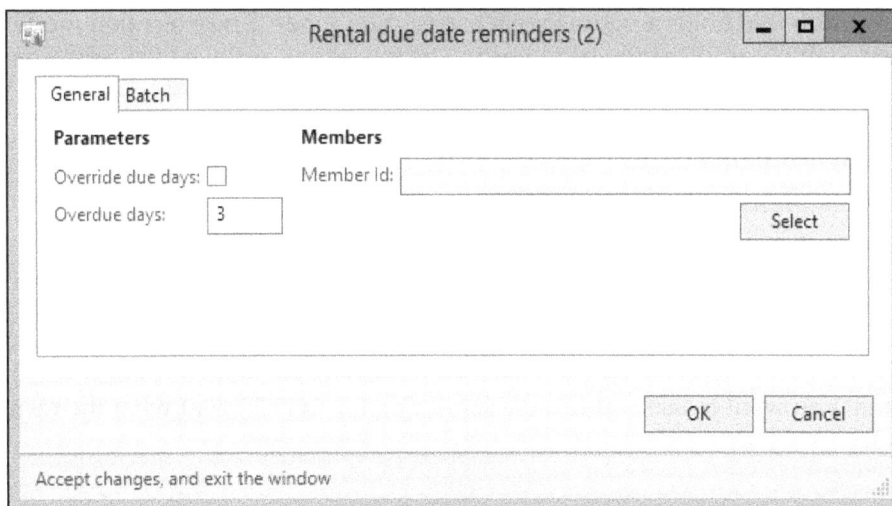

Running a SysOperation service

Because a user is able to run a service by starting it in the user interface, the menu item is an important part of a SysOperation service. As we have seen earlier, the menu item has the following properties that are required by the SysOperation framework:

- A **parameters** property that contains a reference to the service and service operation
- An **enum** parameter that determines the execution mode
- An **object** property where the controller that will be used is specified
- A **label** that will be displayed on the dialog

We will look at the first two properties now and discuss the others later in the chapter.

Service and service operation

The menu item is linked to the service and the service operation in the **Parameters** property. The format in which this parameter should be provided is ServiceClass. ServiceOperation, where ServiceClass is the name of the service class and ServiceOperation is the name of the service operation, separated by a period.

Execution modes

The SysOperation framework allows both synchronous and asynchronous processing. In our example, we used synchronous processing by specifying the execution mode using the **EnumTypeParameter** and **EnumParameter** properties. The **EnumTypeParameter** property is set to **SysOperationExecutionMode**, which is a base enum that holds a value for each execution mode. The execution mode is specified in the **EnumParameter** property. There are four options to choose from:

- **Synchronous**
- **Asynchronous**
- **ReliableAsynchronous**
- **ScheduledBatch**

When the execution mode is not specified, **ReliableAsynchronous** will be used. To change the execution mode of our service, simply change the **EnumParameter** property on the **CVRRentalDueDateReminderService** menu item to the execution mode that you want to use and run the service again. Let's look at what the results would be.

Synchronous

Synchronous execution of a SysOperation service has the same behavior as running a `RunBaseBatch` class. When you execute a SysOperation service synchronously but not in a batch, the client will be unresponsive for the time it takes for the operation to complete. All the other execution modes are forms of an asynchronous execution, including the execution of a synchronous service in the batch. When you enable the **Batch processing** checkbox on the **Batch** tab, a batch job will be created, analogous to the behavior of `RunBaseBatch`.

Asynchronous

When a SysOperation service uses the asynchronous execution mode, the client will still be responsive while the operation is executed. This is useful when you want a process to run in the background.

To run a service asynchronously, the service class must have an associated service node in the AOT. The service node has to be part of the AxClient service group, and the service group must be deployed again after the service is added to the group. If this isn't the case, the service will still run synchronously instead of asynchronously.

ReliableAsynchronous

The **ReliableAsynchronous** execution mode differs from the regular asynchronous mode in that it creates a batch job. This ensures that the service will be executed completely even if the client session in which it was started was destroyed, hence it is *reliable*. The service will be visible among other scheduled batch jobs, but unlike these, it will be deleted when the execution is complete. It is still visible in the batch job history, though.

The ReliableAsynchronous execution mode also differs from regular batches in that the user who executes the services will receive Infolog messages from the service when it is complete. This isn't the case with regular batches where you need to manually check the log on the batch job.

ScheduledBatch

The ScheduledBatch execution mode will schedule a batch job for the SysOperation service. Even when you don't check the **Batch processing** checkbox on the **Batch** tab of the service, it will still be executed in the batch. On the same tab, you can set up the recurrence for the batch job. This will also be used even if the **Batch processing** checkbox isn't checked.

Custom controllers

In the earlier example, we used the SysOperationServiceController class on our menu item to run the services. This is the base controller, but you can create your own controller when there is the need. In this part, we will first take a look at some of the scenarios in which custom controllers can be used, after which, we will create a custom controller.

Usage scenarios

What follows are two of the most common scenarios in which you would use a class that extends SysOperationServiceController. The first is using a controller to initialize a data contract and the second is a scenario in which you override methods of the dialog fields.

Initializing the data contract

A controller can be used to initialize the data in the data contract. This is one of the most common scenarios in which a controller is used and is the scenario that we will demonstrate further on in this chapter. Initializing a data contract is usually done based on the Args object.

The Args object contains information such as the following:

- The execution mode
- The service operation that should be executed
- The menu item from which the controller is started
- The records that are selected when the menu item is executed
- The caller object

Dialog overrides

The dialog that is used by a SysOperation service is generated based on the SysOperationTemplateForm form, the data contracts, and the menu item. In most cases, the default dialog that is generated is sufficient, but in other cases, you'll want to customize the dialog. There are methods on the controller that allow you to do this.

The following table lists the commonly used methods:

Method	Use
parmShowDialog()	Set this to `false` if you want to avoid user interaction. The dialog will not be shown, yet the operation will still run.
parmDialogCaption()	By default, the label of the menu item is used for the caption of the dialog. Use this method to override the label.
caption()	When a batch task is created, this label is used for its description. By default, it is the same as the `parmDialogCaption()` method.
showQueryValues()	When a query is used and this method returns `true`, the fields with ranges and a **Select** button will be shown on the dialog. Return `false` in this method to hide them.
showQuerySelectButton()	This method does the same as the `showQueryValues()` method but only affects the **Select** button.
canGoBatch()	Return `false` in this method to hide the **Batch** tab.
templateForm()	This method returns the form that the dialog is based on. By default, this is the `SysOperationTemplateForm` form, but you can override this method so that another form is used.
parmExecutionMode()	You can either override or set this method before starting the operation to override the execution mode.

Obviously, there are many other methods that you can override, but discussing all of them would take far too long. When you override methods on a controller, always keep in mind that the controller is only part of your solution. Use it wisely and use the other components such as service operations, data contracts, and UI Builder classes wherever they seem appropriate.

Study the code

The SysOperationServiceController class has a lot of documentation on its code that can help you figure out what the methods are for. You can also use the **Type Hierarchy Browser** to work out which classes extend the SysOperationServiceController class and get ideas from them.

Without further ado, let's see how we can create a controller for our example service.

Creating a controller

We want our controller to do the following things:

- Set a query range when the service is started from a form with a selected record

- Set the description of the batch tasks to reflect the record that is being processed

This is something we cannot accomplish with the `SysOperationServiceController` class, so we will have to create our own controller.

Declaration

To create a new controller, open the AOT and create a new class; name it `CVRRentalDueDateReminderController`. Open the class in the X++ editor and extend it from `SysOperationServiceController`. The class declaration should look like the following code:

```
public class CVRRentalDueDateReminderController extends
SysOperationServiceController
{
}
```

The main() method

A controller is started by running a menu item. Because of this, it needs a `main()` method, otherwise nothing will be executed. When creating a controller for your SysOperation service, the `main()` method should be similar to the `main()` method of the `SysOperationServiceController` class, shown as follows:

```
public static void main(Args args)
{
    SysOperationServiceController controller;

    controller = new SysOperationServiceController();
    controller.initializeFromArgs(args);
    controller.startOperation();
}
```

As you can see, a new controller is constructed and is then initialized using the `args` object. This initialization will use the properties of the `args` object to get the execution mode and the service operation that needs to be executed. The controller is run using the `startOperation()` method. You should always use this method to start an operation and refrain from using the run method.

We will create our `main()` method slightly differently, because we will put the `initializeFromArgs` call in a constructor, shown as follows:

```
public static void main(Args _args)
{
    CVRRentalDueDateReminderController
        rentalDueDateReminderController;

    rentalDueDateReminderController =
        CVRRentalDueDateReminderController::newFromArgs(_args);
    rentalDueDateReminderController.startOperation();
}

public static CVRRentalDueDateReminderController newFromArgs(Args
    _args)
{
    CVRRentalDueDateReminderController
        rentalDueDateReminderController;

    // Create a new instance of the controller
    rentalDueDateReminderController = new
        CVRRentalDueDateReminderController();

    // Initialize from args
    // One of the things this will do is read the "parameters"
    // property from the menu item
    rentalDueDateReminderController.initializeFromArgs(_args);

    // Return a new instance of this controller
    return rentalDueDateReminderController;
}
```

As you can see, it's similar to the first `main()` method and paves the way for the additions that we will make next.

Constructor

With the previous methods created, we basically have a custom controller that has the same functionality as the `SysOperationServiceController` class. We will extend the functionality of the `newFromArgs()` method that we created so that the data contract is initialized. The final method will look like the following code:

```
public static CVRRentalDueDateReminderController newFromArgs(Args _
args)
{
```

```
CVRRentalDueDateReminderController
    rentalDueDateReminderController;
CVRRentalDueDateReminderContract
    rentalDueDateReminderContract;
CVRMember                              member;
Query                                  query;

// Create a new instance of the controller
rentalDueDateReminderController = new
    CVRRentalDueDateReminderController();

// Initialize from args
// One of the things this will do is read the "parameters"
// property from the menu item
rentalDueDateReminderController.initializeFromArgs(_args);

// Get the data contract
// The string should be the same as the parameter name!
rentalDueDateReminderContract =
    rentalDueDateReminderController.getDataContractObject(
    '_dueDateReminderContract');

// Check if we are running this from a rental member
if(_args && _args.dataset() == tableNum(CVRMember))
{
    // Cast the record
    member = _args.record();

    // Create new query instance
    query = new query(queryStr(CVRMember));

    // Add a range on the member id
    query.dataSourceTable(tableNum(CVRMember)).
    addRange(fieldNum(CVRMember, Id)).value(queryValue(member.Id));

    // Set the new query on the data contract
    rentalDueDateReminderContract.setQuery(query);

    // Notify the controller that we changed the query. This
        avoids a refresh problem on the dialog
    rentalDueDateReminderController.queryChanged(
    '_dueDateReminderContract.parmQuery', query);
```

```
    }

    // Return a new instance of this controller
    return rentalDueDateReminderController;
}
```

As you can see, you can get the data contract instance using the `getDataContractObject` method:

```
rentalDueDateReminderController.getDataContractObject(
    '_dueDateReminderContract');
```

The string that you pass as a parameter is the name of the data contract parameter of the service operation that is used. It is very important to get this right. It can easily be overlooked, because the compiler does not check the validity of this parameter.

After this, it is simply a matter of setting parameter methods on the data contract. When the service is started from the member form, we use the `Args` variable to set a range on the query.

Menu item

The last thing that we need to do is create a menu item. To create a menu item, perform the following steps:

1. In the Development Workspace, open the AOT.
2. Expand the **Menu Items** node, then right-click on **Action** and click on **New Menu Item**.
3. Rename the menu item to `CVRRentalDueDateReminderServiceCustomCon`.
4. Right-click on the menu item and then click on **Properties**.
5. Set the **Label** property to **Rental due date reminders**.
6. Set **ObjectType** to **Class** and enter `CVRRentalDueDateReminderController` in the **Object** property.
7. In the **Parameters** field, enter `CVRRentalDueDateReminderService.checkDueDates`. This corresponds to the service class and the service operation that we want to use.
8. Set the **EnumTypeParameter** property to **SysOperationExecutionMode** and the **EnumParameter** property to **Synchronous**.
9. Set the **RunOn** property to **Client**.
10. Right-click on the menu item and then click on **Save**.

Testing

Before you start testing, remember to generate CIL by clicking on the **Generate Incremental CIL** button or pressing *Ctrl* + *Shift* + *F7*.

To test if the query range is added when the service is started from the **Members** form, first add the menu item to the CVRMemberListPage form. When you click on the button that is created, you should see that the query range is added based on the record that was selected:

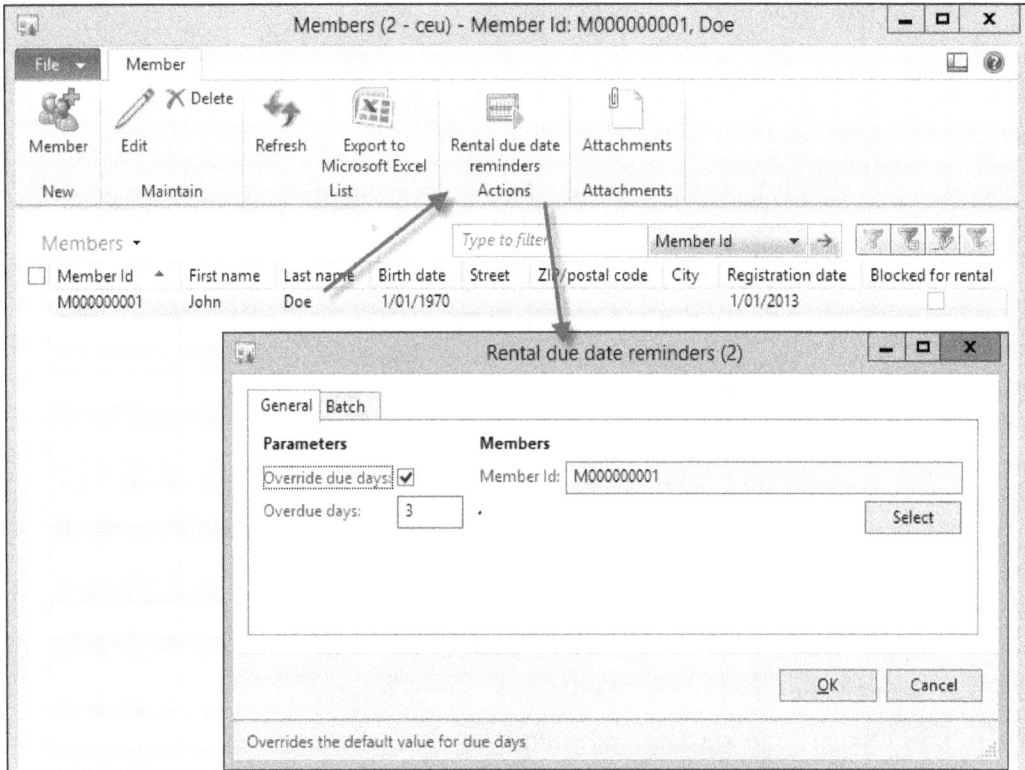

Custom UI Builders

One of the great improvements that the SysOperation framework has over the RunBaseBatch framework is that it generates the dialog for you. Fields on the dialog, for example, are generated based on the data contract. However, if you want to change the dialog that is generated, you can use the UI Builder classes.

When we say custom UI Builders, we mean a class that extends the `SysOperationAutomaticUIBuilder` class. This is the class that generates the dialog based on the data contract of your service operation. By extending this class, you can add your own logic to the building process. Most commonly, this will include logic that does the following:

- Set properties of field controls such as `mandatory` and `enabled`
- Override methods of field controls such as `lookup()` and `modifiedField()`
- Prevent controls from being added by overriding the `addDialogField()` method

When you create your own UI Builder class, you will notice that the possibilities go far beyond what we have just described. Just as with custom controllers, keep in mind that a UI Builder is also just a part of your solution. For example, when you feel that you are adding a lot of controls to your dialog using the UI Builder, consider using a template form on your controller instead. When you're putting a lot of validation code in your UI Builder, consider implementing the validation in the data contract in order to respect the MVC philosophy.

Creating a UI Builder

In this demonstration, we will create a UI Builder for our service. The purpose of this UI Builder is to override the `modifiedField()` method of the checkbox control. It will behave in the following way:

- When the checkbox is checked, the control for the number of overdue days is enabled
- When the checkbox is blank, the control for the number of overdue days is disabled

Declaration

Let's start by creating the UI Builder class. Create a new class and name it `CVRRentalDueDateReminderUIBuilder`. This class will extend `SysOperationAutomaticUIBuilder` as follows:

```
public class CVRRentalDueDateReminderUIBuilder extends
SysOperationAutomaticUIBuilder
{
    DialogField dialogFieldOverrideNumOfDays;
    DialogField dialogFieldNumberOfDueDays;

    CVRRentalDueDateReminderContract reminderContract;
}
```

Note that we have also declared the following three variables that we will use later:

- A dialog field for the checkbox
- A dialog field for the number of overdue days field
- A variable that holds the data contract

The override method

The first method we add is the method that will be executed when the value of the checkbox changes. This method will enable or disable the **Number of Overdue days** field. This is a very simple method that looks like the following code:

```
public boolean overrideNumOfDaysModified(FormCheckBoxControl
_checkBoxControl)
{
    // Enable or disable the number of days field based on the
    // value of the checkbox
    dialogFieldNumberOfDueDays.enabled(_checkBoxControl.value());

    return true;
}
```

As you can see, the code uses the value of the `_checkBoxControl` parameter to set the `enabled` property of the control that holds the number of overdue days.

In this example, the parameter is of the type `FormCheckBoxControl`, because we are overriding a method on a checkbox control. When you override a method on a control of a different type, you should use that type instead, for example, `FormStringControl` for a string control. A full list of controls can be found in the system documentation. In the AOT, navigate to **System Documentation | Classes | FormControl**. Right-click on the **FormControl** node and then navigate to **Add-Ins | Type Hierarchy browser**. When you expand the **FormControl** node, you will see a list of all the control types that are available. You can look these up in the system documentation to see what methods you can override.

The postBuild() method

The `postBuild()` method is called immediately after the dialog has been created, so it is a good place to put the logic that registers override methods. The code that we need to add to this method is shown as follows:

```
public void postBuild()
{
```

```
    super();

     // Retrieve the data contract
    reminderContract = this.dataContractObject();

     // Retrieve the dialog fields
    dialogFieldOverrideNumOfDays      =
        this.bindInfo().getDialogField(reminderContract,
        methodstr(CVRRentalDueDateReminderContract,
        parmOverrideNumOfDays));
    dialogFieldNumberOfDueDays        =
        this.bindInfo().getDialogField(reminderContract,
        methodstr(CVRRentalDueDateReminderContract,
        parmNumberOverdueDays));

     // Register override methods
    dialogFieldOverrideNumOfDays.registerOverrideMethod(methodstr
        (FormCheckBoxControl, modified),
        methodstr(CVRRentalDueDateReminderUIBuilder,
        overrideNumOfDaysModified), this);

     // Call the override already once to support packed value to
     // be sync immediately
    this.overrideNumOfDaysModified(dialogFieldOverrideNumOfDays.
        control());
}
```

Let's go through it step-by-step. The first line retrieves the data contract:

```
reminderContract = this.dataContractObject();
```

Next, we use the data contract together with the bindInfo object to get the controls for the checkbox and the number of the overdue field:

```
dialogFieldOverrideNumOfDays      =
    this.bindInfo().getDialogField(reminderContract,
    methodstr(CVRRentalDueDateReminderContract,
    parmOverrideNumOfDays));
dialogFieldNumberOfDueDays        =
    this.bindInfo().getDialogField(reminderContract,
    methodstr(CVRRentalDueDateReminderContract,
    parmNumberOverdueDays));
```

In the previous code, the `bindInfo()` method returns an object of type `SysOperationUIBindInfo`. This contains information about the dialog controls that the data members are bound to. By providing a reference to the `parmOverrideNumOfDays` and `parmNumberOverdueDays` members when calling the `getDialogField()` method, we get the dialog control that is associated with each member.

After we retrieve the dialog fields, we can register the override method. The following line does just that:

```
dialogFieldOverrideNumOfDays.registerOverrideMethod(methodstr
    (FormCheckBoxControl, modified),
    methodstr(CVRRentalDueDateReminderUIBuilder,
    overrideNumOfDaysModified), this);
```

As you can see, we can use the `registerOverrideMethod()` method to override methods on the dialog fields. We simply point to the method that we want to override (`FormCheckBoxControl.modified`) and the method that needs to be executed (`CVRRentalDueDateReminderUIBuilder.overrideNumOfDaysModified`).

Finally, we initialize the value of the `enabled` property by calling the override method directly. This will make sure that the checkbox reflects the values of the data contract after the dialog is built. Call the method as follows:

```
this.overrideNumOfDaysModified(dialogFieldOverrideNumOfDays.
    control());
```

Linking the UI Builder to the data contract

We have created a UI Builder class, but what remains is linking it to our data contract. That's what we use the `SysOperationContractProcessingAttribute` attribute for. To link the UI Builder class to the data contract, open the `CVRRentalDueDateReminderContract` class in the X++ editor and add the `SysOperationContractProcessingAttribute` to it:

```
[DataContractAttribute
,SysOperationContractProcessingAttribute(classstr(CVRRentalDueDate
    ReminderUIBuilder))]
public class CVRRentalDueDateReminderContract implements
    SysOperationValidatable, SysOperationInitializable
{
    CVRNumberOverdueDays            numberOverdueDays;
    CVROverrideNumberOfOverdueDays  overrideNumOfDays;
    str                             packedQuery;
}
```

Testing

Now that you have added the UI Builder, you can test the service. But before you do that, remember to generate CIL by clicking on the **Generate Incremental CIL** button or pressing *Ctrl + Shift + F7*. When the CIL compilation is complete, right-click on the **CVRRentalDueDateReminderServiceCustomCon** menu item to open the dialog, as shown in the following screenshot:

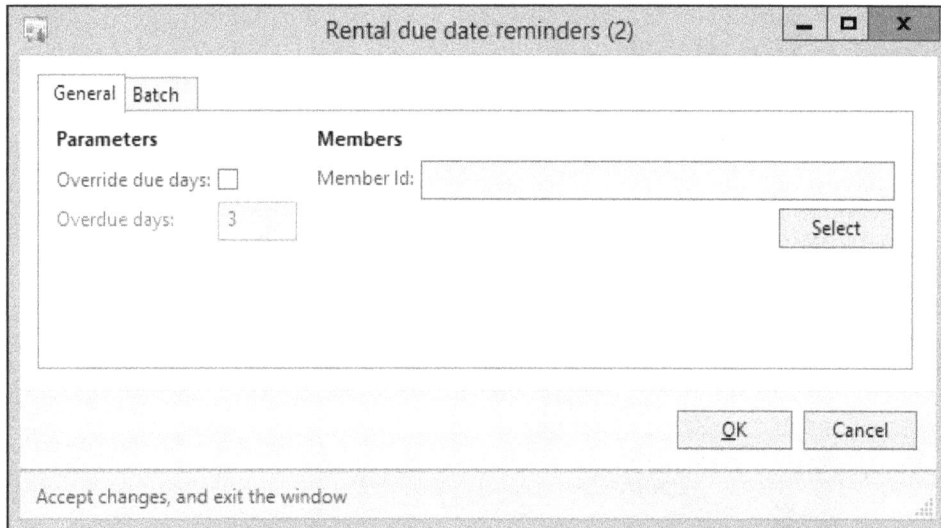

When you check the checkbox, you should see that the **Number of Overdue days** field is enabled. To disable the field, uncheck the checkbox.

Multithreading

Microsoft Dynamics AX 2012 has the ability to run jobs in the batch by leveraging the abilities of the batch framework. The batch framework has two main purposes:

- Enabling the scheduling of jobs.
- Providing a mechanism to split jobs up into smaller parts and run them in parallel. By doing so, the batch job has a larger throughput and the response time is much better.

We want the service that we created earlier to use the same batch framework so that it has better performance. There are different approaches to this, and each has its advantages and disadvantages. The two most commonly used approaches can be described as the following:

- The individual task approach
- The helper approach

The individual task approach

This approach will divide the batch job into a number of work units that are also known as **runtime tasks**. For each work unit, a runtime task will be created. So, you will have a one-to-one relation between work units and runtime tasks.

When your batch job is executed in batch, it is only responsible for creating the tasks for every unit of work to be done. Once the batch job is done creating tasks, it will be finished, and the batch framework will continue to work on the created runtime tasks in parallel. In the following diagram, you can see that a processing task is created for every record, which represents a unit of work:

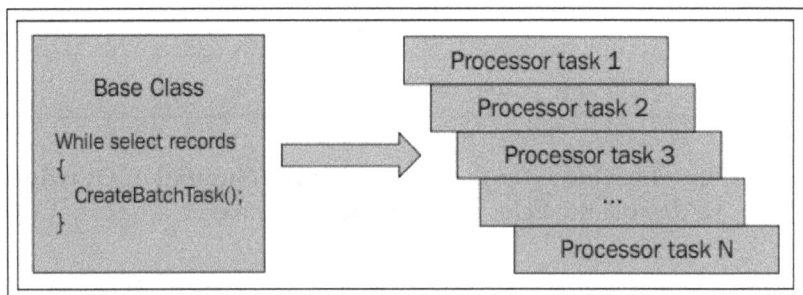

The advantages of using this approach are:

- It scales perfectly along with the schedule of the batch framework. It is possible to set up the batch framework to use a different number of threads depending on a time window during the day. The batch job will scale the number of threads depending on the number of threads that have been set up for that time window and either use or yield resources.
- Assuming that your business logic is well designed, less effort is required to make your batch job multithread-aware.
- You can easily create dependencies between the individual tasks.

The disadvantages of using this approach are:

- As some batch jobs may create a large number of tasks, there will be a lot of records in the batch framework's tables. This will have a negative impact on performance as the framework needs to check dependencies and constraints before running each of the tasks.

- Though this approach is ideal to scale the schedule of the batch framework, you do not have control over the amount of threads that are processing your batch job on each of the batch servers. Once your task is assigned to a batch group picked up by an AOS, all of the free thread slots will be used for the processing of your tasks.

The helper approach

The second approach that you can use to split up the work is by using **helpers**. Instead of creating an individual task for every unit of work to be done, we create a fixed number of threads. This resolves the issue that we faced with the individual tasks where there were too many batch tasks being created in the batch framework tables.

After creating a fixed number of helper threads, we need to introduce a staging table to keep track of the work to be done. The helpers themselves look into this staging table to determine the next thing to be done when they have finished their current task.

The steps to be followed when creating batch jobs that use this approach are as follows:

1. Create a staging table that contains the work list.
2. Create your batch job and let it be responsible for queuing the work in the staging table.
3. Build a worker class that can deal with the processing of one staging table record (contains business logic).
4. Create a helper class that is able to pick the next task and call the worker.
5. Add code to the batch job to spawn helper threads until the desired number of helpers is available.

As for the staging table, you need to provide the following fields in the staging table:

- An identifier field
- A reference field that may point to a record or contain information that helps the workers know what needs to be done
- A status field to keep track of what's done and what needs to be done

Also, keep in mind that helpers must use pessimistic locking to retrieve the records from the staging table. This is to make sure that two helper threads do not select the same record and start working on the same task. In the following diagram, you can see that although a record is created for each unit of work, only 10 helpers are created, independent of the amount of records to be processed in the work queue:

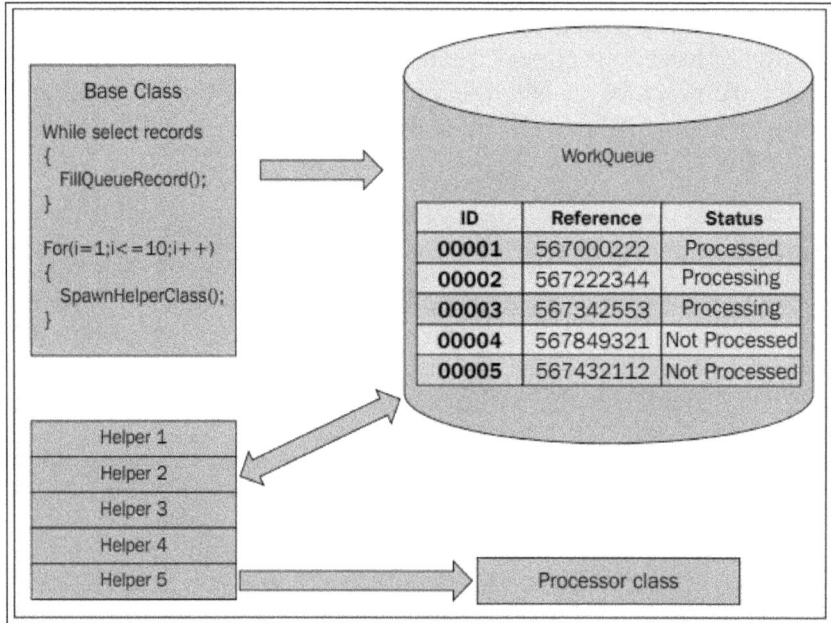

The advantages of using this approach are:

- You have control over the number of threads that are processing your batch job. This can be useful when you want your tasks to leave threads open on the AOS for other batch jobs when scaling the number of threads available for batch processing on the AOS instance.

- The batch tables are not filled with a huge number of tasks as only a fixed number of helper threads are created. This lowers the performance hit when checking dependencies and constraints.

- If you put a little effort into a generic solution for this approach, you can reuse the same staging table for different batch jobs.

The disadvantages of using this approach are:

- Because the number of threads is fixed, this approach does not scale as well as the individual task approach. Scaling up the number of threads on the AOS servers will not result in more working threads or higher throughput.

- It is a little more work to create the staging table needed for the helper threads to keep track of the work to be done as compared to spawning runtime tasks.

- This approach is not suitable to process a huge number of small tasks as maintaining the staging table would have a negative influence on the performance and throughput.

> **Useful link**
>
> If you want to learn more about these two approaches, you can find a series of blog posts on this topic on the MSDN blog of the Dynamics AX Performance Team. The first blog post of the series can be found at `http://blogs.msdn.com/b/axperf/archive/2012/02/24/batch-parallelism-in-ax-part-i.aspx`.

Enabling multithreading

Now that we know the differences between these approaches, we can go ahead and update our SysOperation service to provide multithreading support. Because implementing both approaches would take too long, we will use only the individual task approach. Firstly, we have to extend our service class from the `SysOperationServiceBase` class. The declaration should look like the following code:

```
class CVRRentalDueDateReminderService extends SysOperationServiceBase
{
}
```

This is needed because the `SysOperatonServiceBase` class contains methods that allow us to work with the batch header and check whether the code is running in the batch.

Next, we add a new operation to our service. This operation differs from the existing one because it does not do the work itself; instead, it creates runtime tasks that do the work. The full code listing is as follows:

```
[SysEntryPointAttribute(true)]
public void checkDueDatesMulti(CVRRentalDueDateReminderContract
_dueDateReminderContract)
{
    QueryRun      queryRun;
    CVRMember     cvrMember;

    BatchHeader                              batchHeader;
    SysOperationServiceController            runTaskController;
    CVRRentalDueDateReminderContract         runTaskContract;
```

```
    Query                                    taskQuery;

    // Get the query from the data contract
    queryRun = new QueryRun(_dueDateReminderContract.getQuery());

    // Loop all the members in the query
    while (queryRun.next())
    {
        // Get the current member record
        cvrMember = queryRun.get(tableNum(CVRMember));

        // Create a new controller for the runtime task
        runTaskController = new SysOperationServiceController(
            classStr(CVRRentalDueDateReminderService)
            , methodStr(CVRRentalDueDateReminderService,
            checkDueDates));

        // Get a data contract for the controller
        runTaskContract =
        runTaskController.getDataContractObject('_
dueDateReminderContract');

        // create a query for the task
        taskQuery = new Query(queryStr(CVRMember));
        taskQuery.dataSourceTable(tableNum(CVRMember)).
addRange(fieldNum(C
        VRMember, Id)).value(cvrMember.Id);

        // set variables for the data contract
        runTaskContract.setQuery(taskQuery);
        runTaskContract.parmNumberOverdueDays(
            _dueDateReminderContract.parmNumberOverdueDays());

        // If running in batch
        if(this.isExecutingInBatch())
        {
            // If we do not have a batch header yet
            if(!batchHeader)
            {
                // Get one
                batchHeader = this.getCurrentBatchHeader();
            }

            // Create a runtime task
```

```
        batchHeader.addRuntimeTask(runTaskController,
            this.getCurrentBatchTask().RecId);
    }
    else
    {
        // Not in batch, just run the controller here
        runTaskController.run();
    }
}

// After all of the runtime tasks are created, save the
    batchheader
if (batchHeader)
{
    // Saving the header will create the batch records and add
        dependencies where needed
    batchHeader.save();
}
}
```

Let's break up the code and take a look at it piece by piece. The top part of the method remains roughly the same just up to the query part. We still get the query from the data contract and loop all of the results:

```
// Get the query from the data contract
queryRun = new QueryRun(_dueDateReminderContract.getQuery());

// Loop all the members in the query
while (queryRun.next())
{
    // Get the current member record
    cvrMember = queryRun.get(tableNum(CVRMember));
```

What follows is more interesting. Instead of running our business logic, we create a controller for the runtime task and point to the checkDueDates() method. In this example, we have chosen to reuse the same data contract and service operation that we created earlier to act as the runtime task:

```
runTaskController = new SysOperationServiceController(
classStr(CVRRentalDueDateReminderService),
methodStr(CVRRentalDueDateReminderService, checkDueDates));

    // Get a data contract for the controller
    runTaskContract = runTaskController.getDataContractObject('
_dueDateReminderContract');
```

After creating a controller, a data contract is constructed to pass to the runtime task. We reuse the same contract that is also used by the job service. Because of this, we need to create a query object that contains a range on the member's Id field, as shown in the following code snippet:

```
// Get a data contract for the controller
        runTaskContract =
        runTaskController.getDataContractObject('
_dueDateReminderContract'
        );

        // create a query for the task
        taskQuery = new Query(queryStr(CVRMember));
        taskQuery.dataSourceTable(tableNum(CVRMember)).
        addRange(fieldNum(CVRMember, Id)).value(cvrMember.Id);

        // set variables for the data contract
        runTaskContract.setQuery(taskQuery);
        runTaskContract.parmNumberOverdueDays(
_dueDateReminderContract.parmNumberOverdueDays());
```

What follows is the part that will create the runtime tasks. First, a batch header instance will be constructed if we do not have one already. The batch header class is used to contain the information on the runtime tasks that we add to the running batch job. Once the batch header class is instructed to save this information, the actual records are created in the batch table along with all of the dependencies, as shown in the following code:

```
            // If running in batch
            if(this.isExecutingInBatch())
            {
                // If we do not have a batch header yet
                if(!batchHeader)
                {
                    // Get one
                    batchHeader = this.getCurrentBatchHeader();
                }

                // Create a runtime task
                batchHeader.addRuntimeTask(runTaskController,
                    this.getCurrentBatchTask().RecId);
            }
            else
            {
```

```
            // Not in batch, just run the controller here
            runTaskController.run();
        }
    }

    // After all of the runtime tasks are created, save the
    // batchheader
    if(batchHeader)
    {
        // Saving the header will create the batch records and add
        // dependencies where needed
        batchHeader.save();
    }
```

Summary

It should be clear that the SysOperation framework is not only a replacement for the RunBaseBatch framework, but it also improves upon it. Many of the improvements are due to the implementation of the MVC pattern. This allows for the reuse of many of the components such as the data contracts, service operations, and controllers.

Reusing these components enables the batch processing for existing services and rapid development of new services. More than that, the different execution modes allow these services to run synchronously and asynchronously with little effort by the developers. It is even possible to leverage the power of the batch framework to run the processes in parallel, all in a way that is scalable. This improves the overall performance and user experience.

Up until now, we have always created services in Microsoft Dynamics AX and exposed them to external applications. In the next chapter, we will reverse the roles and consume an external service in Microsoft Dynamics AX 2012.

6
Web Services

For the better part of this book, we have developed services in Microsoft Dynamics AX and exposed them. However, in this chapter, we will see how to consume a web service from Microsoft Dynamics AX 2012.

In the previous versions of Microsoft Dynamics AX, you could add a web service reference in a reference node in the AOT. This generated proxy classes and other artifacts that you could then use to consume the service. In Microsoft Dynamics AX 2012, we no longer have the option to add service references to the AOT. Instead, Microsoft Visual Studio is used to generate all artifacts, which are then added to the AOT.

How this works and how this can be done will all become clear in this chapter.

The following topics will be covered in this chapter:

- **Installing Visual Studio tools**: We have to install additional components because part of the development takes place in Visual Studio 2010. You will learn which components to install and what exactly they do.

- **Visual Studio development**: After introducing the demo service, we will create a reference for the services with the help of Visual Studio. We will take you through this process step-by-step.

- **X++ development**: Finally, we will demonstrate how we can use the Visual Studio project to consume services in Microsoft Dynamics AX. You will also gain an insight into the different deployment modes that are available to deploy the project's output.

Installing Visual Studio tools

Part of the coding that is needed to consume an external service is performed in Visual Studio. This is why we must install both Visual Studio 2010 and Visual Studio tools for Microsoft Dynamics AX 2012 before we can create Visual Studio projects and add them to the AOT. Although you can develop applications that integrate with Microsoft Dynamics AX 2012 using other versions of Visual Studio, such as Visual Studio 2012, Visual Studio tools are only available for Visual Studio 2010.

To install Visual Studio tools, perform the following steps:

1. Run the Microsoft Dynamics AX 2012 setup.
2. Go to the **Install** section and select **Microsoft Dynamics AX Components**.
3. Click on the **Next** button to move to the next screen and select **Add or modify existing components**.
4. Look under the **Developer Tools** node and select **Visual Studio Tools**.
5. Go through the rest of the setup wizard to complete the installation process.

Installing Visual Studio tools will add the following extensions to Visual Studio:

- The **Application Explorer** option that is available in Visual Studio by navigating to **View | Application Explorer**. Enabling it will display the AOT in Visual Studio.

- Two new templates that are available when you create a new project in Visual Studio — **Report Model** and **EP Web Applications**.

- An option to add Visual Studio projects to the AOT. This is the option we're interested in when consuming web services.

Visual Studio development

When consuming a service, the first thing you need to do is create a reference to the service. As this can no longer be done in Microsoft Dynamics AX, we have to use Visual Studio. So, we'll do that, but first we'll examine the service that we are going to consume.

Introducing the USA zip code service

To show you how Microsoft Dynamics AX 2012 enables developers to consume web services, we are going to use an example zip code service. This service is available on the website of RESTful web services: `http://www.restfulwebservices.net/servicecategory.aspx`.

In the zip code service, we have two operations available to use when referencing the WCF version; these are as follows:

- `GetPostCodeDetailByPostCode`: This operation takes a zip code as a parameter and returns a `PostalCode` data contract with all of the information about `PostalCode` we searched for

- `GetPostCodeDetailByPlaceName`: This operation takes names as parameters and also returns a `PostalCode` data contract with the information needed

Creating the Visual Studio proxy library

In Microsoft Dynamics AX 2012, Visual Studio projects can be contained in the AOT. This enables us to use Visual Studio to create a class library project and add it to the AOT. The advantage is that Visual Studio deals with the service reference. It uses the `SvcUtil` tool to create the proxy client and generate the types that are needed to consume the service.

Perform the following steps to create a Visual Studio class library project:

1. In Visual Studio, navigate to **File** | **New** | **Project...**.

2. In the **New Project** window, select **Visual C#** and select the **Class Library** project type.

3. In the **Name** textbox, give the project a name and click on **OK**.

These steps are illustrated in the following screenshot:

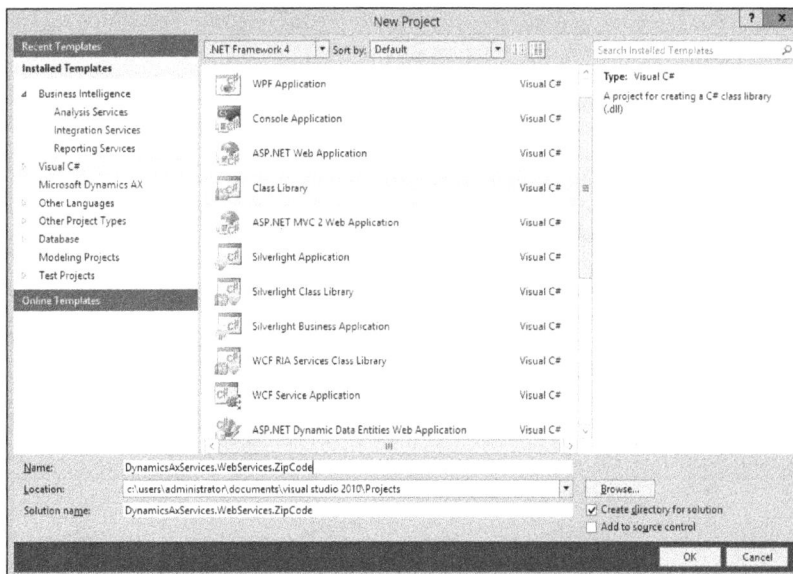

Adding a service reference

Next, we will create a service reference to the USA zip code service. To do this, perform the following steps:

1. Locate the **References** node in the project.

2. Right-click on the **References** node and select **Add Service Reference...** to open the **Add Service Reference** window.

3. In the **Address** drop-down box, specify the following address for the service: `http://www.restfulwebservices.net/wcf/USAZipCodeService.svc?wsdl`. Then, click on **Go**. The address is queried and the two operations mentioned previously are listed. You can expand to the **USAZipCodeService** node to view the service operations.

4. In the **Namespace** dialog box, specify the namespace that you want to use: `USAZipCodeServiceRef`. The **Add Service Reference** window will look like the following screenshot:

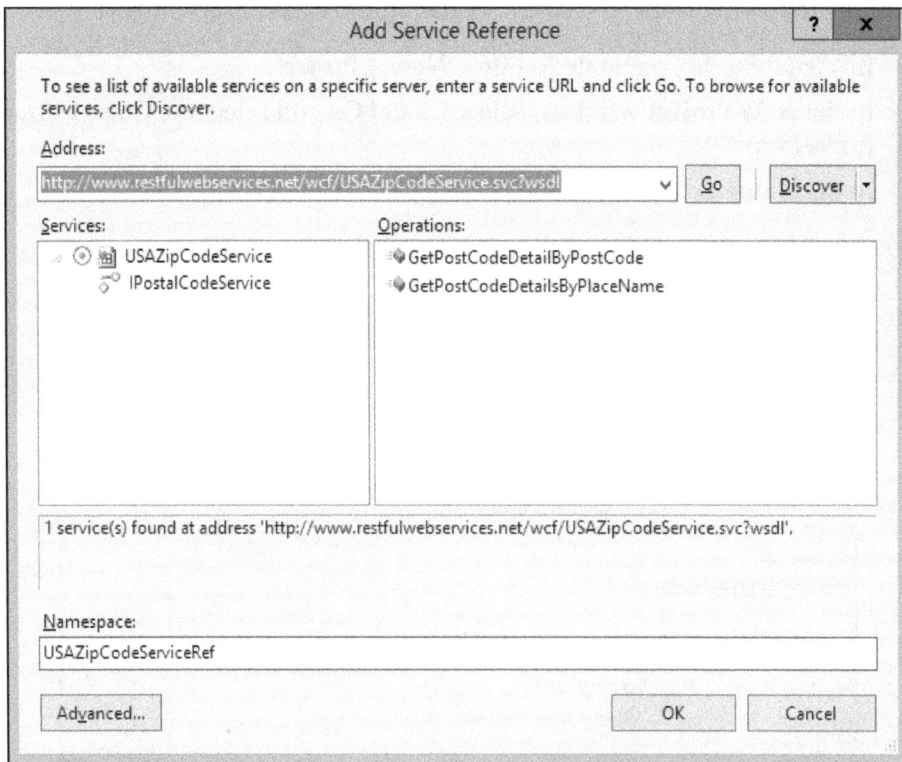

5. Click on **OK**. The service will be added to the **Service References** node.

6. Delete the `Class1.cs` class as we will not need it.

7. To add the project to the AOT, right-click on the project and then click on **Add DynamicsAxServices.WebServices.ZipCode to the AOT**.

8. After the project has been added to the AOT, you can specify the deployment options. In the properties of the project, set **Deploy to Client** and **Deploy to Server** to **Yes**.

9. Finally, right-click on the project and click on **Deploy**.

X++ development

The Visual Studio project and its output have been added to the AOT, so the first stage of development is now complete. You can leave Visual Studio and switch to Microsoft Dynamics AX 2012. The project has been added to the **Visual Studio Projects** node in the AOT. As we have used C#, the project will be in the **C Sharp Projects** node.

Look for the **DynamicsAxServices.WebServices.ZipCode** project and expand some of the nodes to inspect it. It should appear as shown in the following screenshot:

As you can see in the preceding screenshot, this is divided into the following two main components:

- The **Project Content** node contains the actual C# project source such as properties of the project, the service references, an `app.config` file, and C# source files

- The **Project Output** node contains the assemblies that will be deployed, taking into account the deployment options

In order to use the assemblies that have been created and stored in the AOT, we'll have to deploy them. Let's look at the options that are available.

Deploying managed code

When we create a project in Visual Studio and add it to the AOT, the following deployment options are available:

- Deploy to Server
- Deploy to Client
- Deploy to EP

In our earlier example, we enabled deployment on the client and to the server because these are important in the context of services.

Deploy to Server

When you have enabled deployment to the server, the output of the Visual Studio project will be copied to the VSAssemblies subfolder in the bin folder of the AOS directory. The default path is C:\Program Files\Microsoft Dynamics AX\60\ Server\<AOSServer>\Bin\VSAssemblies. After you have deployed assemblies to the server, you should restart the AOS so that they are loaded.

> **Hot swapping**
>
> When hot swapping is enabled on the AOS, restart is not needed after deployment. This feature is added for the convenience of developers but is not recommended for a production environment. For more info, check out the following article on MSDN: *How to: Enable Hot Swapping of Assemblies* (http://msdn.microsoft.com/en-us/library/gg889279.aspx).

Deploy to Client

When you have enabled deployment to the client, the output of the Visual Studio project will be copied to the following folder on the client: %localappdata%\ Microsoft\Dynamics Ax\VSAssemblies. You may have to restart the Microsoft Dynamics AX client after deployment, otherwise the assemblies may not get copied.

The assemblies will be deployed to a client as and when are needed. This comes down to the following three situations:

- When you use IntelliSense
- When you compile code that uses the assembly
- When code runs on the client in which a call is made to the assembly

Obviously, you will want to have the assembly on your client as a developer, otherwise you will not be able to use IntelliSense or compile your code.

Consuming the web service

Now that we have created a service reference in our Visual Studio proxy library and deployed it to Microsoft Dynamics AX, we can use the types in the library from Microsoft Dynamics AX.

First attempt

Let's take a look at the following X++ code that consumes the zip code service to retrieve a place name:

```
static void Consume_GetZipCodePlaceName(Args _args)
{
    DynamicsAxServices.WebServices.ZipCode.USAZipCodeServiceRef
    .PostalCodeServiceClient postalServiceClient;
    DynamicsAxServices.WebServices.ZipCode.USAZipCodeServiceRef
    .PostalCode postalCode;
    System.Exception Exception;

    try
    {
        // Create a service client proxy
        postalServiceClient = new DynamicsAxServices .WebServices.
    ZipCode.USAZipCodeServiceRef .PostalCodeServiceClient();

        // Use the zipcode to find a place name
        postalCode = postalServiceClient.
    GetPostCodeDetailByPostCode("10001"); // 10001 is New York

        // Use the getAnyTypeForObject to marshal the
    System.String to an Ax anyType
        // so that it can be used with info()
        info(strFmt('%1', CLRInterop::
    getAnyTypeForObject(postalCode.get_PlaceName())));
    }
    catch
    {
        // Get the .NET Type Exception
        exception = CLRInterop::getLastException();

        // Go through the inner exceptions
        while(exception)
        {
            // Print the exception to the infolog
```

```
            info(CLRInterop::
    getAnyTypeForObject(exception.ToString()));

            // Get the inner exception for more details
            exception = exception.get_InnerException();
        }
    }
}
```

When we go through the code bit by bit, we can see that a proxy client is created first. Note that this is the managed type that is created by the `SvcUtil` tool when adding the service reference:

```
postalServiceClient = new DynamicsAxServices
    .WebServices.ZipCode.USAZipCodeServiceRef
    .PostalCodeServiceClient();
```

After that, using the following code, we immediately invoke the service operation with a zip code:

```
postalCode = postalServiceClient.
    GetPostCodeDetailByPostCode("10001"); // 10001 is New York
```

Then, there is a simple infolog message that shows the place name using the following code:

```
info(strFmt('%1', CLRInterop::
    getAnyTypeForObject(postalCode.get_PlaceName())));
```

Notice the `CLRInterop::getAnyTypeForObject` method, which is used to marshal between the .NET type `System.String` and the X++ `anyType` type before submitting it to the infolog.

That's it for consuming services. However, we also have some exception handling that handles any .NET exceptions while invoking the external service, as shown in the following code snippet:

```
catch
{
    // Get the .NET Type Exception
    exception = CLRInterop::getLastException();

    // Go through the inner exceptions
    while(exception)
    {
        // Print the exception to the infolog
```

```
              info(CLRInterop::  getAnyTypeForObject(exception.
    ToString()));

              // Get the inner exception for more details
              exception = exception.get_InnerException();
          }
      }
```

Fixing configuration issues

Although the preceding code example should suffice, you will get an error message when running it. The error message is shown in the following screenshot:

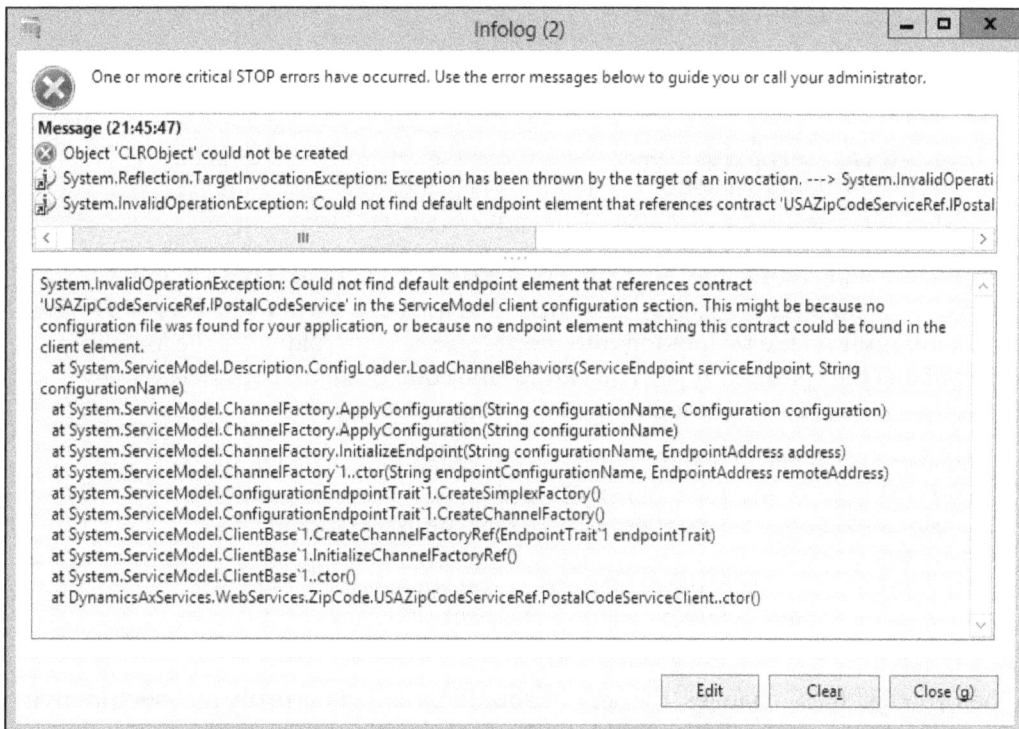

What is going on here is that the service is trying to look for the endpoint's configuration in the application's configuration file but does not find it. This is because Microsoft Dynamics AX is acting as the host application here (Ax32.exe). Therefore, the service tries to open the Ax32.exe.config file and look for the endpoint configuration.

It is clear that putting the configuration details of every service that we want to consume into the `Ax32.exe.config` file is a bit impractical and should be avoided. The solution to this issue is using the `AifUtil` class to create the service client.

Let's change the preceding code so that it uses the `AifUtil` class to point to the right configuration file and see what happens then. Start off by declaring a new variable of the `System.Type` type at the top of the job, as shown in the following code:

```
System.Type type;
```

Take a look at the following line of code:

```
postalServiceClient = new DynamicsAxServices
    .WebServices.ZipCode.USAZipCodeServiceRef
    .PostalCodeServiceClient();
```

Replace the preceding code with the following two lines of code that use the variable that you just declared:

```
type = CLRInterop::getType('DynamicsAxServices.WebServices
    .ZipCode.USAZipCodeServiceRef.PostalCodeServiceClient');
postalServiceClient = AifUtil::createServiceClient(type);
```

The first line will resolve the .NET type of the service client and pass it to the `AifUtil::createServiceClient` method. The `AifUtil` class will then resolve the right configuration file by looking into the `VSAssemblies` folder for the assembly that contains the specified type. You can see the code of the `AifUtil` class's `createServiceClient` method in the following code snippet:

```
vsAssembliesPath = xApplication::getVSAssembliesPath();
configFilePath = Microsoft.Dynamics.IntegrationFramework.
    ServiceReference::GetConfigFilePath(serviceClientType,
vsAssembliesPath);
serviceClient = Microsoft.Dynamics.IntegrationFramework.
    ServiceReference::CreateServiceClient(serviceClientType,
configFilePath);
```

When you test these changes, the service should be called correctly and should give you an infolog message that shows **New York** as the place name.

Deploying between environments

Although the previous code consumes the external service just fine, there is another impractical issue going on when you want to deploy the code across environments.

Suppose that you want to have different versions of your service running on development, test, and production systems. Then, you will probably have three different addresses for each environment. However, the issue here is that you only have one address available in the proxy class library.

To solve this issue, we need to update our X++ code one more time. Start by declaring two new variables that will hold the endpoint and endpoint address:

```
System.ServiceModel.Description.ServiceEndpoint endPoint;
System.ServiceModel.EndpointAddress endPointAddress;
```

You may have to add a reference to the System.ServiceModel assembly to the AOT. To do that, go to the AOT, right-click on the **References** node, and then click on **Add Reference**. Next, select **System.ServiceModel** in the grid, click on **Select**, and finally, click on **OK**.

Then, add the following three lines of code just before the line that invokes the service operation:

```
endPointAddress = new System.ServiceModel.EndpointAddress
    ("http://www.restfulwebservices.net/wcf/USAZipCodeService.svc");
endPoint = postalServiceClient.get_Endpoint();
endPoint.set_Address(endPointAddress);
```

What the preceding code does is that it creates an endpoint address for the service client that is to be used. When the endpoint is created, it replaces the endpoint address that is currently being used by the service client. Note that in the preceding example, the address should be replaced by a parameter that is stored in the system. This way, you can set the endpoint address depending on the parameter value of that environment.

Final result

After all these changes, the code that consumes the services will look as follows:

```
static void Consume_GetZipCodePlaceNameWithEndPoint(Args _args)
{
    DynamicsAxServices.WebServices.ZipCode.USAZipCodeServiceRef.
  PostalCodeServiceClient postalServiceClient;
    DynamicsAxServices.WebServices.ZipCode.
  USAZipCodeServiceRef .PostalCode postalCode;
    System.ServiceModel.Description.ServiceEndpoint endPoint;
    System.ServiceModel.EndpointAddress endPointAddress;
    System.Exception exception;
```

```
    System.Type type;

  try
  {
      // Get the .NET type of the client proxy
      type     = CLRInterop::getType
('DynamicsAxServices.WebServices.ZipCode.
USAZipCodeServiceRef.PostalCodeServiceClient');

      // Let AifUtil create the proxy client because
      // it uses the VSAssemblies path for the config file
      postalServiceClient = AifUtil::createServiceClient(type);

      // Create an endpoint address; this should be a
      // parameter stored in the system
      endPointAddress = new System.ServiceModel.EndpointAddress
("http://www.restfulwebservices.net/wcf/USAZipCodeService.svc");

      // Get the WCF endpoint
      endPoint = postalServiceClient.get_Endpoint();

      // Set the endpoint address.
      endPoint.set_Address(endPointAddress);

      // Use the zipcode to find a place name
      postalCode        = postalServiceClient.
GetPostCodeDetailByPostCode("10001"); // 10001 is New York

      // Use the getAnyTypeForObject to marshal the
      // System.String to an Ax anyType
      // so that it can be used with info()
      info(strFmt('%1', CLRInterop::getAnyTypeForObject
(postalCode.get_PlaceName())));
  }
  catch
  {
      // Get the .NET Type Exception
      exception = CLRInterop::getLastException();

      // Go through the inner exceptions
      while(exception)
      {
          // Print the exception to the infolog
```

```
            info(CLRInterop::getAnyTypeForObject(exception.
    ToString()));

            // Get the inner exception for more details
            exception = exception.get_InnerException();
        }
    }
}
```

Summary

At first sight, the procedure to consume a service in Microsoft Dynamics AX 2012 might seem a bit complex, but once you've done it, you see how easy it really is. Using Visual Studio, you can take advantage of having control over how you create the reference. You can choose whether you want to use message contracts, reuse data types, and so on.

Support for different deployment options also means that it is easier than ever to use managed code. The assemblies are part of the model store and are deployed when needed, so no manual actions are needed to deploy them.

In the next chapter, we will take a closer look at the system services that are available to us. They are new to Microsoft Dynamics AX, so they are easily overlooked when planning for integration. However, because of their flexibility, it is worth considering using them.

7
System Services

With each new release of Microsoft Dynamics AX, new features for developers are added. These features range from wizards that are used to automate repetitive development tasks to support for new technologies such as WCF. From a developer's perspective, you might think that Microsoft is really generous to provide us with all these cool features. This is true to a certain extent, but providing developers with tools can never be an end goal. In reality, these features are added to facilitate new functionalities in Microsoft Dynamics AX.

This is also true for a new set of services that are supported in Microsoft Dynamics AX 2012 known as **system services**. These services are WCF services that allow you to access system information; for example, they are used in the Excel add-in.

This doesn't mean you can't use them in your solutions. On the contrary, in this chapter, we will demonstrate how you can use these services to build your applications.

The following topics will be covered in this chapter:

- **Introducing system services**: We will start with a general description of the four types of system services along with an introduction of the demo application we will build.

- **Metadata service**: The first service we will use is the metadata service, a service that exposes information about the AOT. We will discuss what kind of information can be retrieved and how it can be done.

- **Query service**: Next, we will look at the query service, a service that, as the name suggests, allows you to execute queries on the Microsoft Dynamics AX database and retrieve the results.

- **User session service**: Next, we will learn about the user session service, a service that allows you to obtain a user's session-related information.

- **OData query service**: We will conclude with a demonstration of the OData query service, a service that exposes queries from the AOT in the web feed using the OData protocol.

Introducing system services

System services are automatically installed when the AOS is installed and are available when the AOS instance is running. They are written by Microsoft in managed code and hence they cannot be customized.

As mentioned, there are four system services as follows:

- The metadata service
- The query service
- The user session service
- The OData query service

We will have a detailed discussion of these services later in the chapter. We will not be able to go into every detail of all service operations, but it will be more than enough to get you started. Fortunately, for those who want to dig deeper, these services are well documented on MSDN. For OData in particular, there is a complete documentation available at `http://www.odata.org`.

Presenting a demo application

To demonstrate the usage of different system services, we start with a demo application. The application is a Windows Forms application that contains the following elements:

- A combobox that contains the **Contoso Video Rental** queries
- A DataGridView control to contain the resulting data
- **Previous page** and **Next page** buttons to provide paging of the results
- A button for retrieving titles using the OData query service
- A ListBox control that contains the session information of the calling user

The design of the demo application is shown in the following screenshot:

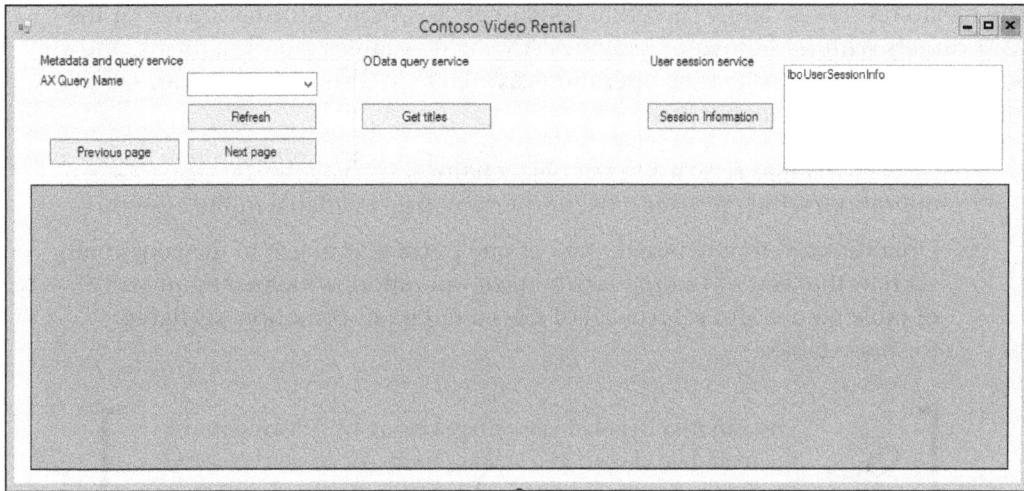

The following Microsoft Dynamics AX services are used in the application, and for each of them, a service reference is created:

- **Metadata service**: `http://DYNAX01:8101/DynamicsAx/Services/MetaDataService`

- **Query service**: `http://DYNAX01:8101/DynamicsAx/Services/QueryService`

- **User session service**: `http://DYNAX01:8101/DynamicsAx/Services/UserSessionService`

- **OData query service**: `http://DYNAX01:8101/DynamicsAx/Services/ODataQueryservice`

When creating the references, you should replace **DYNAX01** with the name of the server on which your AOS is installed and specify the correct port to use, which is `8101` by default. All of the service references we use in the demonstration have been configured to use the `System.Collections.Generic.List` collection type.

The metadata service

The metadata service allows external consumers to obtain information about the AOT objects within Microsoft Dynamics AX, such as tables, queries, forms, and so on. When we take a look at the operations available in the service, we can see the following two types of operations:

- Operations that return a list of object names, such as the `GetQueryNames` operation, which returns a list of query names available in the system

- Operations that return metadata of one particular object to the consumer, such as the `GetTableMetaDataByName` operation, which takes an array of table names and returns all of the metadata information available for these tables

> You can find detailed class diagrams on MSDN describing the metadata classes at `http://msdn.microsoft.com/en-us/library/gg845212`.

Filling the combobox

Let's start by taking a look at the code that is executed when the form loads.

To fill the combobox, we need to use the `GetQueryNames` operation on the metadata service and filter the results to show only the queries that start with CVR. You can use the following code to do this:

```
private void MainForm_Load(object sender, EventArgs e)
{
    // Create a service client
    AxMetadataServiceClient client = new AxMetadataServiceClient();

    // Get queries from Ax that start with CVR
    IList<string> queryNames = client.GetQueryNames()
.Where(queryItem => queryItem.StartsWith("CVR")).ToList();

    // Set the results as the combobox's data source
    cboAxQueryName.DataSource = queryNames;
}
```

First, the service client is created:

```
    AxMetadataServiceClient client = new AxMetadataServiceClient();
```

Then, the following line invokes the operation to retrieve all of the query names. We apply a lambda expression to the `IList` object to filter out the queries that start with `CVR` using the following line:

```
IList<string> queryNames = client.GetQueryNames()
.Where(queryItem => queryItem.StartsWith("CVR")).ToList();
```

Lastly, we just take the result and set it as the data source of the combobox using the following line of code:

```
cboAxQueryName.DataSource = queryNames;
```

When running your application, you should see the following result:

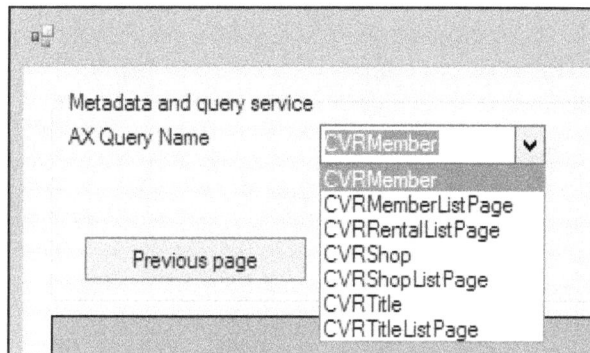

The query service

The query service enables us to retrieve data from Microsoft Dynamics AX without having to use the .NET Business Connector or, even worse, access the SQL database directly.

By using the query service, you can fetch data using any of the following query types:

- **Static query**: This is used to retrieve data using queries that are present in the AOT. We will use this query in the demonstration.

- **User-defined query**: A query can also be created using the `QueryMetadata` class. By doing this, you can create a query in the same way you create queries in X++ code.

- **Dynamic query**: Another way of running a query is by creating an X++ class that extends the `AifQueryBuilder` class. You can invoke the `ExecuteQuery` operation by passing in the name of the query builder class. It is also possible to pass arguments using a class that extends from the `AifQueryBuilderArgs` class.

Fetching data for the grid

Now let's put some code behind the clicked event handler of the **Refresh** button. The idea is to invoke the query service to retrieve the data of the selected query and then put it into the DataGridView control.

Put the following code behind the **Refresh** button's clicked event handler to get the job done:

```
private void cmdRefresh_Click(object sender, EventArgs e)
{
    this.refreshData();
}
```

Before this can work, we obviously need to add a refreshData() method that does the refreshing part. This is put in a separate method to support the reuse of the code when we add paging later on:

```
private void refreshData()
{
    try
    {
        // Determine the selected query / datamember
        string dataMember = cboAxQueryName.Text;
        string queryName = cboAxQueryName.Text;

        // Create a binding source for members
        BindingSource bindingSource = new BindingSource();

        // Set the binding source as the data source for the data grid
        dtgAxData.DataSource = bindingSource;

        // Create a service client
        QueryServiceClient queryClient = new QueryServiceClient();

        // Create an empty paging object
        Paging paging = null;

        // Call the query to retrieve the results
        DataSet dataSet = queryClient.ExecuteStaticQuery(queryName,
        ref paging);

        // Set as the data source of the binding source
        bindingSource.DataSource = dataSet;
        bindingSource.DataMember = dataMember;
    }
```

```
    catch (Exception _ex)
    {
        MessageBox.Show(_ex.Message);
    }
}
```

The first two lines of code sets the chosen query name and the data member. This data member is the actual list that is bound to the binding source. Here, we have the same name as the query because the **CVRMember** table has the same name as the **CVRMember** query object, as shown in the following code:

```
// Determine the selected query / datamember
string dataMember = cboAxQueryName.Text;
string queryName = cboAxQueryName.Text;
```

Next, the binding source is created and set as the data source of the DataGridView control:

```
// Create a binding source for members
BindingSource bindingSource = new BindingSource();

// Set the binding source as the data source for the data grid
dtgAxData.DataSource = bindingSource;
```

Now we can start to think about fetching data from Microsoft Dynamics AX. So, let's create a service client and call the operation to execute the query. Note that for now, we have a variable of the type `Paging` that is set to `null`, as shown in the following code, because we add the paging functionality later in this chapter:

```
// Create a service client
QueryServiceClient queryClient = new QueryServiceClient();

// Create an empty paging object
Paging paging = null;

// Call the query to retrieve the results
DataSet dataSet = queryClient.ExecuteStaticQuery(queryName,
ref paging);
```

Once the dataset containing the resulting records is returned, we can set it as the data source for the binding source.

```
// Set as the data source of the binding source
bindingSource.DataSource = dataSet;
bindingSource.DataMember = dataMember;
```

That's all there is to it. To test the code, run the application and hit the **Refresh** button with the **CVRMember** query selected. The result should look like the following screenshot:

Paging the results

The next thing that we want to enable in our application is paging. To handle large data sets, we can make use of paging to retrieve only a defined number of records at a time. In our example, we want to use pages of ten records.

The first thing to do is to add a member variable to the form that keeps track of the starting position, as shown in the following code:

```
private int nextStartPosition = 1;
```

The code behind the paging buttons is rather simple and will just decrement or increment the starting position for data retrieval by 10. After adjusting the starting position, the data is refreshed by calling the refreshData() method as seen before:

```
private void cmdNextPage_Click(object sender, EventArgs e)
{
    nextStartPosition += 10;
    this.refreshData();
}
private void cmdPreviousPage_Click(object sender, EventArgs e)
{
    nextStartPosition -= 10;
    this.refreshData();
}
```

The code behind the paging buttons is in place, but we still need to add some code to the `refreshData()` method to actually deal with the paging of the data. So, we need to replace the following line of code:

```
// Create an empty paging object
Paging paging = null;
```

Replace it with the following piece of code that tells the query service to only fetch 10 records starting from the currently calculated starting position:

```
// Create a paging object to start at the starting offset and fetch
// 10 records
Paging paging = new PositionBasedPaging()
{
    NumberOfRecordsToFetch = 10,
    StartingPosition = nextStartPosition
};
```

When we now run our application, the result should be as shown in the following screenshot:

Notice that we only have 10 records in our DataGridView control, and by clicking on the **Next page** button, we get to see the next set of records, as shown in the following screenshot:

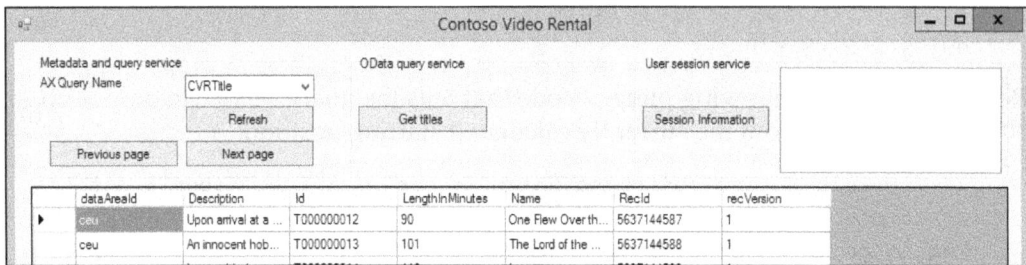

> For paging techniques such as position-based paging to work, you have to use a query that contains at least one sorting field. This field will be used to order the results before the paging is applied. In our demo application, the CVRTitle query has the Id field in the **Order By** node of the query data source. The CVRTitleListPage query does not have a sorting field, which is why it will not work if you try to retrieve all titles using that query.

The user session service

The user session service exposes information about the current user and their session. Although this service is categorized by Microsoft as a system service, technically it isn't. Unlike other system services, the business logic is contained in a service class in the AOT and exposed using a basic port. Consequently, it is also possible to expose this service using an enhanced port, allowing you to further customize the service.

The user session has the following operations:

- GetUserSessionInfo: This returns information about the current session in the form of an instance of the UserSessionInfo class containing the following information: language, currency, company, company time zone, user-preferred time zone, preferred calendar, user ID, whether the user is a system admin, and the locale name.

- GetAccessRights: This returns a collection of the type AccessRight that contains the permissions which the user has on the items that were provided as parameters, such as tables, fields, and menu items.

- ApplyTimeZone: This executes the DateTimeUtil::applyTimeZoneOffs et() method and thereby offsets the utcdatetime value by the amount specified in the timezone parameter.

- RemoveTimeZone: This executes the DateTimeUtil::removeTimeZoneOf fset() method and thereby removes the offset specified by the timezone parameter from the utcdatetime value.

We will use the GetUserSessionInfo and GetAccessRights operations in the following scenario to demonstrate how to use this service.

Retrieving user information

The functionalities that we will add to the form are as follows:

- A button is added to retrieve the user session information
- A ListBox control is added to display the user session information
- General user information such as the company and language is retrieved
- Permissions are retrieved for the query data source

To enable this functionality, override the cmdUserSessionInfo_Click() method using the following code:

```
private void cmdUserSessionInfo_Click(object sender, EventArgs e)
{
    // Create an instance of the usersession client
    UserSessionServiceClient client = new UserSessionServiceClient();

    // Get session information
    UserSessionInfo sessionInfo = client.GetUserSessionInfo(null);

    // Put all of the information in the listbox
    lboUserSessionInfo.Items.Clear();
    lboUserSessionInfo.Items.Add("User : " + sessionInfo.UserId);
    lboUserSessionInfo.Items.Add("Company : " + sessionInfo.Company);
    lboUserSessionInfo.Items.Add("Language : " + sessionInfo.
    AXLanguage);
    lboUserSessionInfo.Items.Add("Currency : " + sessionInfo.
    CurrencyInfo.CurrencyCode);
    lboUserSessionInfo.Items.Add("Administrator : " + sessionInfo.
    IsSysAdmin);

    // Create an access control item for the main table of the
    // selected query
    AccessControlledItemKey key = new AccessControlledItemKey()
    {
        ItemType = AccessControlledType.Table,
        ItemName = cboAxQueryName.Text
```

```
    };

    // Create a list with the item in it
    List<AccessControlledItemKey> keys = new
    List<AccessControlledItemKey>();
    keys.Add(key);

    // Now request the effective access right for this user session on
    // the item
    List<AccessRight> accessRights = client.GetAccessRights(null,
    keys);

    // Get the access rights
    AccessRight accessRight = accessRights.First();

    lboUserSessionInfo.Items.Add("Query access right : " +
accessRight.ToString());
}
```

As you can see, we can divide the code into the following two large parts:

- First, we use the `GetUserSessionInfo` operation to retrieve the session information and use it to add items to the listbox.

- Next, we create a new list object of the type `AccessControlledItemKey` and add an item specifying the table name. Then, we use the `GetAccessRights()` method to retrieve the permissions that the user has on this table and then add them to the list.

To test the code, simply click on the **Session Information** button and the listbox should be filled with the session information, as shown in the following screenshot:

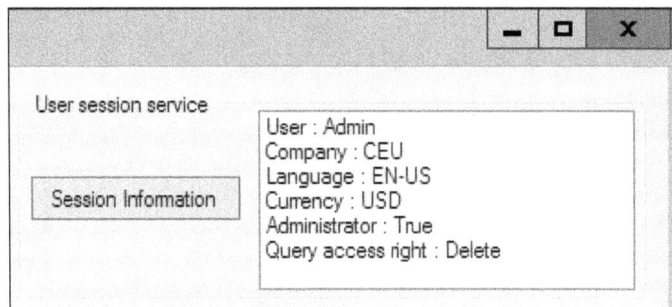

The OData query service

The last system service we will discuss is the OData query service. This service exposes data from Microsoft Dynamics AX using the **Open Data Protocol** (**OData**). This is a web protocol for querying and updating data, although Microsoft Dynamics AX 2012 currently only supports querying data.

The records that result from this querying are published as entries in an **Atom** feed. Atom is a web feed probably best known as being used for subscribing to updates from websites such as blogs. Atom is similar to the better known RSS but standardized, which makes it the obvious choice over RSS. OData also supports **JavaScript Object Notation** (**JSON**) as an alternative to Atom, but that is not supported by Microsoft Dynamics AX 2012.

To demonstrate this service, we will consume it using Internet Explorer and use it in our example application.

Creating and publishing a data source

Exposing data using the OData query service is very straightforward. It consists of the following:

- Creating a query or using an existing one
- Setting up **Document data sources**

Creating a query

So, the first thing to do is to create a query. If you've installed the example code that comes with this book, you already have the query. The query we'll be using is **CVRTitle**. It returns all titles by selecting all records in the **CVRTitle** table and is shown in the following screenshot:

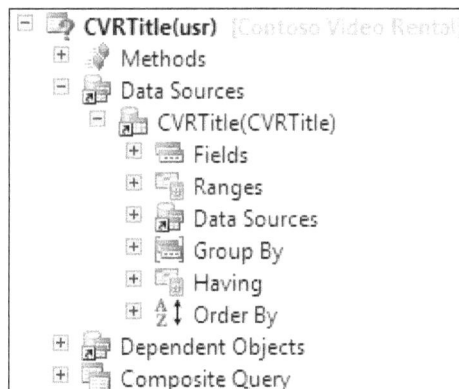

Setting up document data sources

In order to expose the data in the query as an OData feed, perform the following steps:

1. Go to **Organization Administration** | **Setup** | **Document management** | **Document data sources**.

2. Click on the **New** button or press *Ctrl + N* to create a new document data source.

3. Set the **Module** to **Basic** and the **Data source type** to **Query reference**; in the **Data source name** field, enter CVRTitle.

4. Enter some descriptive text in the **Description** field, so you can easily identify your document data source later.

5. Press *Ctrl + S* to save your changes and click on the **Activate** button.

That's all you need to do; your query is now ready to be used in the OData query service. The newly created record is highlighted in the following screenshot:

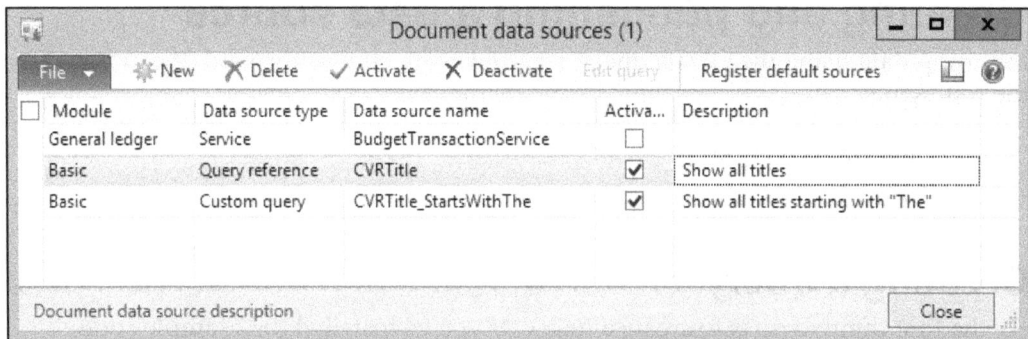

Note that another document data source has also been created named CVRTitle_StartsWithThe. This is so that a list of document data sources is available, which will make the following examples easier to interpret. Try experimenting and creating it yourself. What does selecting the document type **Custom query** do? The answer follows.

Before we take a look at how we can consume this data service, let us examine the fields and buttons on the **Document data source** form first. Depending on what version of Microsoft Dynamics AX 2012 you are using, you will have the following options to choose from:

- **Module**: The **Module** field is an informative field that provides a way to categorize your document data sources.

- **Data source type**: Depending on what version you are using, you will have different options. In R2, there are three options to choose from:

  - **Service**: This allows you to create a document data source using an AIF document service. This is then visible in Microsoft Excel when adding data using the Excel add-in.

  - **Query reference**: This allows you to expose a query using the OData query service. This query will also be available using the Excel add-in.

  - **Custom query**: This is the same as **Query reference**, but when selecting a query, you will have the option to modify that query – for example, by adding ranges – thus limiting the number of records returned by the query. You can edit the query afterwards by clicking on the **Edit query** button.

  In the feature pack release, the **Custom query** option is not available, and the **Query reference** option is named **Query** but its function remains the same.

- **Data source name:** Depending on the **Document source type**, this option allows you to specify either the service or the query to use. When using the **Custom query type**, you can rename the data source name after it is saved.

- **Activated:** This indicates whether the data source is active. Inactive document data sources will not be available for use. You can activate or deactivate a document data source by using this checkbox or the **Activate** and **Deactivate** buttons.

- **Description**: This is only available in R2 and allows for an informative description of the service, which is especially useful when using custom queries.

The **Register default sources** button registers default document data sources. When you extend Microsoft Dynamics AX 2012 and you need to ship document data sources as part of your solution, you can register them here by subscribing to the delegate named `insertDataSources`, which is available on the `DocuDataSourceLoader` class. If you do so, be sure to subscribe to this delegate and not modify any code on existing methods. That way, multiple solutions across different models within the same layer can extend this functionality without you running into problems when importing models.

Consuming the OData query service using Internet Explorer

Because the OData protocol uses technologies such as HTTP and OData, many applications can consume the OData query service. Internet Explorer is such an application and is ideal for us to explore the query we have just exposed.

The OData query service is available at the following URL, where DYNAX01 is the name of the AOS server and 8101 is the service WSDL port that is defined in the **Microsoft Dynamics AX Server Configuration Utility**: http://DYNAX01:8101/ DynamicsAx/Services/ODataQueryservice/.

As you can see in the following screenshot, when you type this URL in Internet Explorer, you are presented with a list of feeds that are exposed as collections, in this case, the **CVRTitle** and **CVRTitle_StartsWithThe** feeds.

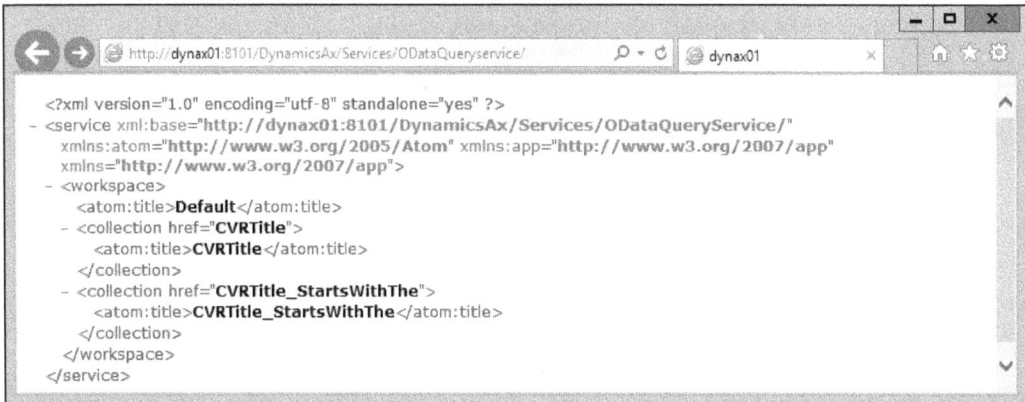

To view the data, simply add the name of the feed after the URL of the OData query service, for example, http://DYNAX01:8101/DynamicsAx/Services/ ODataQueryservice/CVRTitle. As you can see in the following screenshot, a feed is shown with an entry for every one of the 248 titles that are available in the **CVRTitle** table:

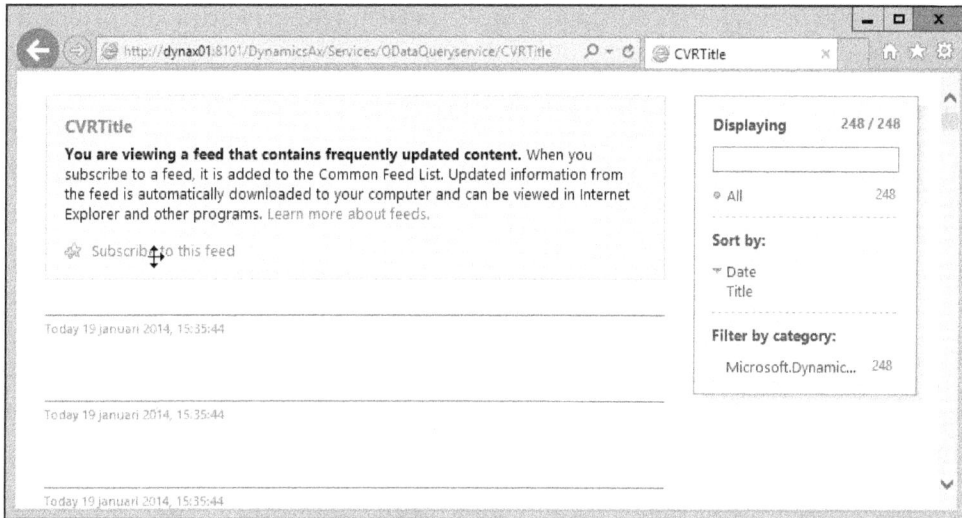

As you can see, not much data is shown in a readable fashion. This is because Internet Explorer tries to render the Atom feed but does not know how to interpret the data in it. To view the Atom feed in XML format, right-click on the page on the browser and click on **View source**. This will open up a text editor showing the file, as shown in the following screenshot:

The preceding screenshot shows part of the document with a header identifying it as an Atom feed and the first entry with the data embedded in the content tag.

Right now, all data from the table is shown, but there is a limit. The default number of results that are returned is 1000 and is set in the ax32serv.exe.config file in the bin directory of the AOS using the ODataQueryPageSize key, shown as follows:

```
<configuration>
    <appSettings>
    <add key="ODataQueryPageSize" value="1000" />
    [...]
</configuration>
```

If you set the value to 20, save the file and refresh the feed in Internet Explorer; you will see that there are only 20 entries in the Atom feed.

Just as regular services expose their metadata using WSDL, the OData query service also exposes a metadata document. Instead of using WSDL, OData uses **Entity data model (EDM)**, which represents its data in **EDMX**, an XML-based file format. You can find this document at http://DYNAX01:8101/DynamicsAx/Services/ODataQueryservice/$metadata. The screenshot of this document is as follows:

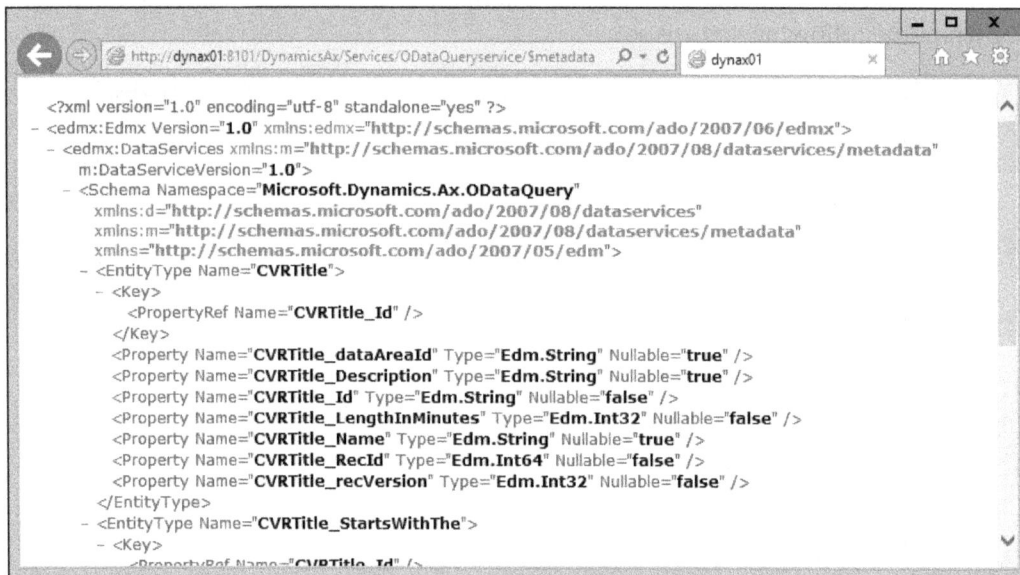

As you can see in the screenshot, the document uses the EDMX namespace and describes the OData service metadata. This is the document that is used when adding a service reference to the OData query service in Visual Studio. In fact, the content of this file is copied to a file with the extension `.edmx` in the subfolder for the service reference in the project folder.

Consuming the OData query service using Visual Studio

For this demonstration, we will expand the functionality of our demo application by creating a button that uses the **CVRTitle** feed exposed by the OData query service to display all titles in the grid. For this, we will use **WCF Data Services**, a component of the .NET framework that will allow us to consume the OData query service.

> More information about WCF Data Services can be found on MSDN at http://msdn.microsoft.com/en-us/library/cc668792.aspx. Note that many features of WCF Data Services are currently not supported by Microsoft Dynamics AX 2012.

Adding a service reference

Before we can consume the service, we first have to add a service reference. We've done this many times over the course of this book, so please refer to the previous chapters on how to do this. Use the following URL when adding the service reference, but replace the AOS name and WSDL port with the ones you want to use: http://dynax01:8101/DynamicsAx/Services/ODataQueryservice/.

When you've installed the sample code and the existing service reference is not working, delete that service reference and recreate it.

Fetching data for the grid

Once the service reference has been added, we can use it to fetch the data. Override the click event of the **Get titles** button as follows:

```
using DynamicsAxServices.SystemServices.UI.ODataQueryService;

private void btnTitles_Click(object sender, EventArgs e)
{
    // Create a binding source
```

```
        BindingSource bindingSource = new BindingSource();

        // Set the binding source as the data source for the data grid
        dtgAxData.DataSource = bindingSource;

        // create a new URI (replace with the URI of your service)
        Uri uri = new Uri("http://localhost:8101/DynamicsAx/Services/
        ODataQueryService/");

        // create the data service context
        ODataQueryService.ODataQueryService context = new
        ODataQueryService.ODataQueryService(uri);

        // set the credentials, in this case pass the credentials of the
        // user that is currently logged on
        context.Credentials = System.Net.CredentialCache.
        DefaultCredentials;

        // bind the CVRTitles feed to the datasource of the grid
        bindingSource.DataSource = context.CVRTitle;
    }
```

As you can see, we start by creating a URI object using the URL of our data service:

```
Uri uri = new Uri("http://localhost:8101/DynamicsAx/Services/
ODataQueryService/");
```

Next, we use that URI to construct the data service context:

```
ODataQueryService.ODataQueryService context = new ODataQueryService.
ODataQueryService(uri);
```

After that, we set the credentials to the user that is currently logged on. This is sufficient for our demo, but you could also pass the credentials of a specific user using the following code:

```
context.Credentials = System.Net.CredentialCache.DefaultCredentials;
```

Finally, we get the feed and bind it to the grid:

```
bindingSource.DataSource = context.CVRTitle;
```

When we compile the project and test the button, we can see that all titles are displayed in the grid, as shown in the following screenshot:

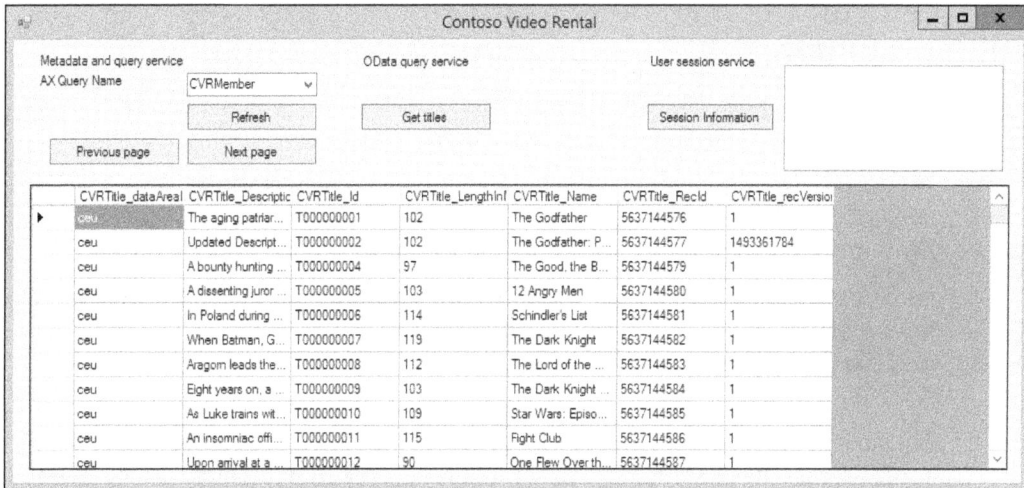

Consuming the OData query service using other applications

We got to know what OData is by consuming it using a web browser, and we've seen how to consume it in .NET, but of course, there are a lot of other applications that can consume an OData data service. Exploring all of these would put the focus too much on these applications. This is not part of the scope of this chapter as we are trying to focus on services, but a few are worth mentioning:

- **Microsoft Excel and PowerPivot**: You can import OData feeds into Excel in the regular grid form, or you can use PowerPivot to create pivot tables and analyze the data. This is well documented on MSDN on the page *Walkthrough: Creating a PowerPivot Data Mash-up [AX 2012]* at `http://technet.microsoft.com/en-us/library/dn198214.aspx`.

- **Microsoft InfoPath**: When creating a form using Microsoft InfoPath, you can use an OData service, for example, to fill lookups for fields. This is explained in the book *Extending Microsoft Dynamics AX 2012 Cookbook, Packt Publishing*.

Limitations

Those who are familiar with OData may notice that the OData query service has a few limitations. It's important to know these and not make assumptions so that you don't run into any surprises. The limitations are as follows:

- **No JSON support**: The OData protocol supports Atom as well as JSON, but Microsoft Dynamics AX 2012 only supports Atom.

- **No create, update, or delete**: With OData, you can also modify data instead of only reading it, but this feature is not supported in Microsoft Dynamics AX 2012.

- **No support for query options**: OData supports query options that allow you to, for example, select only the top five records, select only a specific entry, or sort the feed; however, this feature is not supported in Microsoft Dynamics AX 2012 and using it will result in an error.

- **No support for queries with fetch mode 1:n**: Using a query that has a data source which has its fetch mode set to **1:n** will result in an error in the **event log** for the Feature Pack release and a warning for the R2 release. The latter will automatically convert the **1:n** fetch mode to **1:1**, which is the only fetch mode that is supported.

- **No support for views**: Queries that use views are not supported, and using a view will result in an error.

As you can see, it is quite a list as many key features of OData are not yet supported.

Summary

System services are new in this iteration of Microsoft Dynamics AX, but they are spot on. In this chapter, we have demonstrated that system services are powerful, especially when they are used together.

If you use system services where possible, you're using an out-of-the-box functionality that Microsoft Dynamics AX 2012 offers. This will save you the time that you would spend developing document or custom services, thereby allowing you to focus on more important tasks.

In the next chapter, we will take a break from the development side of services and focus on how to set up Microsoft Dynamics AX 2012 to achieve High Availability for services.

8
High Availability

Today's enterprise applications have evolved from smaller proprietary systems to integrated applications that are always available. In most Microsoft Dynamics AX implementations, we see that there is a multi-company setup where there is a difference in business critical hours between those companies. During business critical hours, the software must be capable of handling different kinds of loads. Outside these hours, there are often nightly processes such as inventory replenishment that are running. These processes too can put a load on the system. Even companies that are based in a single location cannot afford to have much downtime because they run 24/7; for example, hospitals or factories.

All of this results in the need for a system that is available at any time.

In this chapter, we will take a look at precisely that. Starting with a very simple setup, we will modify the architecture of Microsoft Dynamics AX so that it can handle higher loads while avoiding single points of failure.

The first goal of this chapter is for Microsoft Dynamics AX professionals to be able to recognize situations in which a high availability setup is desired. The second goal is for you to be able to configure Microsoft Dynamics AX for high availability. In this chapter, we will cover the following topics:

- **Introducing high availability**: We will start by defining what high availability is and how it relates to redundancy and disaster recovery.

- **Application level load balancing**: Starting with a very basic architecture, we will gradually add components until all Microsoft Dynamics AX components are in place to achieve high availability of the services.

- **Network load balancing**: The final components that we will add to the architecture are network load balancers. These are vital components, especially if you want high availability of services, because they take care of load balancing WCF communication.

Introducing high availability

High availability (HA) means creating a system design for your Microsoft Dynamics AX components in a way that ensures that the system is up and running as close to 100 percent of the time as possible at an acceptable level of performance.

For anyone working with Microsoft Dynamics AX, it is obvious that this is no easy feat. Installing fixes in a best practice way requires restarting the AOS, which means that many components are unavailable. Rolling out one fix per month with a downtime of 5 minutes, for example, would mean a system that is running only 99.99 percent of the time. This, however, can be planned and should have little impact on the business.

However, there are many occasions when the system is unavailable that can't be foreseen, such as the following:

- Power outage
- Server crashes
- Hardware failure
- Network outage
- Security breaches

Fortunately, there are ways to deal with these problems, most of which might already be known to you, such as using **Redundant Array of Inexpensive Disks (RAID)** to protect the system against disk failures or using **Uninterruptable Power Supply (UPS)** to protect the system against power outage. Such automated systems can be complemented by defining procedures that need to be performed manually.

Adding redundancy

A chain is only as strong as its weakest link. In terms of system design, links are the components of your system. When adding redundancy, you strengthen these links by avoiding single points of failure.

Ironically, adding extra components might undermine your efforts to create a high availability environment. These components might just increase the number of points of failure, so consider each component carefully.

Adding redundancy opens the door to load balancing. Adding multiple AOS instances to a cluster is an example of load balancing. This will balance the load over these different instances, adding to the performance of the system. If one of the AOS instances fails, the others will still be available, adding to the reliability of the system.

Another example is a SQL Server in an active/passive mode. Only one SQL Server instance is active at a given time in that configuration, but in case one fails, a failover occurs and the other instance is used.

Disaster recovery

Disaster recovery (**DR**) comes into play when HA fails. This could happen because of natural causes such as fire or flood, human errors, or errors that are introduced on purpose. After a disaster occurs, DR strives to restore the system to a previously acceptable state as soon as possible. This could mean doing simple things such as restoring backups and restarting services, but it could also mean moving all operations to a different physical location altogether. In the case of DR, the level of performance is less important, as its first priority is to restore the system to an operational state.

Putting high availability into practice

In the next sections, we will begin with the simplest architecture and point out the flaws in the design. Gradually, we'll solve them until we have a robust high availability design.

The basic architecture

First, let's take a look at the following diagram, which represents the most basic Microsoft Dynamics AX 2012 design. There is a single AOS instance and the AOS connects to a single SQL Server instance, as shown in the following figure:

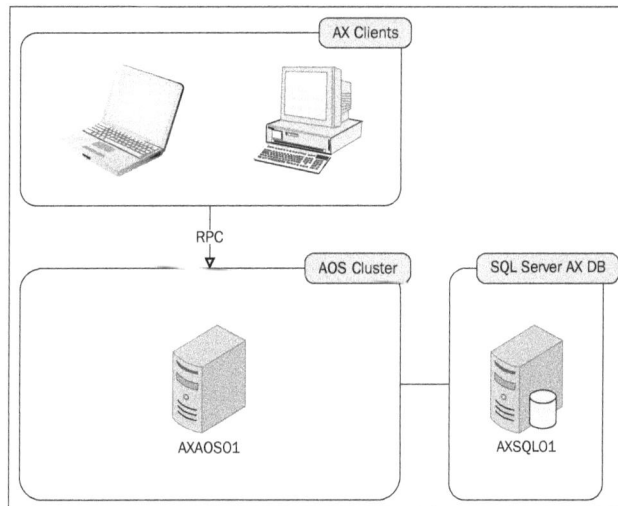

It goes without saying that this is not a good design when it comes to HA. When either the AOS or SQL Server instance has a failure, the whole environment will be out of order.

We will not discuss the SQL Server issues here because we want to focus on the architecture of the AOS instances. These are the most important when it comes to services.

We should begin by adding redundancy for the AOS instance. We will do this by configuring the application level load balancing.

Application-level load balancing

This type of load balancing is configurable from within Microsoft Dynamics AX and has been around for quite some time. It is intended for load balancing **Remote Procedure Call (RPC)** communication between the client and AOS.

Configuring the cluster

The following figure shows us that in order to configure application level load balancing, we have to add multiple AOS instances to a cluster. A new AOS instance (AXAOS02) is placed within a cluster with the existing AOS (AXAOS01):

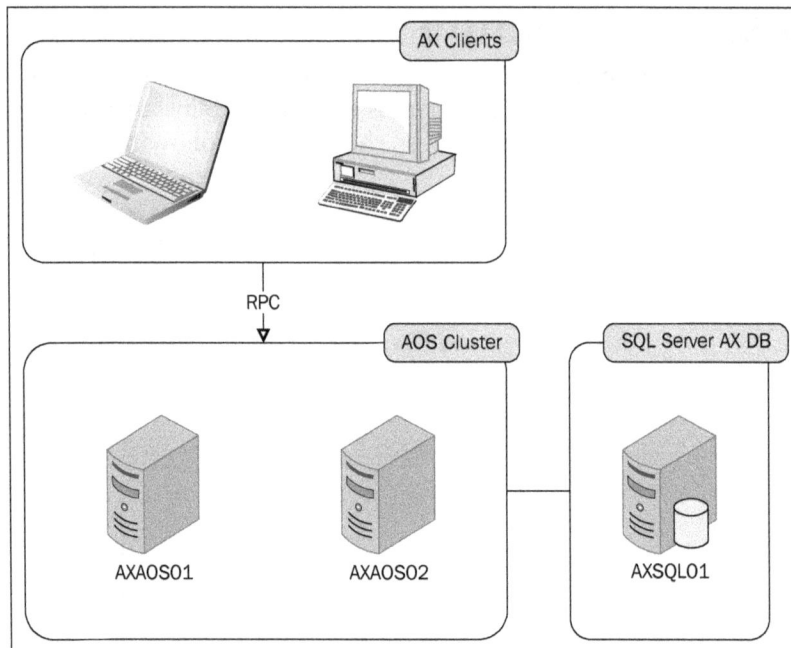

To achieve application level load balancing, perform the following steps:

1. Navigate to **System administration | Setup | System | Cluster configuration**.
2. By default, a non-load-balanced AOS cluster should be available. Create a new record by pressing *Ctrl + N* and add a cluster named `Clustered AOS Instances`. This is a cluster that will support the addition of a load balancer later.
3. Go to the fast tab **Map AOS instances to cluster**.
4. Add the following entries to the grid:

AOS Instance Name	Load balancer	Max Concurrent Sessions	Cluster name
AXAOS01	No	2000	Clustered AOS Instances
AXAOS02	No	2000	Clustered AOS Instances

> Note that once you have created the cluster records in this form, it does not matter which record you are on as the fast tab always shows all of the AOS instances. To assign instances to a cluster, use the drop-down menu on the cluster name field.

5. Restart both the AOS instances.

With both the AOS instances now becoming part of the cluster, we need to make a modification in the client configuration. The clients should be configured to connect to both the AOS instances. To do this, add the second AOS instance to your configuration by performing the given steps:

1. Open **Microsoft Dynamics AX Configuration Utility**.
2. Go to the **Connection** tab.
3. Click on the **Add...** button and enter the AOS details.
4. Click on the **OK** button and verify that both the AOS instances are present.
5. Click on the **Apply** button at the bottom of the utility.

The output looks like the following screenshot:

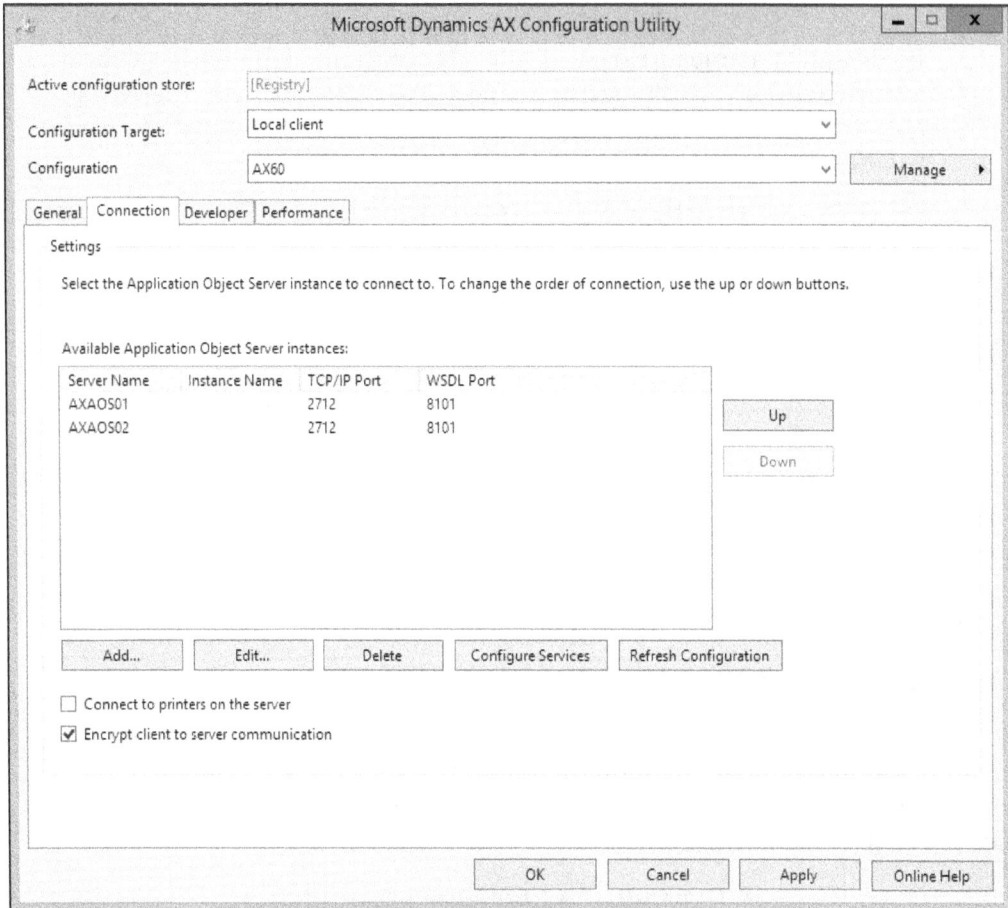

When a client starts using this configuration, the client will send a request to the first AOS in the list. This AOS will respond with a list of active AOS instances in the cluster, sorted by workload. The workload is determined by the number of connected clients divided by the maximum number of allowed clients on that AOS. Then, the client will try to connect to the AOS instances in order, starting with the AOS that has the lowest workload.

This provides us with the following advantages:

- **Scalability**: You can add new instances to the cluster, after which the load is also handled by the new instance
- **Redundancy**: By adding AOS instances to the cluster, more instances remain available in case the other instances fail

Although we have successfully added a second AOS instance to the cluster, there are still some pitfalls to this approach:

- **Maintenance**: Removing or adding AOS instances to the cluster requires the client configuration to be updated.

- **Startup performance**: On startup, the client will go through the list of AOS instances sorted by workload. When the first AOS instance does not respond, the next in the list will be tried, and so on. Because there is a timeout before moving to the next instance, this may result in slower startup times for the client. This is especially inconvenient for services because they tend to log in and log off from Microsoft Dynamics AX more frequently.

- **Overhead**: Each individual AOS acts like a load balancer, which causes overhead for the server.

Adding a dedicated load balancer

To solve the maintenance and startup performance issues, a dedicated load balancer can be used within the cluster. When using a dedicated load balancer, clients connect to that instance. The dedicated load balancer will then point the clients to one of the AOS instances that are not designated as load balancers.

The process to divide the load is as follows. The load balancer maintains a list of all the available AOS instances. To view this list in the Microsoft Dynamics AX client, perform the following steps:

1. Navigate to **System administration | Common | Users | Online users**.
2. Click on the **Server Instances** tab.

It's important to notice the AOS **Status** and **Number of clients** columns here. These fields are used to create a list of AOS instances sorted by workload. When a client makes a request, the load balancer will sort the list by workload in ascending order and use the first AOS to redirect the client.

Using a cluster with a load balancer, AOS has the following benefits:

- **Maintenance**: You can add new instances to the cluster without having to modify the client configuration

- **Performance**: Using a dedicated load balancer frees the other AOS instances from their task of performing load balancing themselves

The following diagram shows us a design using a dedicated load balancing
AOS instance:

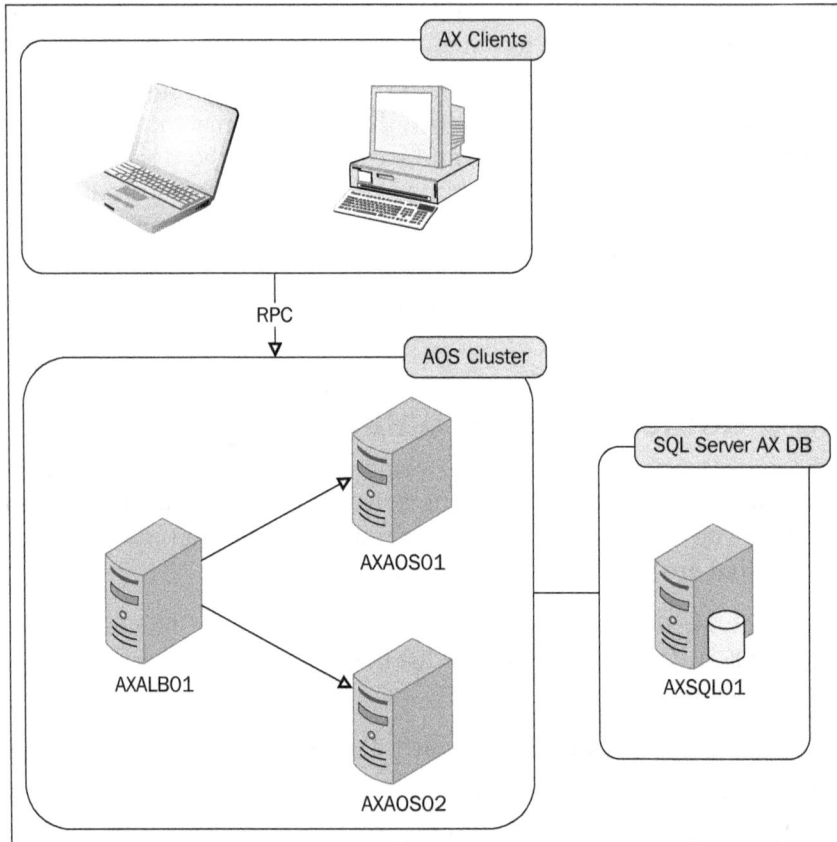

To add a dedicated load balancer, follow the same steps that we used earlier to add
`AXAOS02` to the cluster. Add the following to the list:

AOS Instance Name	Load balancer	Max Concurrent Sessions	Cluster name
AXLB01	Yes	0	Clustered AOS Instances

As you can see, the **Max concurrent sessions** parameter is automatically set to 0 for dedicated load balancers. This is because dedicated load balancers do not accept client connections but only serve the purpose of load balancing. It is also important to note that the dedicated load balancer instance will not consume an AOS license.

Once the load balancer is in place, we need to make an adjustment to the client configuration so that it connects to the dedicated load balancer.

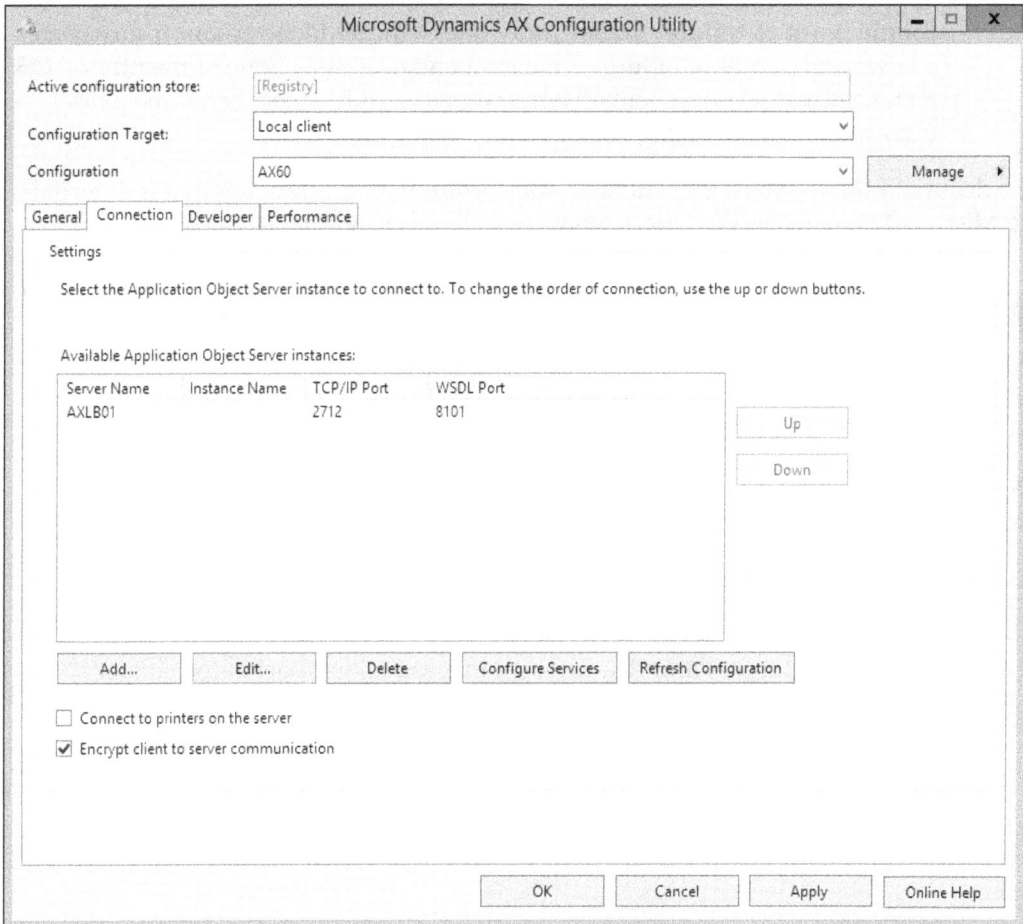

We have now solved the downsides of not using a dedicated load balancer, but we are not out of the woods yet. We have created two new problems:

- **WCF communication**: When using dedicated load balancers, the WCF communication between the client and AOS fails. This is because the WCF client connects directly to a dedicated load balancer that does not accept clients and because the mechanism of application level load balancing only applies to RPC communication.

- **Single point of failure**: Adding only one dedicated load balancer introduces a new single point of failure. If the load balancer fails, none of the other AOS instances will receive clients. Therefore, we should at least add one extra dedicated load balancing AOS instance to the cluster.

To deal with these issues, we will need some kind of load balancing that is external to Microsoft Dynamics AX. This is what we will discuss next.

Network Load Balancing

Microsoft **Network Load Balancing (NLB)** is a feature that you can add in the server versions of Windows. It also allows you to create load balancing clusters, but here, it is on the network level.

NLB enables you to create a cluster and, among many other things, specify the following key components:

- The full name of the cluster, so you are able to refer to the cluster later on
- A dedicated IP address for the cluster
- A list of hostnames and IP addresses that are taking part in the cluster

> For more information on how to install and configure NLB clusters, please refer to the following MSDN page: `http://technet.microsoft.com/en-us/library/cc770558.aspx`.

To further optimize our design for HA, we will need NLB for the following
two reasons:

- Load balancing the Microsoft Dynamics AX dedicated load balancer to avoid
  a single point of failure
- Load balancing services (WCF communication)

NLB for AX load balancers

Let's take a look at the design that we have now. One of the remaining problems is
that although the AXLB01 AOS balances load over the AOS instances, it is the single
point of failure itself now. If the dedicated load balancer fails, none of the clients can
connect to the AOS instances anymore.

So, the first thing to do here is to add at least one extra dedicated load balancer to the
cluster. By doing so, you will avoid the system going down when the dedicated load
balancer is unavailable. Add the following load balancer to the cluster:

AOS Instance Name	Load balancer	Max Concurrent Sessions	Cluster name
AXLB02	Yes	0	Clustered AOS Instances

Now that both the dedicated load balancers are in place, two options are available to
enable clients to connect to the dedicated load balancers:

- **Modify client configuration**: We could add AXLB02 to the list of AOS
  instances within the **Connection** tab of the **Microsoft Dynamics AX
  Configuration Utility**.
- **Use an NLB cluster on the network level**: The better option is to configure
  an NLB cluster. To do that, add a cluster named AXLB in the NLB manager
  and give the cluster its own dedicated IP address. Then, you can also add
  two hosts within the cluster by using the names and ports of the Microsoft
  Dynamics AX load balancers.

We will go with the option of creating an NLB cluster. We will assume that an NLB cluster has been configured as follows:

Cluster Name	Cluster IP	Host Name	Host IP / Port
AXLB	192.168.2.100	AXLB01	192.168.2.101 / TCP 2712
		AXLB02	192.168.2.102 / TCP 2712

The last thing that we need to do is point the clients to the network load balancer instead of the dedicated load balancer.

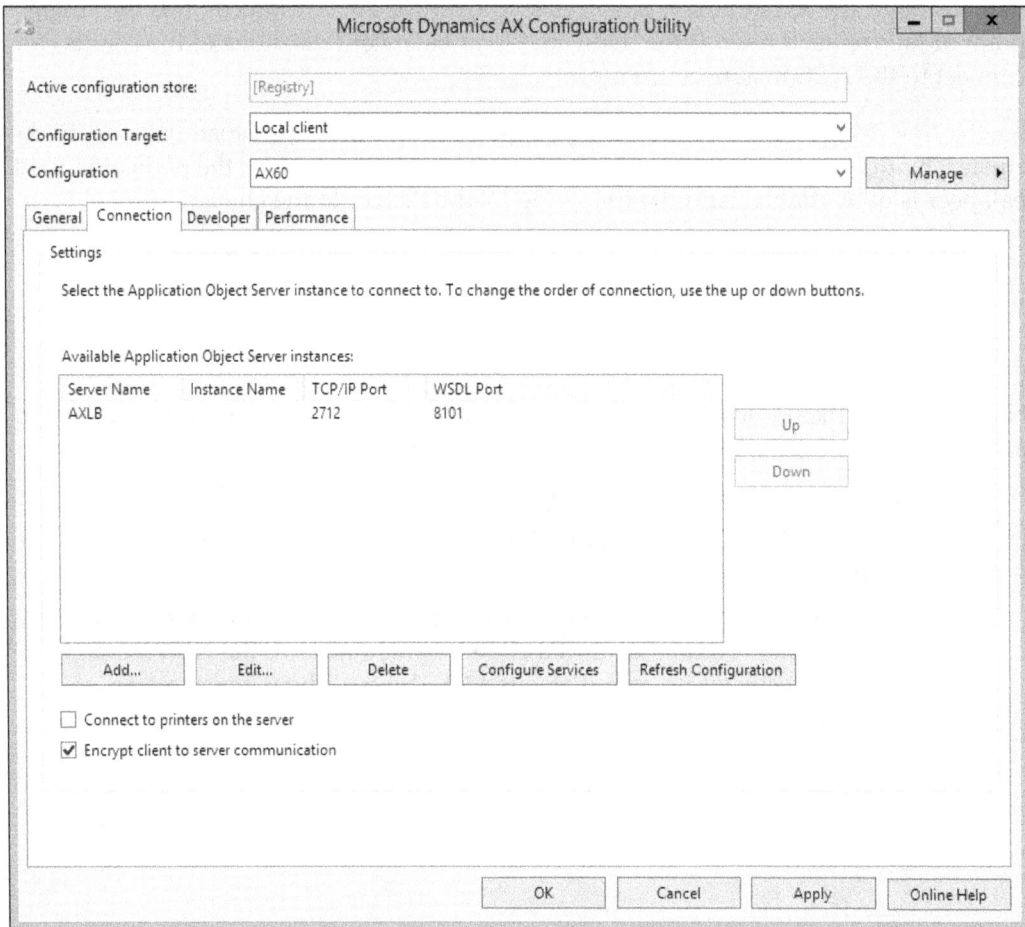

By doing so, all client requests will be made using the AXLB name. The NLB cluster continuously monitors the hosts within the cluster to see if they still respond on their IP address and port. When a client tries to connect to an AOS, the network load balancer chooses a suitable host and forwards the client's request. In our case, this means that AXLB01 or AXLB02 will receive the request.

Once either one of the dedicated load balancers receive the client's request, they will fall back to the application level load balancing to decide which of the client AOS instances will handle the client session.

At this point, our design should look like the following diagram:

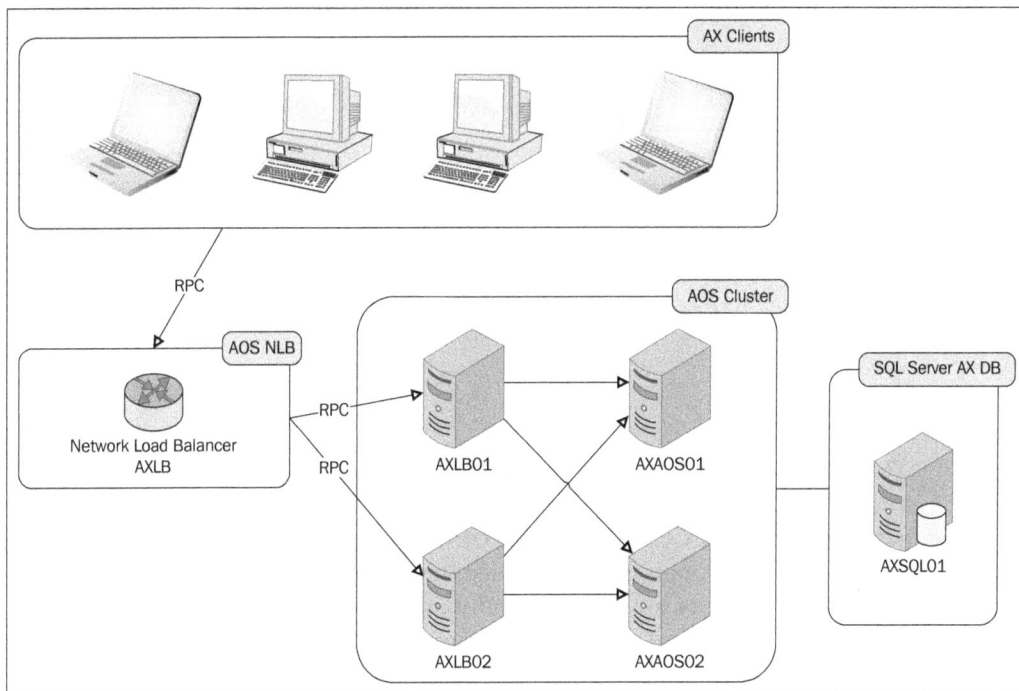

NLB for services

Since the release of Microsoft Dynamics AX 2012, every AOS instance now has two extra ports that are used for WCF services: A WSDL port (8101) and a service endpoint port (8201).

We have gone through several pitfalls so far, but there is actually one pitfall still remaining in our current design. All of the clients connect to AXLB, which is fine for RPC. Requests will be forwarded to one of the dedicated load balancers from which point the application level load balancing takes over to redirect them to the client AOS instance. This, however, does not apply to WCF communication.

When the WCF service clients communicate with the AOS, the request is also made to the AXLB cluster, and it will be rerouted to either AXLB01 or AXLB02. The problem here is that the application level load balancing does not support the load balancing of WCF communication, which causes the service client to try to log on to the dedicated load balancers themselves. When refreshing the service in the **Microsoft Dynamics AX Configuration Utility**, for example, this will result in the following error message:

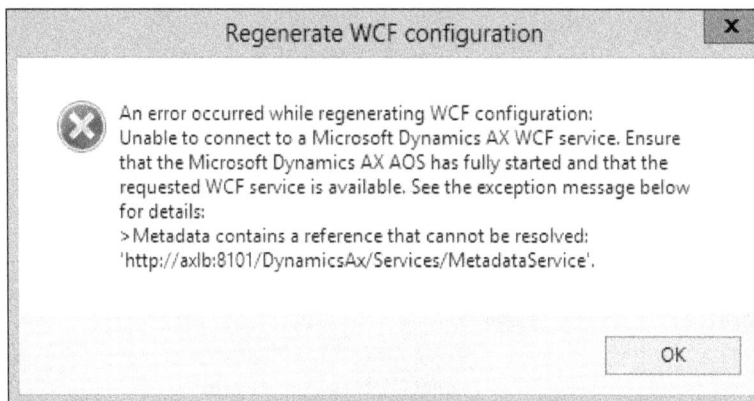

The **Microsoft Dynamics AX Configuration Utility** stores the WCF configuration within the AXC file. If you open it, you will see that the endpoints contain the name of the NLB cluster that points to the dedicated load balancers. This needs to be prevented so that the client does all the WCF communication with the AOS instances directly. To do this, we need to make one last addition to our design, which is shown in the following diagram:

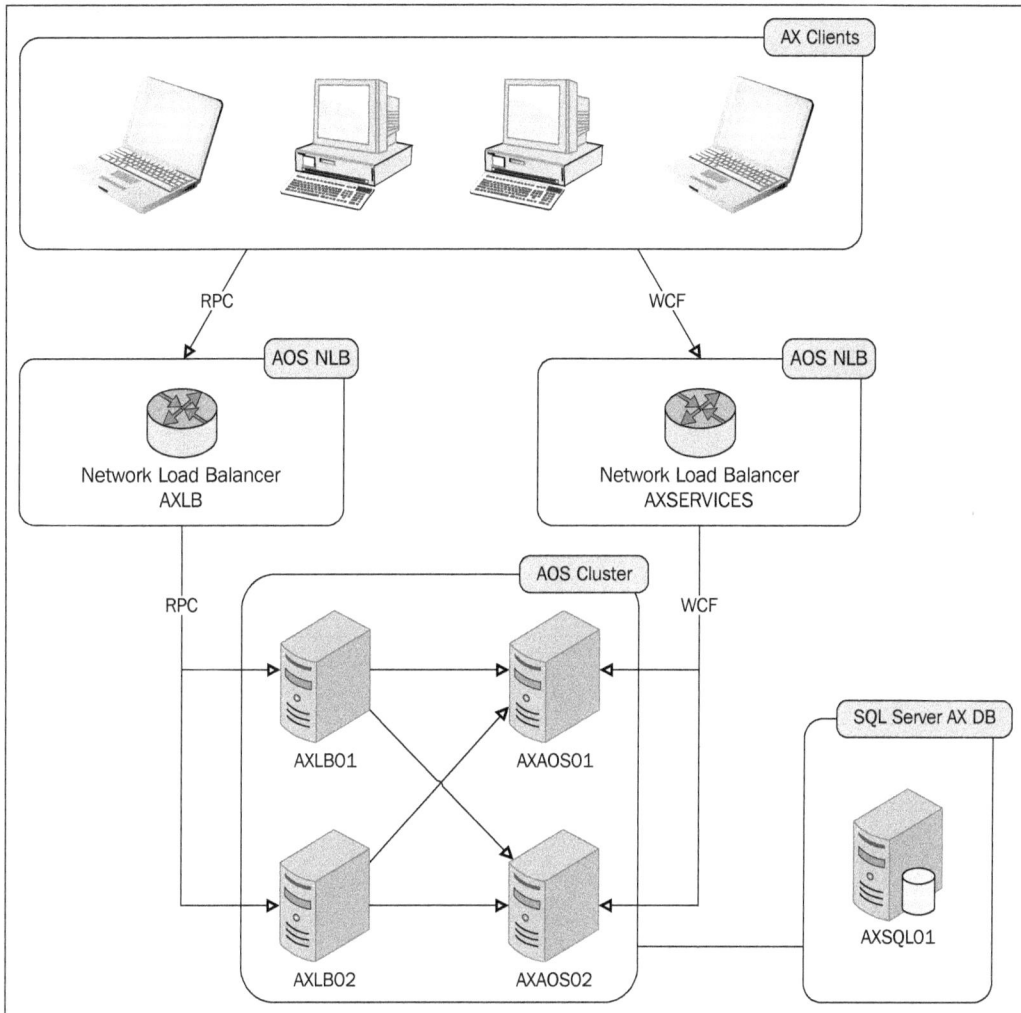

We have added one NLB cluster named AXSERVICES and configured it, as shown in the following table:

Cluster Name	Cluster IP	Host Name	Host IP / Port
AXSERVICES	192.168.2.200	AXAOS01	192.168.2.201 / NetTcp 8201
		AXAOS02	192.168.2.202 / NetTcp 8201

This NLB cluster serves two purposes:

- It routes the service clients directly to the AOS instances (AXAOS01 and AXAOS02) instead of routing them to the dedicated load balancers
- It allows the service communication to be load balanced over the AOS instances

Now we just need a way to make the client connect to AXLB for RPC communication and to AXSERVICES for WCF communication. Unfortunately, only one name can be specified when adding AOS instances in the **Microsoft Dynamics AX Configuration Utility**. To work our way around this, we need to edit the configuration in the registry by performing the following steps:

1. Open up the registry by opening **RegEdit**.
2. Locate the following key for both **HKEY_CURRENT_USER** and **HKEY_LOCAL_MACHINE**: \Software\Microsoft\Dynamics\6.0\ Configuration\<Configuration name>.
3. Add two new string values:

Name	Host IP / Port
Wcflbservername	AXSERVICES
Wcflbwsdlport	8101

4. Start the **Microsoft AX Configuration Utility**. If the utility is already open, close and reopen it.
5. On the **Connection** tab, click on the **Refresh Configuration** button to refresh the WCF configuration.

Now you should not get the error message anymore. If you click on the **Configure** button, the configuration opens and you see that the server name within the endpoint addresses is now replaced with the AXSERVICES NLB instead of AXLB.

```
<endpoint address="net.tcp://AXSERVICES:
   8201/DynamicsAx/Services/MetadataService"
   binding="netTcpBinding" bindingConfiguration=
   "MetadataServiceEndpoint" contract="Microsoft.Dynamics.
   AX.Framework.Services.Metadata.Service.IAxMetadataService"
   name="MetadataServiceEndpoint">
   <identity>
     <userPrincipalName value="s_ax_aos@AX2K12DOMAIN.local" />
   </identity>
</endpoint>
```

Summary

At the beginning of this chapter, we started with the simplest of system designs for Microsoft Dynamics AX 2012. We have learned why this design does not provide what's needed for high availability of Microsoft Dynamics AX.

Step-by-step, we have adjusted the design to work our way around various issues. This includes introducing redundancy and scaling out the AOS instances for better load balancing.

The design that was demonstrated in this chapter can be easily implemented for any project and will help you make sure that Microsoft Dynamics AX 2012 is not the weakest link. This will greatly improve the overall reliability of the system.

In the next chapter, we will take a look at the tools that we can use for the tracing and debugging of services.

9
Tracing and Debugging

Most Microsoft Dynamics AX developers are very familiar with debugging using the Microsoft Dynamics AX debugger. However, because services are compiled to CIL, you'll spend a lot more time with the Visual Studio debugger. Some find this off-putting, but the debugging process is actually very straightforward.

Developers may be used to debugging, but tracing is another story. Probably one of the most underused features of Microsoft Dynamics AX 2012 is the **Tracing cockpit**, which is first and foremost a tool for measuring performance. This is something you should always do when developing with Microsoft Dynamics AX, including when using its services. You can also use it to extract tracing information about X++ code from an environment where debugging is not an option and then study it using the **Microsoft Dynamics AX Trace parser**.

In a live environment, it is better to use WCF tracing; it has less performance overhead and provides you with a wealth of information that helps you when troubleshooting problems.

In this chapter, we will introduce these tools and look at when and how they can be used.

The following topics will be covered in this chapter:

- **Using the Microsoft Dynamics AX debugger**: We start by using the debugger that Microsoft Dynamics AX developers are most familiar with.
- **Using the Visual Studio debugger**: As code running in services in Microsoft Dynamics AX is compiled into CIL, a lot of debugging will be done in Visual Studio. We'll see how to set this up and use the Visual Studio debugger.
- **Using the Tracing cockpit**: The Tracing cockpit is a tool that allows you to collect tracing information about X++ code. We will see how it is used and how we can interpret the output.

- **Using the integration port logging mode**: Integration ports provide a way to log messages that are sent from and to Microsoft Dynamics AX 2012. This can be especially helpful for troubleshooting services when you have pipeline components that are transforming messages. We will look at how to set this up.

- **Using WCF message logging and tracing**: Sometimes debugging is not an option, and that's when message logging and tracing comes very handy. We will set up WCF message logging and tracing and look at how we can interpret the output.

Installing development tools

This chapter uses a number of development tools that can be installed using the Microsoft Dynamics AX setup. These tools are listed in the setup wizard under the **Development tools** node and consist of the following:

- **Debugger**: This is the Microsoft Dynamics AX 2012 debugger used to debug X++ code running on the client and server.

- **Visual Studio tools**: As discussed in *Chapter 6, Web Services*, installing the Visual Studio tools will add a number of extensions to Visual Studio. This includes the Application Explorer, which we will use to set breakpoints to debug code running in CIL.

- **Trace Parser**: This installs the Microsoft Dynamics AX 2012 Trace Parser, which is used to analyze trace files generated by the Tracing cockpit.

> If you are having trouble installing or configuring these components, refer to the Microsoft Dynamics AX 2012 Installation Guide at http://www.microsoft.com/en-us/download/details.aspx?id=12687.

From here on, we assume that you have successfully installed these components and configured both client and server components to allow the debugging of code running on the client, server, and CIL.

Using the Microsoft Dynamics AX 2012 debugger

The Microsoft Dynamics AX 2012 debugger has long been the only debugging tool available for developers and is specially designed to debug X++ code running on both the Microsoft Dynamics AX client and the AOS. It cannot debug code running in CIL.

If services are running in CIL and the debugger is unable to debug them, how can it be useful? We'll take a look at two scenarios: debugging the SysOperation framework and testing service operations.

Debugging the SysOperation framework

Although the SysOperation framework uses services running in CIL, it still has components that run on the client. These components include:

- The controller class
- The UI builder class
- The data contract, which includes the initialization and validation of the data

All of these have to be debugged using the Dynamics AX debugger. The only component that runs in CIL and has to be debugged using Visual Studio is the service operation. However, there is a way around this as follows:

1. In the development workspace, go to **Tools** | **Options**.
2. On the **Development** tab, expand the **General** FastTab.
3. Uncheck the option **Execute business operations in CIL**.

These steps will allow you to debug your SysOperation service using the Dynamics AX debugger. This, however, will only work when the execution mode is synchronous or asynchronous. A SysOperation service running in the reliable asynchronous mode or in a batch will still be executed in CIL. Don't forget to enable this option again after you are done debugging.

Using the Microsoft AX debugger to debug SysOperation services has the following advantages:

- The debugger provides the best support for X++ specific types, such as container
- The debugger shows useful information, such as the current user and the TTS level

- You do not have to compile your code to CIL each time you change your code
- The debugger will not cause the AOS to hang and be unresponsive until the debugging session has ended, as is the case with the Visual Studio debugger

Testing service operations

Troubleshooting services can be quite complex due to the large number of components involved. Sometimes, you just want to get rid of this complexity in order to confirm that your service operation is working properly. To do this, you can simply create a job in the AOT that calls your service operation.

When we apply this to the `getAllTtitles` operation of the `CVRTitleService` service, it looks like the following code snippet:

```
static void XPPGetAllTitles(Args _args)
{
    CVRTitleService         titleService;
    List                    titles;
    ListEnumerator          enumerator;
    CVRTitleDataContract    cVRTitleDataContract;

    // create new instance of the title service
    titleService = new CVRTitleService();

    // get the list of titles from te service
    titles = titleService.getAllTitles().parmTitleList();

    // create an enumerator and loop the results
    enumerator = titles.getEnumerator();

    while(enumerator.moveNext())
    {
        // get the current title from the list
        cVRTitleDataContract = enumerator.current();

        // show titleId and description in infolog
        info(strFmt("%1: %2", cVRTitleDataContract.parmId(),
        cVRTitleDataContract.parmDescription()));
    }
}
```

As you can see, the code is similar to what you would write in .NET; only it runs within Microsoft Dynamics AX 2012 and not in CIL. Due to this, you will be able to take advantage of the debugging capabilities of the Dynamics AX debugger when debugging this code.

Keep in mind that some scenarios are not supported in CIL. These include the functions `evalbuf()` and `runbuf()`, but other code might also behave differently when run in CIL as compared to p-code. That is why, you should not rely solely on this method when testing and always test your code in CIL as well.

If you suspect that the code will behave differently when compiled in CIL as opposed to p-code, you can test it easily using a class. Start by creating a new class in the AOT as follows:

```
class CVRTestCodeInCIL
{
}
```

Then, add a method that contains the code you want to test. It should be static and take a container as a parameter. In this case, we test whether the `evalbuf()` function runs in CIL as follows:

```
public static void run(container _c)
{
    // assert permission
    new ExecutePermission().assert();

    // run evalbuf
    info(EvalBuf("1 + 1"));

    // revert assertion of permissions
    CodeAccessPermission::revertAssert();
}
```

Finally, add a `main()` method that runs the code both in p-code and CIL, making sure it runs on server:

```
public static server void main(Args args)
{
    container con;

    // test in p-code
    CVRTestCodeInCIL::run(con);

    // test in CIL
    new XppILExecutePermission().assert();
    runClassMethodIL(classStr(CVRTestCodeInCIL), staticMethodStr(
    CVRTestCodeInCIL, run), con);
    CodeAccessPermission::revertAssert();
}
```

The output for the code that runs in p-code will be **2**, but for the code that runs in CIL, you'll get an error. Sometimes, the difference is more subtle, so checking your code in this manner can prove crucial when troubleshooting these kinds of problems.

Using the Visual Studio debugger

When your code runs in CIL, you can only debug it using the Visual Studio debugger. Of course, you should have Visual Studio 2010 installed, along with the Visual Studio tools that come with the Microsoft Dynamics AX 2012 installer.

Launching Visual Studio

To start Visual Studio with the intention of debugging the CIL code, perform the following steps:

1. Open the **Microsoft Dynamics AX Configuration Utility**.

2. In the **Configuration Target** combobox, select **Local client**.

3. In the **Configuration** combobox, select the configuration that points to the AOS you want to debug. Then click on **OK** to close the utility.

4. Right-click on the Visual Studio 2010 icon and click on **Run as administrator**.

Visual Studio will launch, and you should see Visual Studio along with the **Application Explorer** window as shown in the following screenshot:

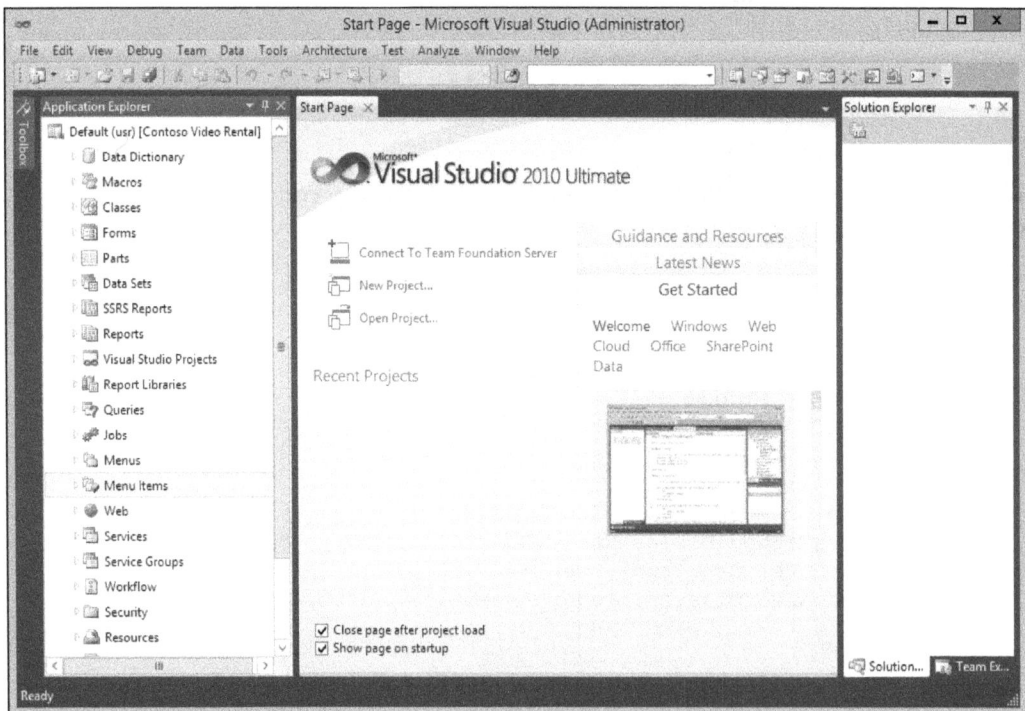

If you can't see the **Application Explorer** window, activate it by going to **View |
Application Explorer** or using the shortcut *Ctrl + D + Enter*.

The **Application Explorer** window shows you the AOT. At the top of the window,
you can see the layer and model that the user is working in. The word **Default**
indicates that the active client configuration was used by Visual Studio to determine
which AOS to connect to.

It is also possible to connect to other AOSes by performing the following steps:

1. Create a new shortcut to Visual Studio 2010, for example, on your desktop.
2. Right-click on the shortcut, then click on **Properties**.
3. Edit the **Target** property as follows by adding either a reference to an AXC
   file or the name of the configuration you want to use:
   1. When you want to use an AXC file, add the `/AxConfig "C:\<locati
      on>\<yourconfiguration>.axc"` reference.
   2. When you want to point to the configuration named `AX60Debug`, add
      the `/AxConfig AX60Debug` reference.

When you start Visual Studio 2010 using the shortcut you just created, you
should see the name of the configuration instead of **Default** in the **Application
Explorer** window.

Attaching the debugger to the AOS

Starting Visual Studio with the **Application Explorer** window connected to the
right AOS isn't enough to start debugging. You must also point Visual Studio to the
process you want to debug. In our case, this is `Ax32Serv.exe`, which is the process of
the AOS.

You can do this in Visual Studio by going to **Debug | Attach to Process...**. The following screenshot will appear:

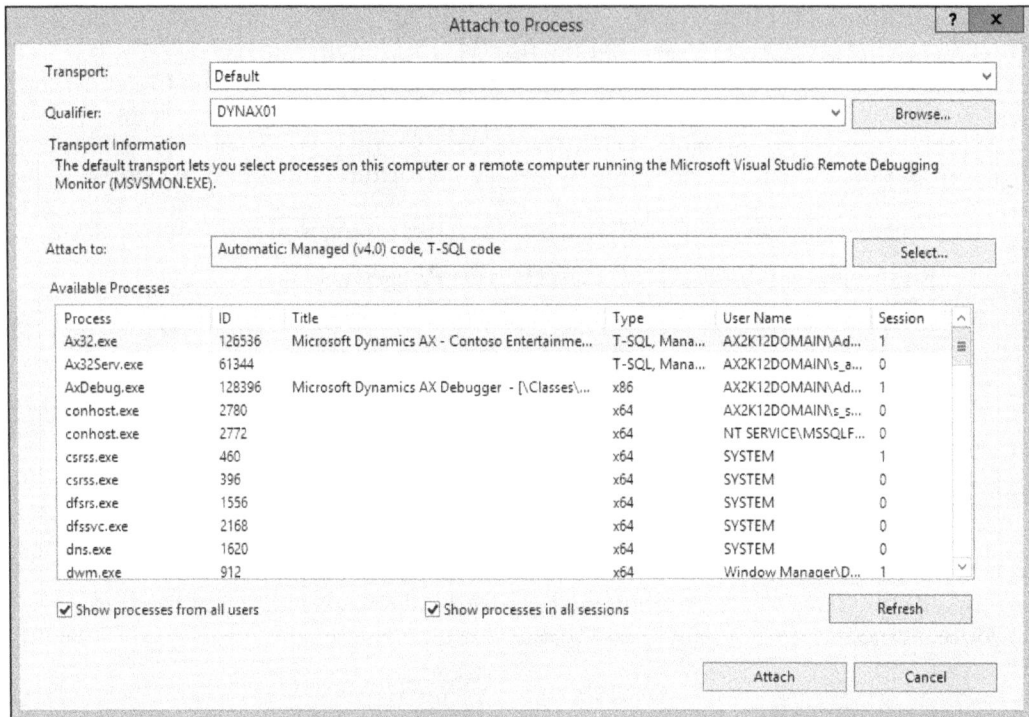

As you can see, it lists processes that are running, including `Ax32Serv.exe`. If you do not see the process, enable the **Show processes from all users** and **Show processes in all sessions** checkboxes.

When you have more than one AOS server running, you can identify the process by hovering your mouse cursor over the process. It will show the path of the process as seen in the following screenshot:

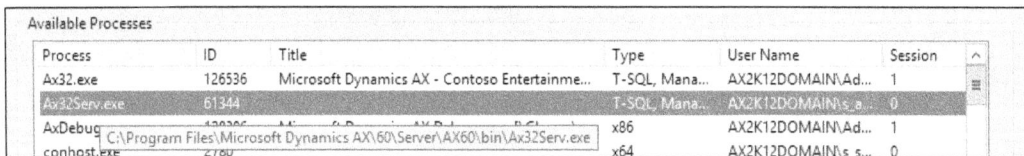

Alternatively, you can also look up the process ID on the **Services** tab of the Windows **Task Manager**. As you can see in the following screenshot, the ID of the process in the **Attach to Process** window is the same as the PID in the task manager, allowing you to identify the process:

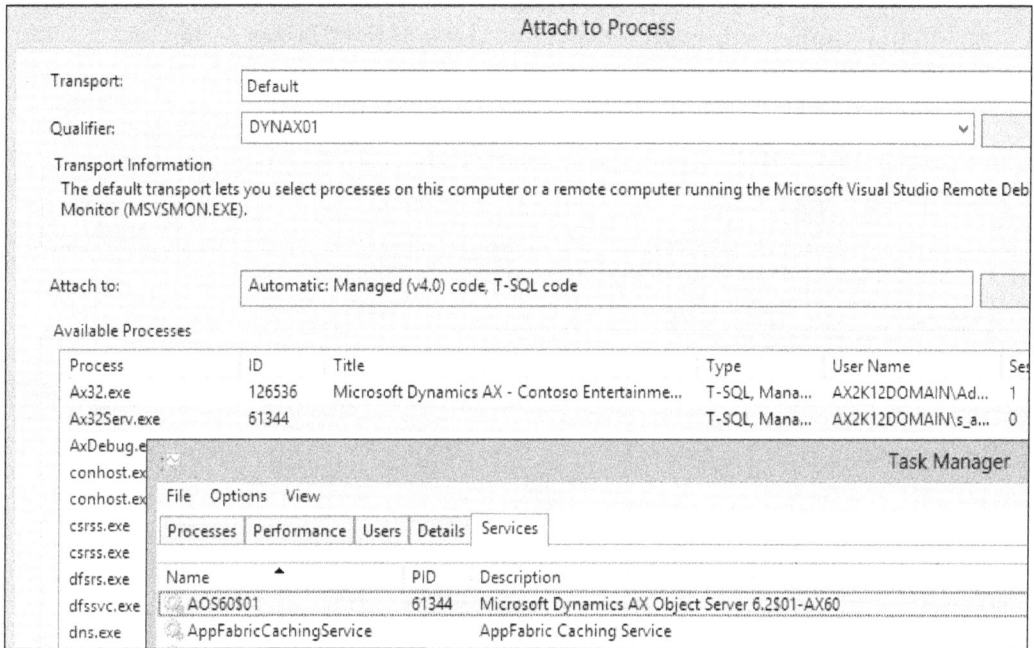

Once you have determined the correct process, click on the **Attach** button. This will display the following **Attach Security Warning** screen:

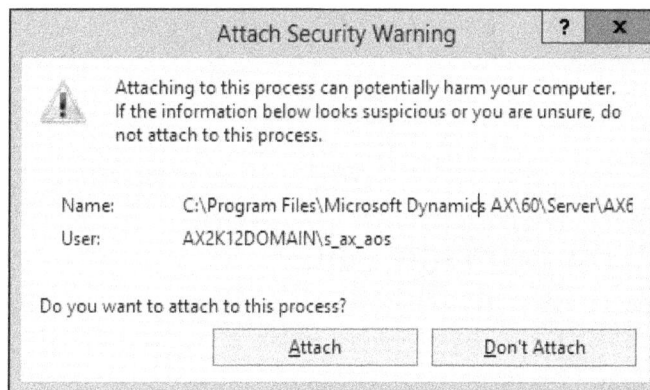

Clicking on the **Attach** button will attach the Visual Studio debugger to the AOS process, so we are now ready to set some breakpoints, which is what we will do next.

Setting breakpoints

Setting breakpoints in the Application Explorer is as easy as setting breakpoints in the AOT. As an example, we will debug the **Title** service that we created in *Chapter 4, Custom Services*. Perform the following steps to set a breakpoint for this service:

1. In the **Application Explorer** window, expand the **Classes** node.

2. Navigate to the **CVRTitleService** class and expand that node.

3. Double-click on the **getAllTitles** method; this will show you the source code of that method.

4. To set a breakpoint for this method, position your cursor on the line where you wish to set a breakpoint and press *F9*. Alternatively, click on the margin to the left of the code to enable or disable breakpoints.

The result should look as follows:

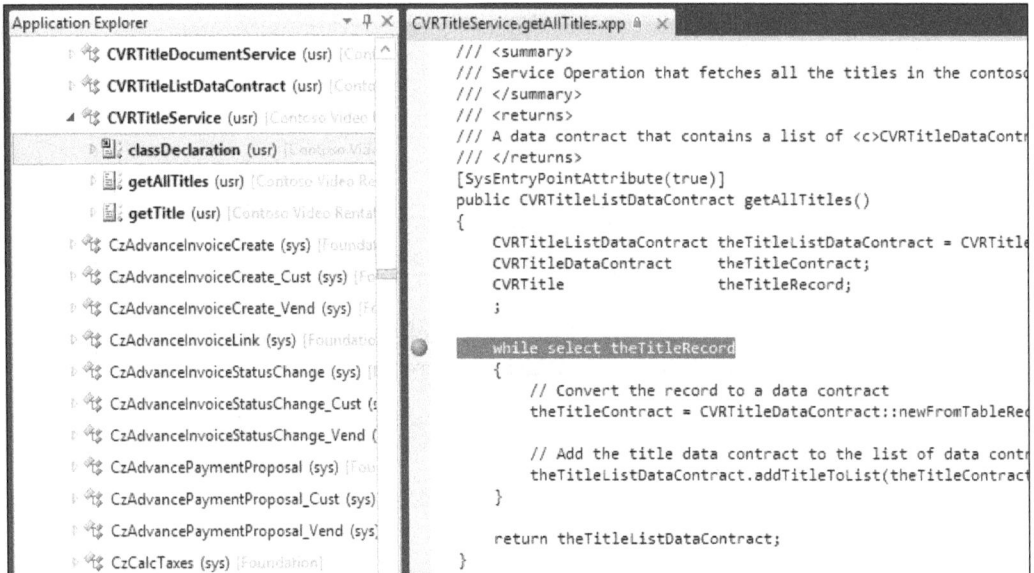

Debugging a service call

With the debugger attached and a breakpoint set, we are ready to run our service. To run the Title service, perform the following steps:

1. Open a new instance of Visual Studio 2010.

2. Go to **File | Open | Project/Solution**.

3. Select the solution `VisualStudio\Chapter4\DynamicsAxServices.`
`Custom\DynamicsAxServices.Custom.sln`. This solution is part of
the code that can be downloaded for this book.

4. In the Solution Explorer, right-click on the **DynamicsAxServices.Custom.
Titles** project and then click on **Set as StartUp Project**.

5. Press *F5* to run the project.

The instance of Visual Studio where we had set a breakpoint will pop up because
the breakpoint was hit. The next line of code that will be executed is indicated with
a yellow arrow, just as is the case in the Dynamics AX debugger, as seen in the
following screenshot:

```
CVRTitleService.getAllTitles.xpp
    /// <summary>
    /// Service Operation that fetches all the titles in the contoso video rental store
    /// </summary>
    /// <returns>
    /// A data contract that contains a list of <c>CVRTitleDataContract</c> contracts
    /// </returns>
    [SysEntryPointAttribute(true)]
    public CVRTitleListDataContract getAllTitles()
    {
        CVRTitleListDataContract theTitleListDataContract = CVRTitleListDataContract::construct();
        CVRTitleDataContract    theTitleContract;
        CVRTitle                theTitleRecord;
        ;

        while select theTitleRecord
        {
            // Convert the record to a data contract
            theTitleContract = CVRTitleDataContract::newFromTableRecord(theTitleRecord);

            // Add the title data contract to the list of data contracts
            theTitleListDataContract.addTitleToList(theTitleContract);
        }

        return theTitleListDataContract;
```

Locals	
Name	Value
this	{Dynamics.Ax.Application.CVRTitleService}
theTitleListDataContract	{Dynamics.Ax.Application.CVRTitleListDataContract}
theTitleContract	null
theTitleRecord	{Dynamics.Ax.Application.CVRTitle}

Call Stack

Name

Dynamics.Ax.Application.dll533.netmodule!Dynamics.Ax.Application.CVRTitleService.GetallTitles() Line 15

[External Code]

As you can see, it shows the X++ source code, the call stack, and all the variables with their values. The shortcuts used for debugging, such as *F10* and *F11*, are the same in Visual Studio as in the Dynamics AX debugger, so the experience for any Microsoft Dynamics AX developer from here on is going to be very straightforward.

Note that during the debugging of the CIL code, the AOS server will be unresponsive. This will cause other clients that are connected to the instance on which you are debugging to also hang. Because of this, you should only debug CIL on a developer machine. This is also one of the reasons why Microsoft recommends a development topology where every developer has his own development environment.

> **Remote debugging**
>
> If you don't want to install Visual Studio on every AOS server that you want to debug, you can use remote debugging with Visual Studio. After a simple setup, the process of debugging will be the same as on a local AOS. For information on how to set this up, visit the *How to: Set Up Remote Debugging* page on MSDN at http://msdn.microsoft.com/en-us/library/bt727f1t(v=vs.100).aspx.

Using the Tracing cockpit

Although performance is quite important, it is often not given much thought until there are performance problems. Sometimes, efforts to improve performance are deliberately postponed until later in the project in order to free resources for other tasks. On the other hand, many developers may feel that performance should be given more attention but are unsure how.

This brings us to the Tracing cockpit and the Microsoft Dynamics AX Trace Parser. These are perhaps the most underused and underrated tools available to Microsoft Dynamics AX developers, but they are tools that developers should be using on a daily basis. Before you submit your code for testing, consider using the Tracing cockpit so you can detect and fix obvious performance problems before they cause any real problems.

The Tracing cockpit is a tool used to measure the overall performance of your code. When it is running, it collects information such as the time spent on each method, the number of round trips made to the database, and the time it took to execute those calls. This information is stored in an **ETL (Event Trace Log)** file, which can be interpreted by the Microsoft Dynamics AX Trace Parser. Although it is not purposely built for tracing services, it is useful to improve the performance of your services. That's why we will take a look at it next.

Collecting a trace

We will use the Title service as an example, so open the `DynamicsAxServices.Custom.sln` solution in Visual Studio. This is the same solution we used to test the Visual Studio debugger. It is important that you set up everything to right before the point when you want to start your trace. As you can imagine, tracing every X++ method and SQL statement that is executed could lead to a large amount of data. This would take up a lot of hard disk space and would be too time consuming for you to analyze.

With the Visual Studio project ready to run, open the developer workspace in the Microsoft Dynamics AX client and go to **Tools | Tracing cockpit**. You should see a screen similar to the following:

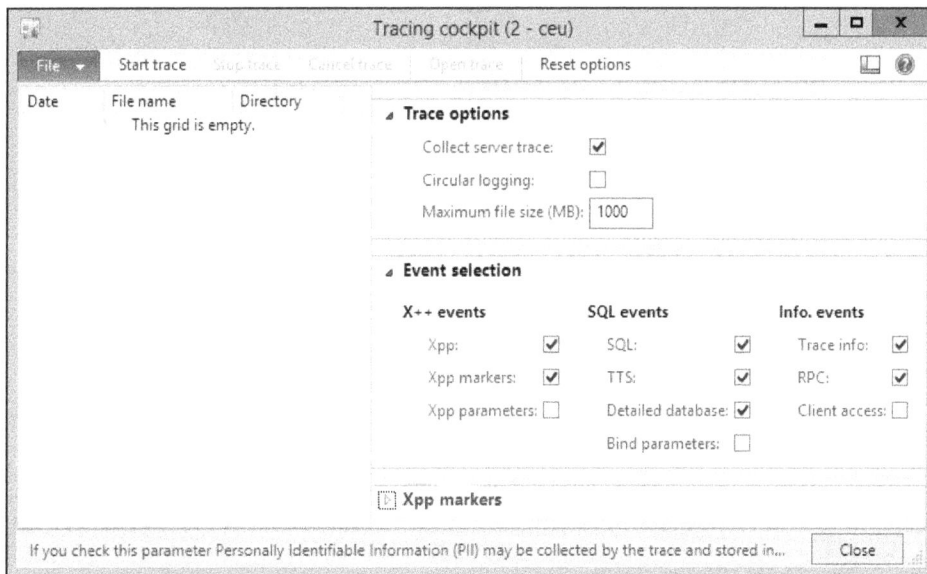

On the right-hand side are the different options you can configure. We won't go over them all because the default options suffice most of the time. One option that is very interesting is the **Bind parameters** option. With this parameter disabled, the SQL statements that are traced will have the values in the `where` clauses replaced by a question mark. This ensures that no sensitive data ends up in the trace file. When you want to see the real values that were used, enable this option. This then allows you to copy the statement from the trace and run it using a query on Microsoft SQL Server, at which point you can examine it further using the tracing options that Microsoft SQL Server has.

When you are done configuring the options, click on the **Start trace** button. Specify a filename and click on **Save**. Next, go to Visual Studio and press *F5* to run the project. When it has finished running, return to the Tracing cockpit and click on **Stop trace**. A new record will be created as shown in the following screenshot:

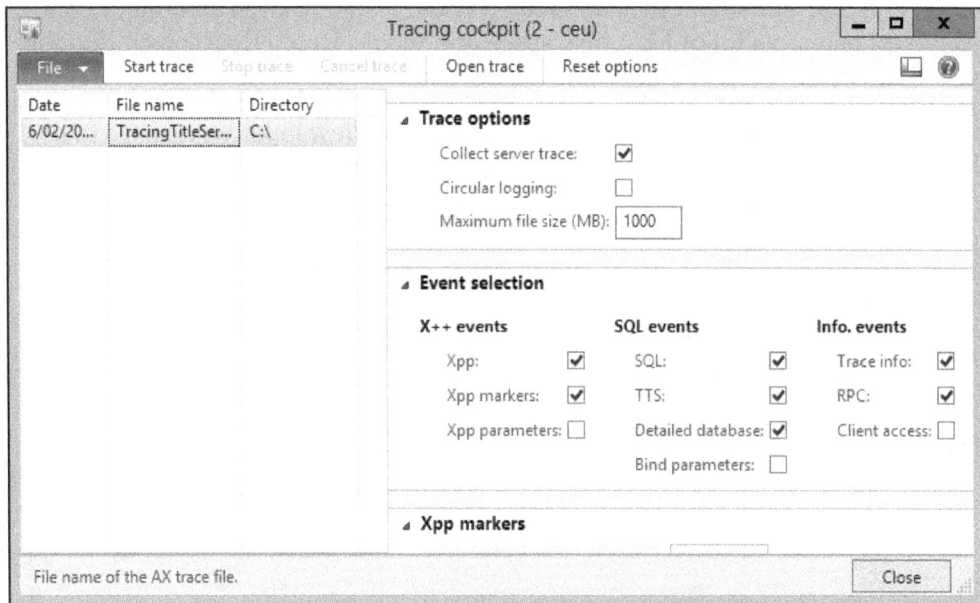

To view the trace, click on the **Open trace** button. If this is the first time you are opening a trace file using the Microsoft Dynamics AX Trace Parser, you will see the following screen:

What happens is that the Microsoft Dynamics AX Trace Parser tries to import the trace file into a database for analysis. Because this is the first time you are importing a trace, no database exists yet; so, create a database by specifying the server you want to create a database on in the **Server name** field. In the **Select or enter a database name** field, enter the name of the database you want to use. If you specified a nonexisting database, a new database will be created with that name, which is **AXTrace** in our case. Click on the **Register** button to register the database. Confirm the creation of the database when prompted.

After a short time, depending on how large the trace file is, you will be presented with the following screen:

Microsoft Dynamics AX Trace Parser - TracingTitleService (1)

File Edit View Help

Session:

Overview

Top 5 X++ Methods by Inclusive Duration

Class	Count	Inclusive (ms)	Exclusive (ms)	RPC	Database Calls
SysTraceCockpit::Sy...	1	42,07	0,37	0	0
CVRTitleService::get...	1	23,03	9,66	0	1
Info::callTimeOut	24	19,07	3,17	0	0
TabPageMarkers::Fo...	1	14,52	11,02	0	0
DictClass::callObject	24	12,58	0,41	0	0

Top 5 X++ Methods by Exclusive Duration

Class	Count	Inclusive (ms)	Exclusive (ms)	RPC	Database Calls
ServerVersionOK	20	11,28	11,28	20	0
TabPageMarkers::Fo...	1	14,52	11,02	0	0
CVRTitleService::get...	1	23,03	9,66	0	1
GroupKeywords::For...	1	7,60	7,60	0	0
ButtonResetOptions::...	1	6,09	5,79	0	0

Top 5 SQL Queries by Inclusive Duration

Statement	Count	Inclusive (ms)
SELECT T1.ID,T1.NAME,T1.ENABLE,T1.DEL_STARTUPMENU,T1.STATUSLIN...	1	1,97
SELECT T1.VERSION,T1.RECID FROM SYSBREAKPOINTLIST T1 WHERE ((M...	1	1,33
{call CREATEUSERSESSIONS(?,?,?,?,?,?,?,?,?,?,?,?,?,?,?,?,?,?,?)}	1	0,90
SELECT T1.ID,T1.NAME,T1.DESCRIPTION,T1.LENGTHINMINUTES,T1.RECVE...	1	0,84

Registered database: DYNAX01\AXTrace

As you can see, a summary of the most costly X++ methods and SQL queries has been presented. From this, we can already observe the following:

- The service operation took 23.03 milliseconds to complete and retrieved all the titles using one database call

- The database call to retrieve the titles took 0.84 milliseconds

If you want to see the details of the trace, select the appropriate session from the **Session** drop-down box. This will allow you to view many more tracing details.

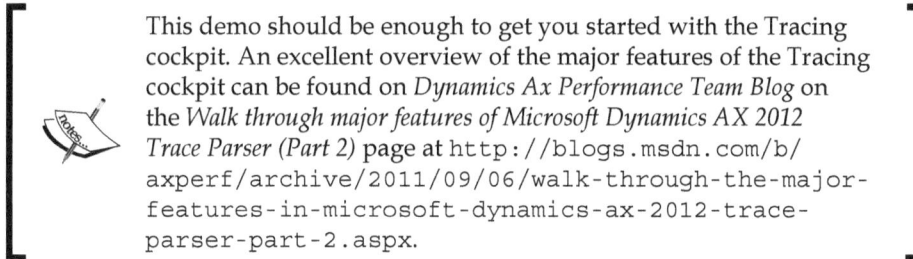

> This demo should be enough to get you started with the Tracing cockpit. An excellent overview of the major features of the Tracing cockpit can be found on *Dynamics Ax Performance Team Blog* on the *Walk through major features of Microsoft Dynamics AX 2012 Trace Parser (Part 2)* page at `http://blogs.msdn.com/b/axperf/archive/2011/09/06/walk-through-the-major-features-in-microsoft-dynamics-ax-2012-trace-parser-part-2.aspx`.

Using the integration port logging mode

Microsoft Dynamics AX 2012 provides the out-of-the-box logging of messages by configuring the logging mode parameter on integration ports. This is available on both basic and enhanced, inbound and outbound ports, and for document services as well as custom services.

Logging is disabled by default. As always, when adding logging to any process, take a moment and think about whether adding logging is really necessary. Also consider the level of detail that is required as this will have an impact on the performance of your service. The **Logging mode** parameter on integration ports provides the following options in the descending order of their level of detail:

- **All document versions**: When selected, a version of the document is stored every time a document is modified by a pipeline component

- **Original document**: When selected, only the original document before it has been modified by the pipeline components is stored

- **Message header only**: Select this option when you want to store only the header of the documents

For this demonstration, we will activate logging on the **CVRDocumentServicesEnhanced** inbound integration port that we created and configured in *Chapter 3*, *AIF Document Services*. We will see which logging occurs when the `Find()` method is invoked from our demo .NET application.

Configuring the logging mode

The first thing we need to do is activate logging on the integration port as it is disabled by default. In this example, we will log the original document only because we haven't configured any pipeline components anyway. Perform the following steps to set the logging mode:

1. Go to **System administration** | **Setup** | **Services and Application Integration Framework** | **Inbound Ports**.

2. Select the **CVRDocumentServicesEnhanced** port. When the port is active, click on the **Deactivate** button to deactivate it.

3. On the **Troubleshooting** fast tab, set the **Logging mode** parameter to **Original document**.

4. Activate the **CVRDocumentServicesEnhanced** port.

Consulting the log

In our demo in *Chapter 3, AIF Document Services*, we used the Find() method to retrieve all the titles longer than 110 minutes. The code we used to invoke this service looks like the following code snippet:

```
static void getTitles_Find()
{
    // Variable to hold the title document
    AxdCVRTitle titleDocument = new AxdCVRTitle();

    // Create a criteria element that selects titles that run over 110
    // minutes
    QueryCriteria criteria = Program.createSingleCriteria("CVRTitle" ,
"LengthInMinutes", Operator.Greater, "110", null);

    // Create a client for as long as we need to
    using (CVRTitleDocumentServiceClient client = new
CVRTitleDocumentServiceClient())
    {
        // Find the titles that match the criteria
        titleDocument = client.find(null, criteria);

        // Loop all the titles
        foreach (AxdEntity_CVRTitle title in titleDocument.CVRTitle)
        {
            // Report the results to the console window
```

```
            Console.WriteLine(title.Id + ' ' + title.Name + ' ' +
            title.LengthInMinutes);
        }
    }
}
```

With logging enabled, let's see what information is logged after we have invoked this code. To consult the log, go to **System administration** | **Periodic** | **Services and Application Integration Framework** | **History**. You should see the following form:

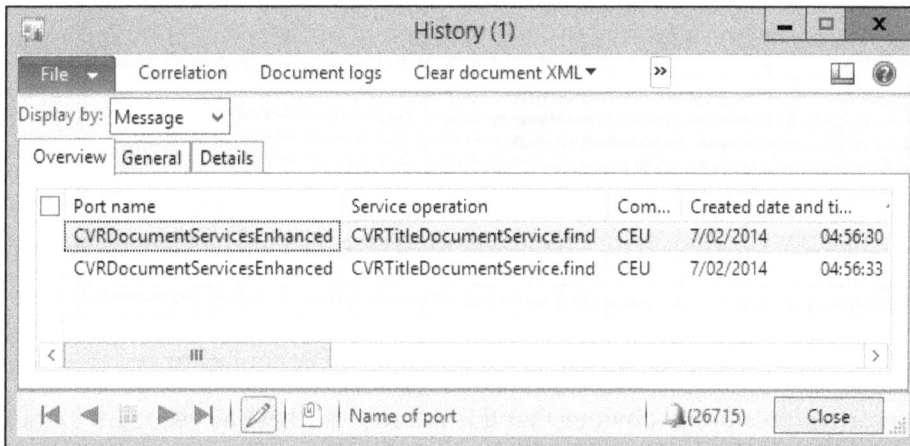

This screen shows all the messages that were logged by the Application Integration Framework. The ordering of this screen isn't particularly good, so it's usually best to sort the messages by created date and time as seen in the previous screenshot. As you can see, two records are present. This is because two messages were sent: a request from the .NET application to the AOS and a reply from the AOS to the .NET application. To see what data was transferred in the body of each message, click on the **Document logs** button. The following screenshot will pop up:

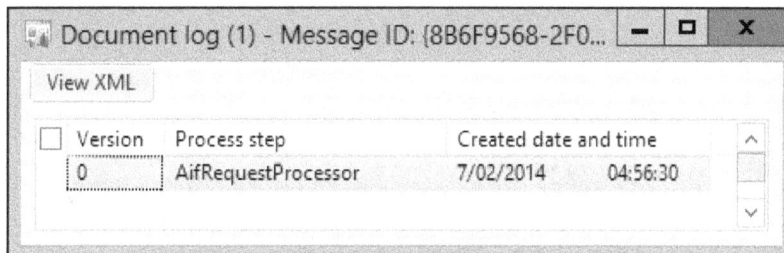

In this screenshot, a record of every step that we want to log is listed. Because we indicated that we only want the original document, only one record is listed. To view the data from the message, click on the **View XML** button; we will arrive at the following screenshot:

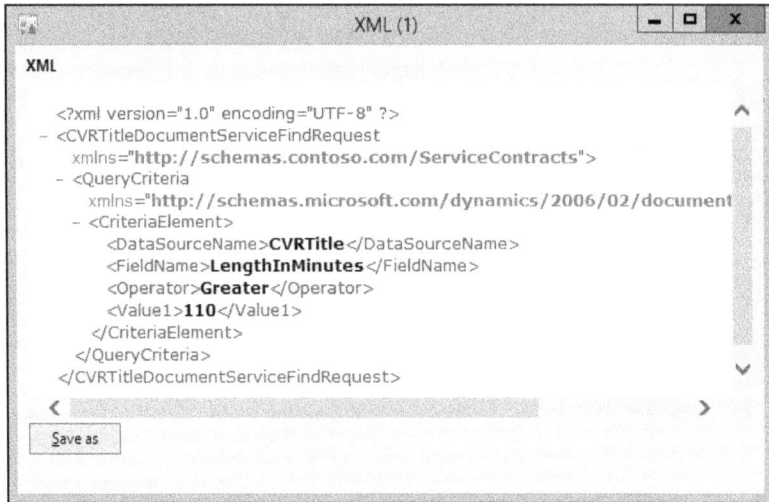

As you can see, it is pretty obvious that this is a request that has been sent to the AOS to retrieve all the titles longer than 110 minutes. The **QueryCriteria** node in the XML matches the object that we constructed in the .NET application perfectly. To view the data that was returned, you can perform the same steps for the second record that is present in the **History** form. In the following screenshot, you can clearly see that it contains a list of CVRTitle records:

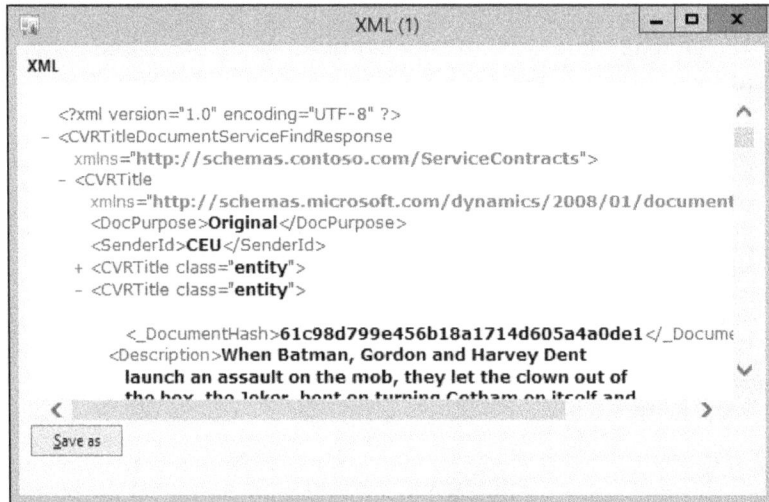

Using WCF message logging and tracing

WCF provides a number of diagnostics features that can help you troubleshoot your applications. We will look at two of these: **message logging** and **tracing**.

- **Message logging**: This enables you to log all the messages that are sent and received by the AOS. It allows you to see what data and parameters are in the messages being exchanged. In this way, it is similar to the logging functionality on the integration port, but it is all handled by WCF.

- **Tracing**: This allows you to look at how messages flow between the client and service. Techniques such as activity propagation and correlation of messages allow you to keep track of the entire conversation between the client and service both at the service and transport level.

Both of these output to the .svclog files that you can analyze using the Service Configuration Editor.

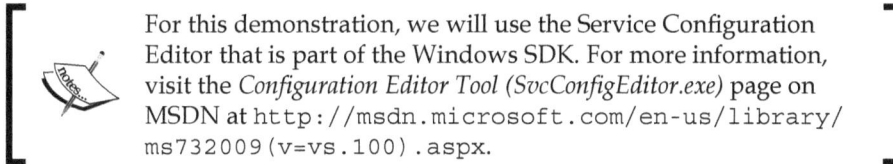

> For this demonstration, we will use the Service Configuration Editor that is part of the Windows SDK. For more information, visit the *Configuration Editor Tool (SvcConfigEditor.exe)* page on MSDN at http://msdn.microsoft.com/en-us/library/ms732009(v=vs.100).aspx.

Configuring message logging and tracing

Message logging and tracing are both configured in the same place, so you will configure them both at the same time. To do this, modify the configuration file of the AOS by performing the following steps:

1. Start the **Service Configuration Editor**.
2. Go to **File | Open | Config File…** or press *Ctrl + O*.
3. Select the **Ax32Serv.exe.config** process from the bin directory of your AOS, for example, C:\Program Files\Microsoft Dynamics AX\60\Server\AX60\bin\Ax32Serv.exe.config.
4. When you are prompted with a warning, click on **Yes** to continue with opening the file.
5. Navigate to the **Diagnostics** node and highlight it.
6. On the right-hand side, click on **Enable MessageLogging** and **Enable Tracing**.
7. Select the **Message Logging** node located under the **Diagnostics** node.
8. On the right-hand side, set **LogEntireMessage** to **True**.
9. Press *Ctrl + S* to save the configuration.

The result should look like the following screenshot:

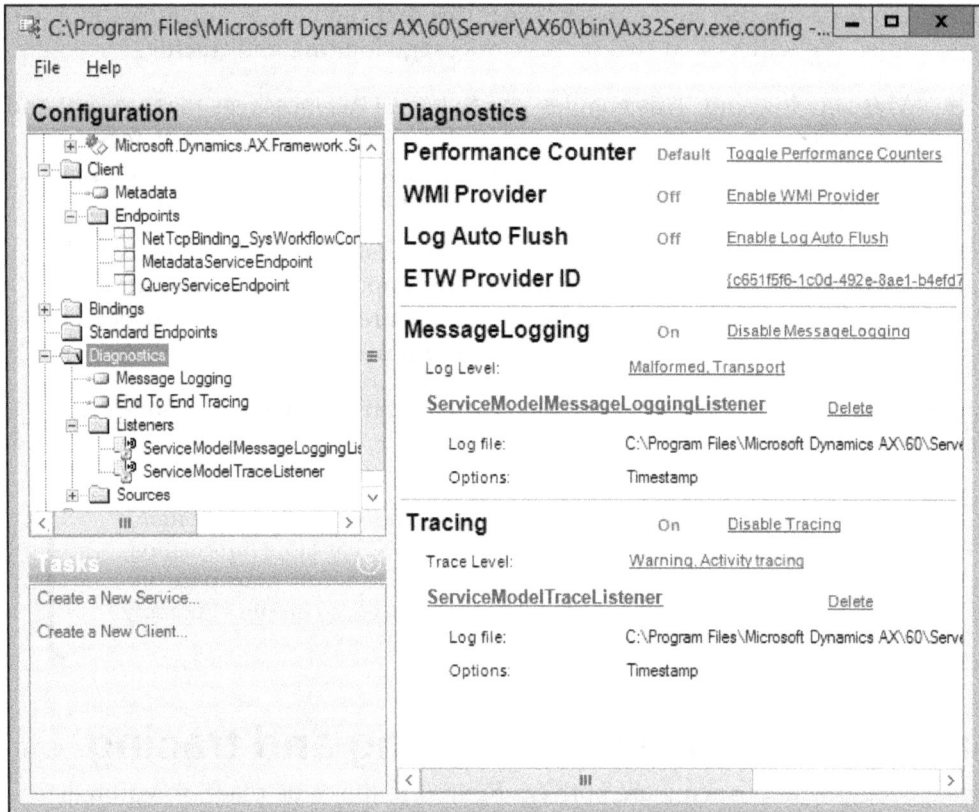

As you can see, both message logging and tracing are now active. What this did was add the following nodes to the configuration file:

```
<system.diagnostics>
  <sources>
    <source propagateActivity="true" name="System.ServiceModel"
    switchValue="Warning,ActivityTracing">
      <listeners>
        <add type="System.Diagnostics.DefaultTraceListener"
        name="Default">
          <filter type="" />
        </add>
        <add name="ServiceModelTraceListener">
          <filter type="" />
        </add>
      </listeners>
```

```
      </source>
      <source name="System.ServiceModel.MessageLogging"
      switchValue="Warning,ActivityTracing">
        <listeners>
          <add type="System.Diagnostics.DefaultTraceListener"
          name="Default">
            <filter type="" />
          </add>
          <add name="ServiceModelMessageLoggingListener">
            <filter type="" />
          </add>
        </listeners>
      </source>
    </sources>
    <sharedListeners>
      <add initializeData="C:\Program Files\Microsoft Dynamics AX\60\
      Server\AX60\bin\Ax32Serv_messages.svclog"
        type="System.Diagnostics.XmlWriterTraceListener, System,
        Version=4.0.0.0, Culture=neutral,
        PublicKeyToken=b77a5c561934e089"
        name="ServiceModelMessageLoggingListener"
        traceOutputOptions="Timestamp">
        <filter type="" />
      </add>
      <add initializeData="C:\Program Files\Microsoft Dynamics AX\60\
      Server\AX60\bin\Ax32Serv_tracelog.svclog"
        type="System.Diagnostics.XmlWriterTraceListener, System,
        Version=4.0.0.0, Culture=neutral,
        PublicKeyToken=b77a5c561934e089"
        name="ServiceModelTraceListener" traceOutputOptions="Timestamp">
        <filter type="" />
      </add>
    </sharedListeners>
    <switches>
      <add name="ServiceTraceLevel" value="Off" />
    </switches>
    <trace autoflush="false" indentsize="4">
      <listeners>
        <add initializeData="Dynamics AX Services"
        type="System.Diagnostics.EventLogTraceListener"
          name="AxTraceListener">
          <filter type="" />
        </add>
      </listeners>
    </trace>
</system.diagnostics>
```

Analyzing service traces

Before you can take a look at the trace files, you first have to make sure to generate some service communication. In order to do this, execute the **getAllTitles** service operation of **CVRTitleService** as you have done many times in this chapter.

Analyzing message logging

The WCF trace file containing the message logging is located in the `bin` directory of the AOS where tracing has been enabled. The name of the file is `Ax32Serv_messages.svclog`. Double-click on it and it will open using the **Microsoft Service Trace Viewer**, as shown in the following screenshot:

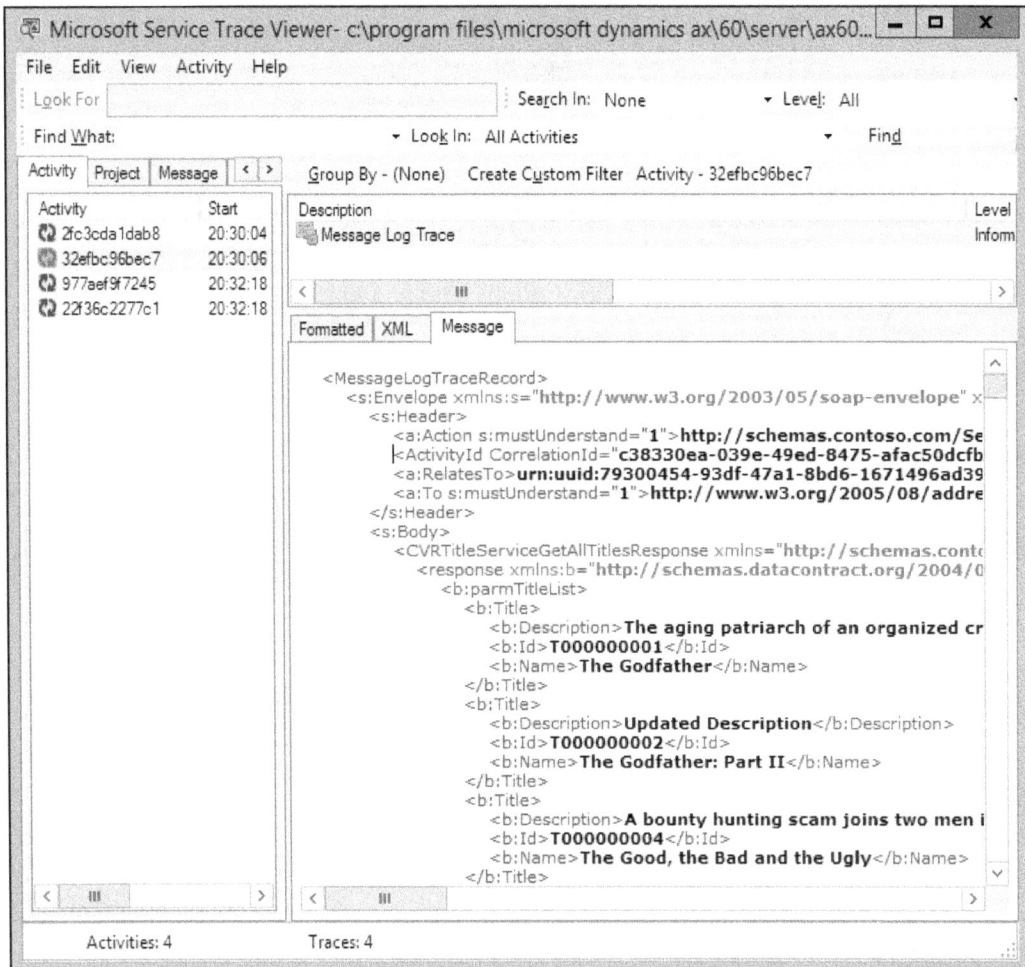

As you can see from the previous screenshot, the message that corresponds to the reply that the AOS sent to the .NET application has been selected. You can see the header and also the data of the message because we already set the **LogEntireMessage** property to **True**.

Analyzing tracing

The WCF trace file containing the tracing data is located in the `bin` directory of the AOS where the tracing has been enabled. The name of the file is `Ax32Serv_tracing.svclog`. Double-click on it and it will open using the **Microsoft Service Trace Viewer**, as shown in the following screenshot:

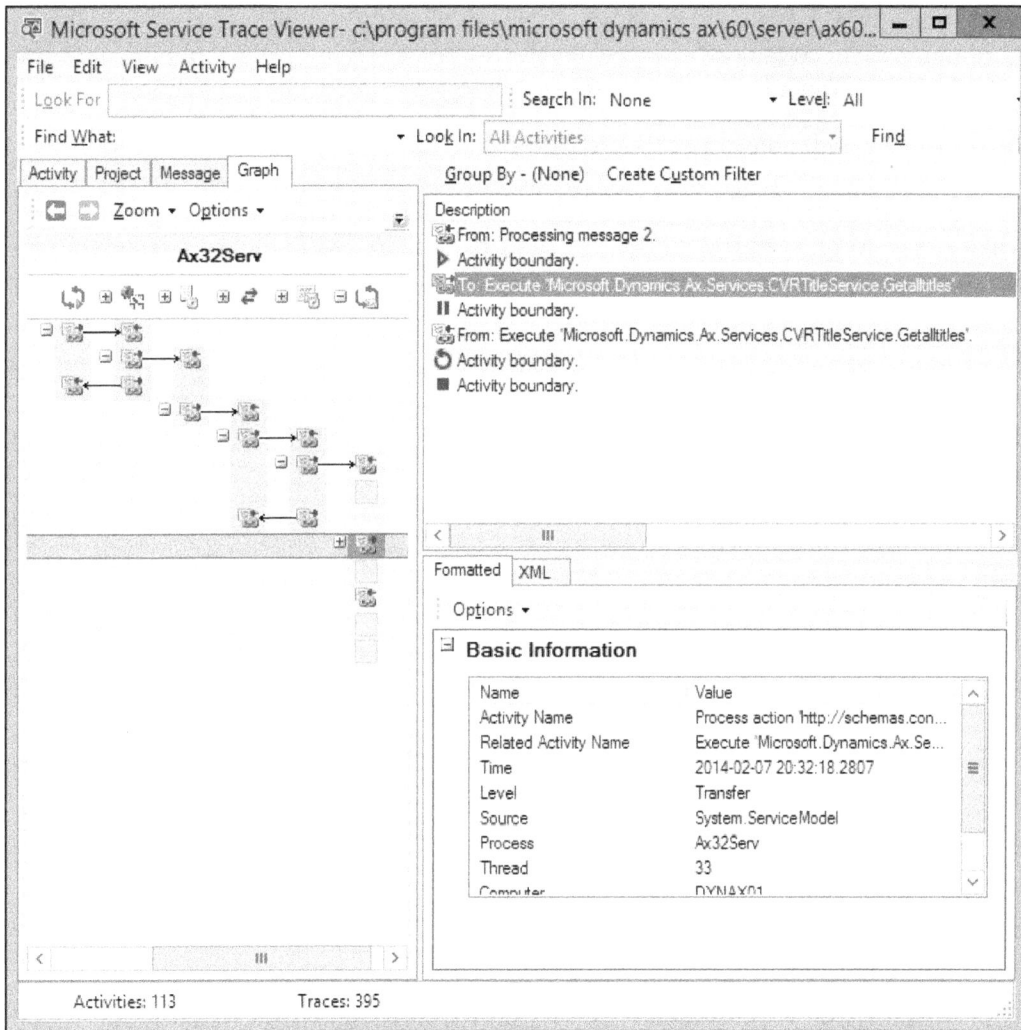

While message logging gives emphasis to the content of the messages, tracing focuses more on the events that occur and the correlation between them. When combined with a trace from the client side, it allows you to trace WCF from end to end.

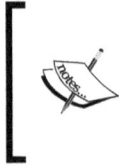

> There is much more to WCF message logging and tracing than we can cover here. For an in-depth view on how to configure it the best for your implementation, visit the *Diagnostic Tracing and Message Logging* page on MSDN at `http://msdn.microsoft.com/en-us/library/dd788183.aspx`.

Summary

Although a lot of code now runs in CIL, the Microsoft Dynamics AX debugger is still very useful. It even has some advantages over the Visual Studio debugger.

On the other hand, you can't get around the fact that you'll be using the Visual Studio debugger on many occasions. Although it is a bit more troublesome to get started with the first time, compared to the Dynamics AX debugger, the procedure will quickly become second nature to you. When compared to the previous iterations of Microsoft Dynamics AX, the Visual Studio debugger makes debugging the Application Integration Framework and its batches much easier.

The Tracing cockpit doesn't have features that are related to services in particular, but nevertheless, it is very helpful for testing the performance of your services during development. After deployment to a live environment, troubleshooting is better facilitated using WCF message logging and tracing.

Installing the Demo Application

In this book, we use a demo application called **Contoso Video Rental** (CVR). It contains sample functionality to create movie titles, shops, rentals, and so on. In order to run the code, you must first install the CVR model into Microsoft Dynamics AX; the following sections will show you how to do this.

Prerequisites

To use the sample code in this book, the following prerequisites must be available:

- Microsoft Visual Studio 2010
- Microsoft Dynamics AX 2012
- Microsoft Dynamics AX 2012 Management Utilities

A full list of software requirements can be found in the Microsoft Dynamics AX 2012 system requirements document available for download at `http://www.microsoft.com/en-us/download/details.aspx?`.

Dynamics AX 2012 models

There are two models available: `CVR_R2.axmodel` and `CVR_Base_R2.axmodel`. Both these models are built on Microsoft Dynamics AX 2012 R2 with the build number 6.2.158.0, as shown in the following screenshot:

CVR_Base_R2.axmodel	AXMODEL File	64 KB
CVR_R2.axmodel	AXMODEL File	140 KB

The `CVR_Base_R2` model contains all CVR demo application objects (tables, forms, and so on). When you install this model, you can follow all of this book's examples step-by-step to complete the application. The `CVR_R2` model contains everything the `CVR_Base_R2` model contains but also all examples already completed.

There is also a folder named `old`, which contains the models that were included in the previous iteration of this book. If you are on the Feature Pack release, you could use these models, but we recommend that you import the XPO file instead and downgrade it.

The models are installed by using PowerShell or AxUtil. The following sections will show you how to install the model of your choice.

Using PowerShell

1. In the **Start** menu, navigate to **All Programs | Administrative Tools** and click on **Microsoft Dynamics AX Management Shell**.

2. At the PowerShell command prompt (`PS C:\>`), type the following command (make sure that you pass in the full path of the model file to avoid being in the wrong directory):

```
Install-AXModel -File "<Model filename>" -Details
```

Using AxUtil

1. Open the **Command Prompt**.

2. Navigate to the directory for the management utilities. Typically, the location of this directory is `%ProgramFiles%\Microsoft Dynamics AX\60\ManagementUtilities`.

3. Enter the following command to import the model:

```
Axutil import /file:"<Model filename>" /verbose
```

After importing a model file into the model store, it is important to do a full compilation of the AOT and a full CIL generation.

Dynamics AX XPO file

There is also an XPO (`SharedProject_ContosoVideoRental.xpo`) that you can use to selectively import objects. This XPO contains all objects used and created throughout the book.

Code snippets

Every code snippet that is mentioned in the book is also available in separate TXT files in the `CodeSnippets` folder. You can use them to copy and paste code so that you don't have to type everything yourself. Files that start with `XPP` contain X++ code and should be used in Microsoft Dynamics AX 2012. Files that start with `CS` contain C# code and should be processed using Visual Studio.

Initializing number sequences

Before you can work with the demo application, you need to initialize the number sequences using the following steps:

1. Go to AOT and run the job named `InitializeCVRNumberReference`.
2. When the job is finished, navigate to **Contoso Video Rental | Setup | Parameters**.
3. Then, select a number sequence for each number sequence reference.

You can create your own number sequences first by right clicking on the **Number sequence code** field and choosing **View Details**. Create your number sequences there and then use them on the parameters form.

Visual Studio code

All examples in the book that are coded in Visual Studio are contained in the `VisualStudio` folder.

Opening the samples

There is a folder for each of the chapters that contains the Visual Studio sample code. You can just go ahead and open the samples by opening the solution files with Visual Studio 2010, shown as follows:

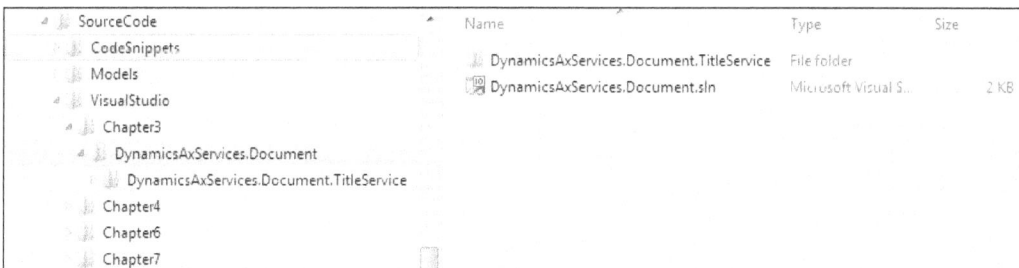

Modifying the service references

Some of the Visual Studio projects contain references to services that we created while building the samples. All of these references are created using an address that points to localhost, so it should also be working for you. If you have an AOS that is not installed as the first AOS on your machine, you will need to configure the service reference address:

1. Right-click on the service reference and choose **Configure Service Reference...**:

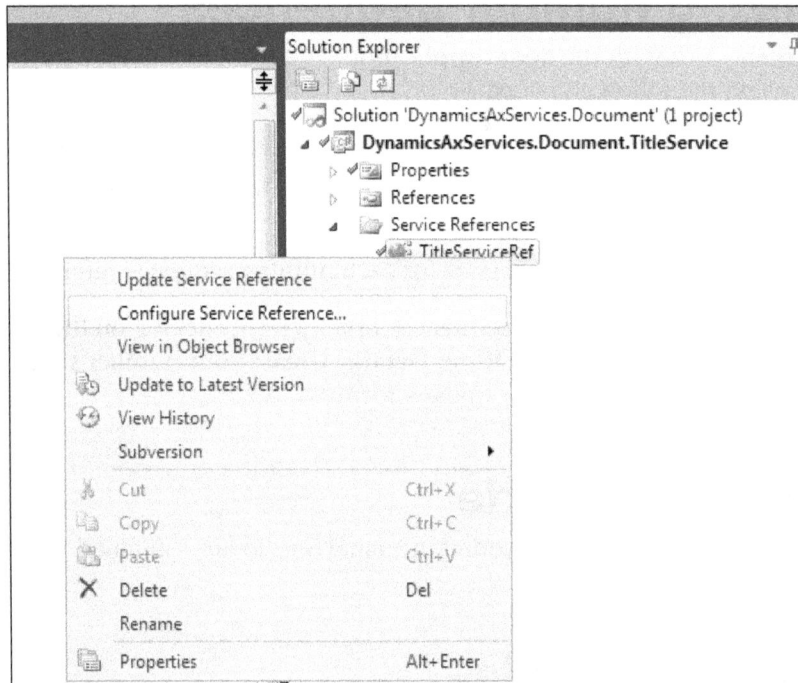

2. In the **Address** field, enter the address that you want to use:

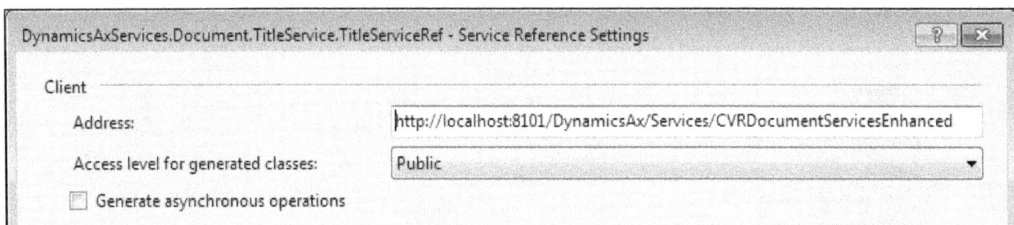

If you do not need to configure the service references, you still need to perform an update of the service references. This is to make sure that the app.config file contains the correct settings for your system. The steps to perform the update of the service references are as follows:

1. Right-click on the service reference and choose **Update Service Reference...**.
2. Verify that the app.config file contains the correct settings.

Sample data

In *Chapter 3, AIF Document Services*, we test the Create operation of a document service by importing an XML file that contains a number of movie titles. This file is located at SourceCode\VisualStudio\Chapter3\DynamicsAxServices. Document\DynamicsAxServices.Document.TitleService\Resources. Copy the TitleDemoData.xml file to C:\temp, and you will be able to import the data using the example console application as described in the chapter.

Index

Thank you for buying
Microsoft Dynamics AX 2012 R2 Services

About Packt Publishing

Packt, pronounced 'packed', published its first book "Mastering phpMyAdmin for Effective MySQL Management" in April 2004 and subsequently continued to specialize in publishing highly focused books on specific technologies and solutions.

Our books and publications share the experiences of your fellow IT professionals in adapting and customizing today's systems, applications, and frameworks. Our solution based books give you the knowledge and power to customize the software and technologies you're using to get the job done. Packt books are more specific and less general than the IT books you have seen in the past. Our unique business model allows us to bring you more focused information, giving you more of what you need to know, and less of what you don't.

Packt is a modern, yet unique publishing company, which focuses on producing quality, cutting-edge books for communities of developers, administrators, and newbies alike. For more information, please visit our website: www.packtpub.com.

About Packt Enterprise

In 2010, Packt launched two new brands, Packt Enterprise and Packt Open Source, in order to continue its focus on specialization. This book is part of the Packt Enterprise brand, home to books published on enterprise software – software created by major vendors, including (but not limited to) IBM, Microsoft and Oracle, often for use in other corporations. Its titles will offer information relevant to a range of users of this software, including administrators, developers, architects, and end users.

Writing for Packt

We welcome all inquiries from people who are interested in authoring. Book proposals should be sent to author@packtpub.com. If your book idea is still at an early stage and you would like to discuss it first before writing a formal book proposal, contact us; one of our commissioning editors will get in touch with you.

We're not just looking for published authors; if you have strong technical skills but no writing experience, our experienced editors can help you develop a writing career, or simply get some additional reward for your expertise.

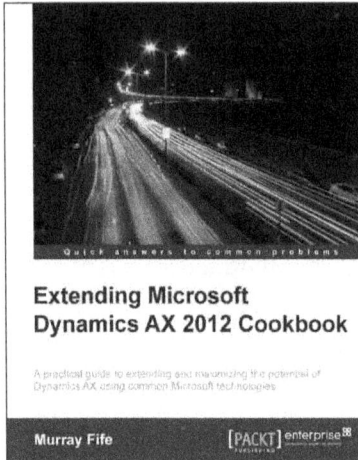

Extending Microsoft Dynamics
AX 2012 Cookbook

ISBN: 978-1-78216-833-1   Paperback: 314 pages

A practical guide to extending and maximizing the potential of Dynamics AX using common Microsoft technologies

1. Extend Dynamics in a cost-effective manner by using tools you already have.

2. Solve common business problems with the valuable features of Dynamics AX.

3. Follow practical and easy-to-grasp examples, illustrations, and coding to make the most out of Dynamics AX in your business scenario.

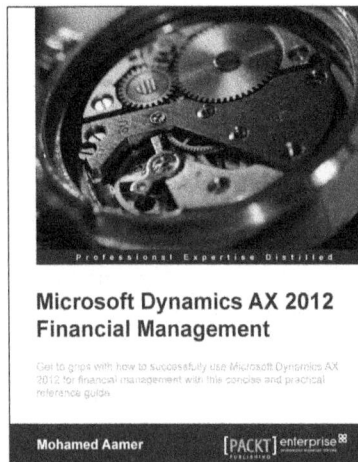

Microsoft Dynamics AX 2012
Financial Management

ISBN: 978-1-78217-720-3   Paperback: 168 pages

Get to grips with how to successfully use Microsoft Dynamics AX 2012 for financial management with this concise and practical reference guide

1. Understand the financial management aspects in Microsoft Dynamics AX.

2. Successfully configure and set up your software.

3. Learn about real-life business requirements and their solutions.

4. Get to know the tips and tricks you can utilize during analysis, design, deployment, and operation phases in a project lifecycle.

Please check **www.PacktPub.com** for information on our titles

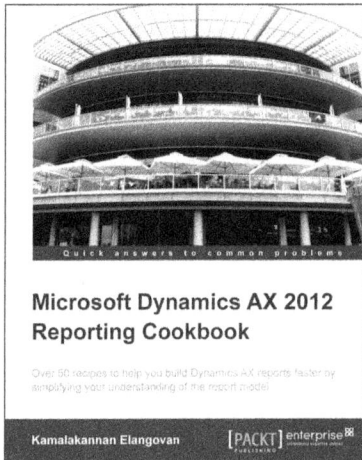

Microsoft Dynamics AX 2012 Reporting Cookbook

ISBN: 978-1-84968-772-0   Paperback: 314 pages

Over 50 recipes to help you build Dynamics AX reports faster by simplifying your understanding of the report model

1. Practical recipes for creating and managing reports.

2. Illustrated step-by-step examples that can be adopted in real time.

3. Complete explanations of the report model and program model for reports.

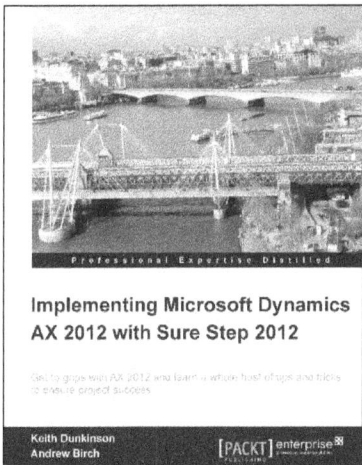

Implementing Microsoft Dynamics AX 2012 with Sure Step 2012

ISBN: 978-1-84968-704-1   Paperback: 234 pages

Get to grips with AX 2012 and learn a whole host of tips and tricks to ensure project success

1. Get the confidence to implement AX 2012 projects effectively using the Sure Step 2012 Methodology.

2. Packed with practical real-world examples as well as helpful diagrams and images that make learning easier for you.

3. Dive deep into AX 2012 to learn key technical concepts to implement and manage a project.

Please check **www.PacktPub.com** for information on our titles

www.ingramcontent.com/pod-product-compliance
Lightning Source LLC
Chambersburg PA
CBHW061359210326

41598CB00035B/6032